your first
NOVEL

a published author and a top agent
share the keys to achieving your dream

Ann Rittenberg and Laura Whitcomb
foreword by Dennis Lehane

W
**WRITER'S
DIGEST**
writersdigestbooks.com
Cincinnati, Ohio

Distributed in Canada by Fraser Direct, 100 Armstrong Avenue, Georgetown, ON, Canada L7G 5S4, Tel: (905) 877-4411. Distributed in the U.K. and Europe by David & Charles, Brunel House, Newton Abbot, Devon, TQ12 4PU, England, Tel: (+44) 1626 323200, Fax: (+44) 1626 323319, E-mail: mail@davidandcharles.co.uk. Distributed in Australia by Capricorn Link, P.O. Box 704, Windsor, NSW 2756 Australia, Tel: (02) 4577-3555.

Visit our Web site at www.writersdigest.com for information on more resources for writers.

To receive a free weekly e-mail newsletter delivering tips and updates about writing and about Writer's Digest products, register directly at our Web site at http://newsletters.fw-publications.com.

10 09 08 07 06   5 4 3 2 1

Library of Congress Cataloging-in-Publication Data

Rittenberg, Ann

Your first novel : a published author and a top agent share the keys to achieving your dream / Ann Rittenberg and Laura Whitcomb ; foreword by Dennis Lehane.

    p. cm.

  Includes index.

  ISBN-13: 978-1-58297-386-9 (hardcover : alk. paper)

  ISBN-10: 1-58297-386-5 (hardcover : alk. paper)

  ISBN-13: 978-1-58297-388-3 (pbk. : alk. paper)

  ISBN-10: 1-58297-388-1 (pbk. : alk. paper)

  1. Fiction--Authorship. 2. Fiction--Marketing. 3. Authorship--Marketing. I. Whitcomb, Laura. II. Title.

PN3365 .R57

808.3--dc22

2006014687

Edited by Kelly Nickell

Interior designed by Claudean Wheeler

Cover designed by Grace Ring

Production coordinated by Robin Richie

Ann Rittenberg photograph © Alissa Sherry;
Laura Whitcomb photograph © Coughlin-Glaser Photography

fw

F•W PUBLICATIONS, INC.

DEDICATIONS

ANN RITTENBERG

For my father, John R. Garman (1930–1969), and for Paul and our three daughters, Polly, Julia, and Gracie—booklovers all.

LAURA WHITCOMB

For my sister, Cynthia, who made the writing life impossible to resist.

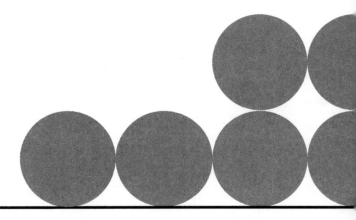

ACKNOWLEDGMENTS

ANN RITTENBERG

Our editor, Kelly Nickell, gave us this idea and then made the book better in every way with insight, humor, and sure-handed guidance. The writers and publishing people quoted in this book gave generously and unhesitatingly of their time, knowledge, and experience. The Brooklyn Writers Space gave me a quiet place to write. My mother, Ann Pitcher, nurtured a bookworm with a love of reading, a house full of books, and, always, a library card. Laura Whitcomb's unstinting support and patience—not to mention her wonderful writing—make her the ideal client and the best possible co-author. Penn Whaling, my incomparably elegant assistant, kept the office humming along and supported the project enthusiastically, as did Ted Gideonse, who made me believe I could do it. Julian Bach taught me how to be an agent and believed in me unconditionally and generously. Dennis Lehane offered support from the very beginning and wrote a wonderful foreword without blinking an eye. Best of all, my clients enchant me with the places their imaginations take them—they're the reason why publishing is still, to me, a place of endless possibility.

LAURA WHITCOMB

Thanks to my family and friends for all the love and support. My Writers Support Group for inspiration. Oregon Literary Arts for the fellowship. The Lake Oswego public library for research assistance. Penn Whaling for all her help. All the wonderful writers I quoted in this book for their brilliant contributions to literature. Kelly Nickell for her excellent editing. And Ann Rittenberg for being a fantastic agent and writing partner.

TABLE OF CONTENTS

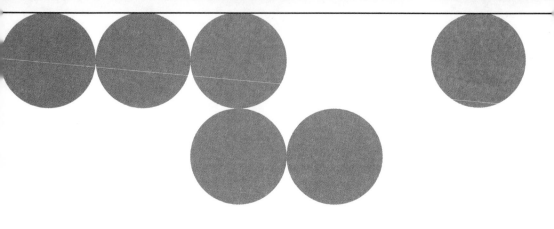

PART II: PUBLISHING YOUR NOVEL
BY ANN RITTENBERG

FOREWORD

I decided to become a fiction writer when I was twenty. An odd choice, believe me. Where I grew up, storytelling was something you did in bars, not a career option. Working for a utility was a career—good benefits, nice pension, and it was really hard to get fired. But writing? It just wasn't done. But after I'd dropped out of two colleges and my parents were losing patience and probably the hope that I'd ever amount to anything, I took stock of myself and realized two very important things:

1. Writing was the one thing I always loved doing that I was actually good at.
2. I sucked at everything else.

Sad, but true. I have no other marketable talents. I played a few sports well, but other kids played them demonstrably better. I dreamed of being a pilot or a doctor, but I'm terrible at math and don't particularly like science. I considered becoming a journalist (safety major number one, college number one) but discovered I wasn't fond enough of facts (dropout number one). Next I decided to become an English professor (safety major number two, college number two) but discovered that while I did indeed love reading books, I didn't much enjoy talking about them (dropout number two). So I took a big breath and went off to my third college to major in creative writing and hopefully make a living telling stories.

It sounds so heartwarming in retrospect—the young lad off to make his fortune with nothing in his pockets but some lint and a dream. How Algeresque, how *American*. Truth was, though, I was petrified. *No one did this.* The people I grew up with became electricians, firemen, social workers, cops, contractors; some even got rich, but no one became a *writer*. So there I was, 1,300 miles from home, terrified, but also certain that there was no going back. Third college, third major, three strikes you're out. One night I went back to my dorm room, wrote the following on a piece of paper and taped it above my desk:

"No one cares."

It sounds so cold. It looks cold. But it wasn't meant that way, not entirely. What I was telling myself was that if I failed, no one would care. If I never published, no one would notice. If I never fulfilled my dream, it wouldn't make a bit of difference to anyone else on the planet. "No one cares" meant no one was watching, no one was keeping score, no one was judging. I was free. Utterly (and at times, it seemed, inconsolably) free. And that purified the writing process; it made it about the words and me. That's it—nothing else in the equation.

The words and you. That's all this is about. If you're reading this, you must have made some kind of decision to become a writer. Good. Congratulations. Right about now you're probably composed of equal parts terror and courage, and I commend you on the latter because it is not easy to think you have something to say to the world. Or to think the world might want to hear it. That's a tall order. As to the terror, remember that it's about the words and you. Hemingway said it was a matter of writing the truest sentence you know. You then follow that true sentence with another, and so on. The late short story writer Andre Dubus used to read his drafts into a tape recorder and play the words back to himself until they had achieved the sound of "fork tines against a wine glass," whereupon he knew the story was ready to send out. Successful writing entails more than the sound of the words or even the truth of them—it entails depth of character, depth of insight and structure, authentic dialogue, and a certain sense of dramatic inevitability—but the foundation is the words. And you.

Think about it: You have never existed in the world of literature before. Your voice, your vision, your unique stamp. I've read or seen a few hundred Westerns but I felt as if I were discovering the form for the first time when I read Cormac McCarthy's *Blood Meridian*. This country has the South and then we have Flannery O'Connor's South. I've read Nadine Gordimer's and J.M. Coetzee's novels of South Africa and they are equally indelible, yet neither could have been written by the other. In great writing, the teller and the tale become so inextricably linked that to attempt to discern where one begins and the other ends is to court farce. So the next time you look in the mirror and think of your own writing, remember that the face staring back at you is your most potent weapon. It's the thing you bring to the table that no one else can.

So now that I've made you feel good, let me deliver some different news: Wanting it and earning it are two totally different things. You are to be commended for even attempting to travel a road as potentially heartbreaking and forlorn as the one the aspiring writer travels. But once the commendations are given, the work begins. You roll up your sleeves and you learn how to write. And that takes time. And toil. Too often aspiring writers ask, "How do I get published?" (Often the ones who ask this are the last ones who should. They're akin to a first-year med school student who asks, "When do I get to perform an angioplasty?") The answer to "How do I get published?" is simple—not easy, but simple: Learn how to write well.

If you learn how to write well, you will get published. The cart follows the horse. Simple. Not easy, mind you, because the learning *is* hard. It separates the men from the boys, the women from the girls, the authentic from the poseurs. If you are writing merely to get published, and you equate publishing with seeing your name in lights, with adoration, with your very self-worth, you are writing for the wrong reasons. E.L. Doctorow has said that a writer's duty is to be true to the times in which he lives. David Mamet, in his book on craft, *Three Uses of the Knife*, says that the duty of art is to celebrate truth. Not triumph, not order, not the status quo, just truth. And the truth he's talking about is the organic truth of the work itself, the truth that you, through the creation of your narrative, discover and raise up to the light of day.

Now while that may sound portentous or even pretentious, it is the job. If not, why else are you writing? There are hundreds of easier ways to make money. Thousands of better methods by which to self-actualize. Millions of less taxing ways to entertain oneself. You should write because you can't not write. You should write because some stray scrap of your soul is trying to manifest itself verbally. You should write because story is your preferred method by which to make order out of the chaos we call existence. You should write because even though the process terrifies you, the absence of that process terrifies you more. Which is to say, you have to love it. Unconditional love and, often, unrequited. There is no guarantee it will love you back. No guarantee you'll ever make a living at it. No guarantee that anyone but you and yours will ever see your words. That's why it can't be about anything temporal—the publishing, the parties, the name in lights. Only the words. And the truth you find in them.

If you reach that mental place and you live it, chances are you'll get better. If you get better and you keep putting one foot in front of the other, chances are you could get good. And if you get good, make no mistake, there are editors and agents—right now, at this very moment— salivating to read good work. I have heard of agents and editors who don't care about the quality of the prose but care only about commercial potential and the bottom line. I assume these are crass people with shriveled dreams and tiny hearts but I can only assume, because in my twelve years in this business, I've never met one of this clan. The editors and agents I have met all want the same thing: They want to be delighted. Engaged. Taken in hand by a confident voice and led down a path of vivid sights and sounds to a place they've never quite been before. They want prose that is clean and concrete and quietly poetic. They want a narrative that unfolds and unfurls and evolves. They want characters whose authenticity is so unquestionable it serves as a form of seduction. They want, as Ann Rittenberg, my own agent (and co-author of this book), often says, to fall in love.

To make them fall in love, you need a toolbox, like a carpenter needs a toolbox to build a house. You will need to learn how to use those tools, to apply them and reapply them so consistently that you reach a state of effortless facility. (We all know what a hammer is for; we all know how to drive a nail; but have you ever watched a master carpenter drive a nail? He barely looks at it yet he drives it home, straight and true, in two or three swings of the hammer.) The tools are in this book, as are the exercises by which you can work toward a mastery of them. Laura Whitcomb and Ann Rittenberg have done a fine job compiling your toolbox for you, and I'll let them show you how to use it.

But let me just add this about the toolbox: Don't reach for the band saw before you've proven you can use a screwdriver. An unfortunate affliction that besets a lot of aspiring writers is one I've dubbed the Ticking-Clock Syndrome. You feel time sweeping past (*tick, tick, tick*) and your loved ones are starting to wonder when you're actually going to, you know, publish something (*tick, tick, tick*), and maybe you came to this writing thing later in life, around the time you realized just how limited our time on Earth is (*tick, tick, tick*), so while you would like to learn how to use every tool in the toolbox, you'd also like to get out there and build the damn house (*tick, tick, tick, tick*). So maybe, you think, you could take a shortcut or two, just shave a year off the process, hell, maybe two.

To which I say: I understand. I do. I empathize. But please remember the tortoise and the hare. This is a marathon, not a sprint. Please remember the part about wanting something vs. earning it. And please remember the "no one cares" part, because if you show your work before it is ready, before it has the power to make someone fall in love, no one will care that you confused wanting it and earning it. They'll just reject it. And on that day, you'll say, "Darn. I wish I'd waited. What was I thinking?"

Ticking-Clock Syndrome extends beyond the point where you may or may not be ready to publish. Once the disease has taken root, it becomes a self-perpetuating virus, one that extends to all aspects of your career. You get over that first hurdle—you land an agent. Wow. An agent. But instead of enjoying it, you immediately begin wondering why that agent hasn't placed your book with a major publisher yet. I mean, it's been, like, three weeks! What are they doing up there—sipping lattes when they should be selling your book? How dare they!

From that point on, nothing's ever good enough. Let's say your book gets accepted. Your dream has just come true. But you don't even notice because Ticking-Clock Syndrome has already convinced you that not only should the book be published, it should be published as Big Noise, the Next Bestseller. You should be feted, sitting up front at the National Book Awards, not schlepping from strip-mall bookstore to strip-mall bookstore where the only readers who approach your signing table do so to ask where they can find the latest Grisham. (Yes, Virginia, this does happen. A lot.) You become agitated, worried all the time, convinced there's a conspiracy (oh, you'd never use that word, not out loud) to keep *your* voice from your public. And you start searching around for another agent, another editor, another publisher, someone who will appreciate your brilliance. Because you worked too hard to get here, you sacrificed too much, there were far too many lonely nights. A few years and a few publishers and agents later, your calls aren't getting returned. You never had that Big Noise. You can't even book an appearance at the strip mall. How did this happen? It happened because you forgot something you learned in kindergarten, without knowing you learned it, and have known implicitly ever since:

All business is personal.

Ticking-Clock Syndrome is not your agent's problem or your editor's (unless you make it thus). It's your problem. And those who show no loyalty give up the right to expect any in return. I know what you're thinking right now: *But that's so easy for you to say, Lehane. You've had a bestseller. You're on easy street. Why, you were a success right out of the gate.*

Here's what a success I was out of the gate: Within a year of landing Ann Rittenberg as my agent, the Chicago agency she worked for was bought out by a much bigger agency. Ann called me and said that this bigger agency would probably take me on as a client, but she was going back to New York to start her own agency out of a basement in Brooklyn. She'd understand if I didn't want to join her. She would. The big agency was all set up; they had the contacts, they had the infrastructure, they could fast-track me, if they so chose, and sell my book. A Brooklyn basement on the other hand … A woman starting over, if not from scratch, then certainly from, well, a basement. But this same woman, let's remember, had read my book and fallen in love with it. She had believed. Up until that point, with the exception of a few teachers and friends, *no one* cared. She cared. She was the first one outside of my rather limited circle to say "Your words matter." What sort of price do you put on that? What sort of price do you put on selling out another's faith in you? And how do you buy it back once you realize you shouldn't have sold it?

So we went to Brooklyn. When four different publishers said they'd take the book if I'd just change one major component (my female protagonist was also a battered wife; apparently there are no battered wives in America), I held my ground. And Ann supported me. No money coming in, a growing pile of rejections, and my agent said, "Stick to your guns. She's a great character."

The book finally landed with Claire Wachtel, an editor at Harcourt Brace, who took it over her boss's objections for the whopping sum of … well, less than minimum wage. But I was going to be published, and Claire risked her job to help facilitate that dream. Then Claire got "downsized" (it wasn't my fault, really, I swear), and my book was published and sold a few thousand copies. When I had fulfilled my contract with Harcourt Brace, I followed Claire to William Morrow & Company. She and Ann and I sat down and came up with a career plan. Here was how I sold myself:

"I will never write a bestseller. You two get that, don't you?"

They got it. My aesthetic vision was too dark, and I had no desire to climb on the hamster wheel of a book a year. Bye-bye bestseller. We decided then and there that the operating principles of my career would be consistency and longevity. Ann and I would never rake Morrow over the coals in contract negotiations; Claire and Morrow would never ask that I write any kind of book except the best I was capable of at the time.

And so it went—through books that didn't quite live up to financial expectations, through corporate takeovers and big-name agents who would try to draw me away from Ann over drinks, through rumors of rival publishers prepared to make mind-boggling offers, through my decision to walk away from a detective series just as it was reaching a tangible level of success so I could write my dream book about a large-scale tragedy affecting small-scale lives in a fictitious neighborhood of Boston.

When that book was released, it climbed the *New York Times* best-seller list and stayed there for a dozen weeks. I was surprised. Hell, I was stunned. Claire was not surprised; Morrow and its parent company, HarperCollins, were not surprised; Ann was not surprised. They'd put in the work, you see, ten years of pushing slowly uphill to achieve my "overnight success."

Why?

Because I stuck by them and they stuck by me.

Because I didn't drive them crazy with Ticking-Clock Syndrome.

Because they loved the words.

And maybe most of all because good agents and good editors and good publishers (and they're out there, believe me) want to believe in the same collective dream: If you put in the work, they'll put in the work; if you care about the words, they'll care about the words; and if you make them fall in love, they'll do their best to make sure the world (or the small part of the world that still reads) falls in love, too.

—Dennis Lehane, author of *Mystic River*

PART ONE

writing your
NOVEL

CHAPTER ONE:

preparations

LISTENING FOR THE IDEA

In the beginning there is only the idea. If you are reading this book, you want to write a novel. If you want to write a novel, you already have an idea, whether you realize it or not. When the first storytellers stood up in their caves and moved closer to the fire, when they looked into the eyes of that first audience and said, "Now listen to me," they did so because they had a story to tell. This is the time to call your idea out of the shadows. Even if you've never written a line of fiction in your life, you can start now. Begin by writing down your idea. So far, it might be only a single sentence, but write it down all the same.

Your idea might be a character you want to follow, a setting that haunts you, or a scene that keeps playing in your mind. A writer gets ideas from everywhere—by watching people pass in the crosswalks, by elaborating on childhood memories, by retelling nightmares, or by taking pieces of history and contemplating alternate outcomes. Inside you there is already the seed of a story that drives you to move closer to the fire and speak. Give it a name. Not a title—that comes later. Just name it, so it will know its master. "Hunted preacher" it might be called, or "Underwater schoolroom."

Your idea might be an overview of the whole tale or just a glimpse. Michael Crichton conceived of *The Andromeda Strain* by reading a footnote in one of his college textbooks. Most of my ideas start out as a single moment: A man waits in the woods for his beloved. A child sits in a bush listening to fairies no one else hears. A woman watches the farmhand praying. If the moment is meant to grow into a whole idea, it will follow you around and beg to be picked up.

Stephen King came to write *The Dead Zone* by imagining the last moment in the story—a lone gunman attempts to assassinate a popular presidential candidate. Under what circumstances could the assassin be right? Be the hero? Your idea could be the last moment of the story, or it could be the first. You see a man answering the phone, a ransom must be paid or his wife will be killed—only he has never been married. It could be a climactic moment from somewhere in the middle of the plot. You don't know why, but a woman in uniform is running through a stream, trying to get to her village before the enemy arrives.

Some ideas start as a character or a set of characters. You keep imagining a healer who is haunted by a past failure, three sisters building a bridge, the husband of a woman on death row who writes notes on the backs of their wedding pictures because she will not speak to him. You keep seeing your character and picturing her in various situations or imagining him telling his story aloud.

Some ideas start as a setting—a place so vivid in your mind that you can smell the damp hay, hear the submarine engines humming, or taste the volcano ash in the air. If the little desert town you grew up in, or the South American nightlife you adored on vacation, or the sinister factory where your aunt worked for thirty years keeps creeping into your daydreams or nightmares, it might become the setting of your novel. Of course, you don't need to have visited a place to write about it. You can create settings from scratch. J.K. Rowling conjured up Hogwarts as she stared out her train window somewhere between Manchester and London.

As a writer, you should always carry paper and pen. When your idea shows up, write it down. More pieces of the story will follow if you welcome the first. Write everything down. Don't worry about fitting the elements together yet. Just take notes. Your muse is brainstorming.

Once you get in the habit of collecting ideas, you'll find that they will come more often and more clearly. Sometimes ideas wake you up in the morning, nagging to be written down. Ideas open up like flowers in the steam while you take a shower. They evolve into other species of themselves while you drive to work. Ideas hide at the back of your mind, then slide forward when you hear a certain strain of music or smell burning leaves.

I like ideas that sit next to me during a play and nag my pen to scratch notes in the program margins, dictating phrases that help me recall the idea later. "Confuses cat with dead son," it will whisper. "Write that down."

I like characters who loiter on top of the television or under my seat at the movies and tell me how they would behave in the same situation—"Not me. I could never walk away from a crying woman," says my character. "And, by the way, I've never been able to wear a wristwatch. They stop working or run backwards. Why do you think that is?"

I like settings that keep house behind my eyes, appearing like ghosts when I blink, that can be heard like a phantom ocean in the cup of my hand. I like settings you can smell as you fall asleep—the creek of the bamboo in a tropical cemetery. The scent of hot wax floating from the cathedral doorway. The red ember of a cigar throbbing like the eye of a cyclops in a darkened office.

Often ideas come from seeing something in a new way or combining two elements you had never pictured together before. While watching a movie you might hear a line of dialogue spoken by a priest and imagine it spoken by a prostitute. What if those words from the lips of a serial killer came from the lips of a four-year-old boy as his mother tucks him into bed? What kind of story would you have if a Rhett Butler type wasn't coupled with a Scarlett O'Hara but a Boo Radley? Imagine Sam Spade locking horns with Eleanor Roosevelt, or a partnership between Lady Macbeth and Joan of Arc.

Think about the kinds of moments you love best in your favorite novels. If you read mostly mysteries, you might love the moment when the first clue contradicts the current theory of whodunit. If you read romances, it might be the first physical contact. If you read horror stories, it might be the satisfaction of stopping the monster/alien virus/psychopath at the last possible second. This is what I call the "that oughta do it" moment. One of my favorite moments is the first time our protagonist (or main character) comes across something that can't be explained without the introduction of the supernatural—the "wait a minute now" moment. Another favorite of mine is the moment when a character reveals something about herself that makes her real, a surprise expansion into three dimensions.

If you have a favorite kind of scene in the novels you read, that might be the place to start with your own story. Ask yourself, "What is my 'that oughta do it' moment? Where is my 'wait a minute now' scene?" If you are starting with a character, imagine what that character wants the most, then imagine the failure and success moments for him. If your idea is only a setting so far, imagine what kind of problems that setting might imply—you see a garden between two skyscrapers in Chicago. Does someone want to buy the space from the reluctant owner? What is growing there? Who designed the stepping stones? Who was married there? Who hides there? What is buried there?

Write down every idea and make a file folder or envelope in which to keep them safe. These are the fragments of your novel that will fit together later. Imagine taking a story and ripping it up, tossing the scraps like confetti. It's like that, only backwards. You are gathering the bits of the story you will one day hold in your hands.

PREPARING THE LEFT BRAIN

You have a split personality—everyone does—your right brain controls your creative side, and your left brain controls your logical side. Some people call them the writer and the editor. Or the artist and the critic. Whatever you call them, you'll want to keep them on good terms with each other because you'll need them both.

When you prepare to write, you need to satisfy your left brain's desire for organization, correctness, and good old-fashioned work ethic. When your left brain is given more than half the control, though, it becomes judgmental and starts calling your right brain an undisciplined dreamer, doomed to failure. You want to keep your left brain in line, but you don't want to kill it. If it weren't for your left brain, you'd rarely get any work done and what you did produce would be unstructured and riddled with mistakes. You don't want to shut down your left brain—you want to keep your left brain happy so it will allow your right brain to fly free.

THE NECESSITY OF READING

Reading feeds both sides of the brain. To the right brain, reading is the air, the water, the rich soil where your spirit grows. Your right brain reads to escape into worlds unknown and fall in love with people who don't even exist. It's magic.

To your left brain, reading is exercise, analysis, and research. The left brain likes the cerebral calisthenics of reading. But remember, you are what you eat. If you only read bad writing, your brain will unconsciously give out what it's been given.

Read the kind of novels you admire. The more your mind hears what great writing sounds like, the better equipped you'll be to produce great writing of your own. Some beginning writers wonder why they have to read at all. Why not use that extra time to write? *Warning*: If you are the only writer you want to read, you will be stumbling over your ego for months and years to come. Get a grip. We can all learn from other authors.

The left brain also likes to analyze what works and what doesn't in the fiction you read. When you read a novel you love, write down some notes on why it got to you. You fell for the hero. You were so scared you stayed up all night to find who murdered the nun. You couldn't get those foster children out of your head because they were so sad and funny.

When you read a novel that disappoints you or drives you crazy, try to figure out why it failed. Where did the author go wrong? Usually you'll know exactly why. The love story was not believable. The dialogue was awkward. The protagonist wasn't likable. The ending has been done to death.

Go into detail: Why was the hero unlikable? He didn't care about the wounded woman. He was dishonest with his partner for no good reason. He did everything for his own benefit until the last three pages—by that point it was too late, you already hated him.

When you write your own novel, you will now have these notes in the back of your mind. You'll write protagonists who are worth caring about because you'll remember how author A succeeded and author B failed.

Read novels in your chosen genre—novels written for the audience to which you want to sell your own story. If you want to write romances, read the best romance novels. If you want to write Westerns, read them. You need to research what's out there and what is doing well. You should always write the story you feel called to write and write it the best way you can, but you should also be well informed on what your potential fans desire.

Give yourself permission to close the cover halfway through if a book is doing nothing for you. Give up and start something else. Life's too short. You will never read everything, so choose books that are giving you the most help. You don't need to put off starting to write your own novel until you've read every bestseller in your genre, but if you haven't been much of a reader so far, start now, read every day, and never stop.

PRACTICING THE CRAFT: LEFT-BRAIN EXERCISES

Only about one out of every billion humans will sit down one day, having never written a word, and produce a masterpiece. Writing is mostly practice. Think of the number of laps a track star runs before she breaks a record, or the number of hours a dancer spends at the barre before he's ready for a performance. There's nothing wrong with hoping your first draft will be brilliant—hope is required—but know that it's normal to need to practice before you succeed.

Some baseball coaches use a training trick on their players, a machine that shoots tennis balls at 150 mph. Each ball is painted with a colored number. The player at bat has to call out the label on the ball (red three, blue seven) before he swings. This exercise improves one's batting average because it brings back the basics—keep your eye on the ball. The player stops thinking about every detail—his grip, the distance to the pitcher's mound, the angle of his shoulders, the turn of his hips, or the spacing of his feet. Writing exercises do the same thing—they give you something else to focus on so you don't trip over this word or that comma. You want to keep your eye on your idea.

Here are some exercises to warm up your right brain and satisfy your left brain's desire for a workout.

• **Timed Writing Sessions.** Find a timer—your watch alarm, an egg timer, but not an hourglass—you want it to make noise so you don't break concentration by glancing up to see if you've gone on too long. Set the timer to fifteen minutes and start writing. It doesn't matter what you write—no one need ever see it. You can write about your characters or what you dreamed the night before. The trick is to keep your fingers moving on the keys or your pencil scratching on the paper. Don't worry about spelling or punctuation. Don't stop to think or rewrite. Just write at full speed. Now read it. You might end up with a great sentence or idea for your novel, or you might have nothing you want to save, but it doesn't matter. The point was to warm you up.

• **Journals.** Write in a journal or diary each day before starting to work on your novel. It doesn't matter if you write a list of what happened the day before or your innermost fantasies—the act of putting words on paper is warming you up.

• **Vocalization.** You can literally talk aloud to yourself, or you can dialogue with yourself or your characters on paper. Talk to your novel. Ask where it hurts. Don't be surprised when it starts answering back. Play truth or dare with your hero. Play twenty questions with your villain.

• **Books on Tape.** You can turn your commute to the office into a grown-up story time. Browse your public library. Look for research materials, novels in your genre, writers who inspire you.

• **First Lines.** Take a stack of novels and read only the first sentence of each.

The year that Buttercup was born, the most beautiful woman in the world was a French scullery maid named Annette.

> —*The Princess Bride*, by William Goldman

I grew up in a small southern town which was different from most other towns because it contained an insane asylum.

> —*Lilith*, by J.R. Salamanca

The church was all heat and white sunlight, dust and the smell of dry grass and manure pushing in through flung-open doors.

> —*The Blackbirder*, by James L. Nelson

Her body moved with the frankness that comes from solitary habits.

> —*Prodigal Summer*, by Barbara Kingsolver

It is a truth universally acknowledged, that a single man in possession of a good fortune must be in want of a wife.

> —*Pride and Prejudice*, by Jane Austen

Getting through the night is becoming harder and harder; last evening, I had the uneasy feeling that some men were trying to break into my room to shampoo me.

> —*Without Feathers*, by Woody Allen

Randomly opening a novel and choosing any line can also work, but the magic of first lines is that the author is setting the stage for you and trying to hook you in. As you prepare to start writing, think: "What is it about my own story that will draw the reader in?"

• **First-Line Story Starters.** This time choose a novel, copy down the first line, and continue to write your own version of what comes next. Go for five minutes. Again, no one needs to see it but you, so let your imagination run wild.

• **Word Association.** Write down one word and then write down another word that the first word brings to mind, and create a chain of single words or phrases in this way. For example:

novel, book, shelf, cupboard, hiding place, stowaway, tall ship, storm, tempest, magic, curse, secret, clue, code, puzzle, joke, seltzer bottle ...

Often this process leads to an idea for a scene, as in this imaginary list for Charles Dickens's *A Christmas Carol*.

> Snow, winter, Christmas, high spirits, ghosts, the past, the Ghost of Christmas Past, the ghost takes Scrooge to his childhood, Scrooge sees his classmates but they can't see or hear him, he sees himself as a child sitting alone and unwanted, the schoolhouse is not quite deserted—a solitary child, neglected by his friends is left there still.

• **Back Reading.** Reread some of what you've already written before you start writing for the day. Hemingway used to read everything he'd written the previous day before he'd add any new material.

RESEARCH

Research is not only a good way to pacify the left brain; for most novels it is a necessity. You might be writing a veiled memoir from your high school days that needs no research, but even then there will probably be at least one thing you'll need to learn about to make the story more vivid. One of the characters might be into something you don't know enough about—reptiles as pets, chess tournaments, making model castles. Details make the story come alive.

Often research involves a broader scope. Unless you're already a Civil War buff, if your story takes place in South Carolina in 1864, you'll need to research it. And some research needs to be done in advance. You will probably not want to start chapter one of a book about a carpenter in nineteenth-century China if you know nothing about that world. On the other hand, it's fine to start writing about your high school days before you start researching model castles.

Research can be dangerous. Some people have so much fun checking out library books, surfing the Web, and taking notes that they never get to the actual writing of the novel itself. If you are prone to this kind of compulsion, either give your research a time line (I will research for two weeks and then start my outline) or give your writing a time line (I will write for one hour every morning before I open my research book). You can always go back and fix things later.

The one kind of research that must be done before page 1 is the kind that colors the whole novel, the kind that determines the makeup of your protagonist. To find out what your hero believes and cares about, to know what his wounds and fears are, you might have to research the background of your setting in history and culture. A teacher in Victorian London will have a different psychological outlook than a teacher in Renaissance Florence, even if they both teach math. You can't just insert a different year and city later on—you need to know what makes your protagonist tick before you write her first thought.

Another danger of research is fixating on accuracy. Of course you want your story to be believable, but remember, this is fiction. You're a storyteller. If you can't find a single book or encyclopedia entry or Internet citation or magazine article that tells you exactly what the ladies' room of a Harlem Renaissance movie theater looks like, move on. You're not writing a nonfiction book on 1920s rest rooms. Make a logical leap from the closest thing you can find.

If you are new to research, here is a general list of resources and examples of what you might find in each area.

Resources

For an example of treasures you might find using various resources, let's use the fictional topic of American carnival performer Jack Cross, magician and psychic, 1851–1944, and see what kinds of sources we might expect to find were he an actual person.

LIBRARY BOOKS, MAGAZINES, FILMS
- book on history of American carnival life
- magazine article on sideshow psychics
- video on turn-of-the-century magicians

INTERNET SEARCHES
- Web site article on the 1901 Robbinsen Circus (Cross was member 1903–1923)

REFERENCE LIBRARIANS
- help in finding interlibrary loan of rare book of carnival photography, 1850–1950 (Cross in three photos)

NEW AND USED BOOKSELLERS

- Borders—new book on Depression-era circus life
- Powell's—used book on hoaxes and deceptions (Cross mentioned in Dubb Family circus scandal of 1901)
- Abebooks.com—used copy of out-of-print book on 1920s show business art includes Jack Cross's tent drop from 1877

EYEWITNESS INTERVIEWS

- phone interview with historian Jon Thuess, who saw Cross perform in 1941

NEWSPAPER ARCHIVES

- microfilm newspaper from 1939 Fort Worth, Texas, with article on Moslowski Carnival (Cross a member, 1937–1944) causing church protest

MUSEUMS

- exhibit on Civil War photographer William A. Watts, county art museum, photos of 1869 carnival life

HISTORICAL SITES

- Leer Hills, Idaho, site of last West Coast performance of Moslowski carnival with Cross performing

COLLEGES AND UNIVERSITIES (LIBRARIES, STAFF, FACULTY)

- rare magazine article from 1941 on psychics found at Trudey College in Meadow, Oregon
- interesting book on 1930s fear of Satan in Washington State University library
- short interview with history professor Epetha Kiley on Depression-era slang

If you need assistance with any of these types of resources, ask the reference staff at your local library for advice. They can not only help you find things but teach you how to refine searches when you're working on your own. Sometimes it's just a matter of knowing what keywords to use or putting your keywords in a different order.

You might be tempted to read as many novels as you can that share your own story's location and period of history or subject. There's nothing wrong with that. It's good to know what's already out there, but don't go overboard. You don't have to read every novel ever written that has an army chaplain in it before you write your own. And remember—if you are reading every novel you can find on New York in the 1920s hoping that in one of them someone will walk into a ladies' room in a movie house in Harlem and describe it for you, you're wasting precious writing time. It's probably better, for instance, to read three carefully chosen nonfiction books on career circus clowns than to read twenty books in which the characters visit the circus. (If you are afraid of getting too many other novelists' ideas in your head, by all means stick to nonfiction research.)

PREPARING THE RIGHT BRAIN

Your right brain is your creator, your free spirit, your passionate artist. The right brain is the heart of your writing self. If your right brain is given too much power, it starts calling your left brain an evil dictator. You want to keep your right brain in check, but you don't want to shut it down. If it wasn't for your right brain, your left brain would write a book with three hundred pages of perfect spelling and grammar and zero emotion. The goal is for the left and right brains to live in harmony.

FINDING INSPIRATION: RIGHT-BRAIN EXERCISES

One way we prepare the right brain for writing is to feed it, and your creator/free spirit/artist hungers for inspiration. I picture inspiration in three categories—writing, career, and life. The following exercises stir your imagination by focusing on these three areas, and remind you why you want to be a novelist.

• **The List.** Make a list of one hundred things you love. Woody Allen has his protagonist in the film *Manhattan* lie on a couch with a handheld tape recorder and list Things That Make Life Worth Living. A hundred sounds like a lot. Just start writing—it's contagious. Especially if you play the game with somebody else and you read back parts of your lists to each other. Hearing what someone else loves reminds you of your own delights. For example:

- hot baths
- Monday Night Football
- blue lights on airport runways
- Marx Brothers movies
- fresh lobster
- the smell of libraries
- when the weather turns cold

Anything, even strange things that you would not normally confess to liking, can go on your list. If you don't want to show it to anyone, don't. It's for your right brain only.

- using old college term papers as kindling
- watching reruns of *Seinfeld*
- reading the Sunday paper in bed
- watching the neighbor's cat stalk a squirrel
- wearing sweats all day on New Year's

Include things you love that you want to see in your novel.

- rainy nights
- mysteries unfolding through dreams
- World War II songs
- 1960s cars
- nun with Tourette's syndrome
- dinosaur bones
- lost letters found

- **Hand Copying.** Choose one of your favorite pieces of writing (no more than 300 words) and copy it by hand. You can copy poetry, a paragraph from a novel, a passage from a play, the lyrics to a song—but choose writing to which you aspire. The process of writing out great words, feeling them travel from your eye to your brain, down your arm, into your hand, and onto the paper will train you to recognize fine writing. You'll know what it feels like. This exercise might sound strange, but it's effective. Try it at least once. Some favorite passages that I have copied in the past include: the speech in which Salieri describes hearing Mozart's music for the first time from the play *Amadeus*, the first page of Mary Stewart's novel *The Crystal Cave*, and the poem "Choose Something Like a Star," by Robert Frost.

- **More Vocalization.** A variation on the exercise on page 15 is simply to read aloud a short passage of writing you consider superb right before you start your own writing for the day. The difference between this and the reading exercise we looked at earlier for the left brain (in which you chose a book off the shelf randomly) is that here you are choosing your favorite moments. It carries a ritual power because you are making a statement—this is great writing and I am choosing to read it out loud because I want to write like this.

- **Career Inspiration.** Career inspiration feeds the worker in you. There's nothing wrong with encouraging your business sense. There are times when seemingly noncreative tasks like retyping your revisions, going to the post office, or making copies can inspire you to focus on your career as a writer.

- **Positive Feedback.** If there is any truth to quantum physics, it couldn't hurt to give the universe and yourself some positive feedback in advance. Take the file folder or manila envelope or cardboard box you keep your manuscript in and, with a bold marking pen, label it with success. Call it names you hope it lives up to someday. "Excellent," "Brilliant," "Superb," "Breathtaking," even "Award Winning" or "Critically Acclaimed."

- **Cover Art.** Take a few minutes and sketch a design for the cover of your novel. When you walk through bookstores or flip through book club catalogs, take a look at what's out there and fantasize your perfect cover. Will it be a watercolor landscape or a comic book cartoon? Will it have bold print and bright colors like an Elmore Leonard book? Will it have a faded photograph or a Da Vinci–like sketch? Your real cover will probably look nothing like the one you create here, but that's fine—this is a visualization exercise to draw your success to you.

• **Rave Reviews.** Pretend you are a book critic and write yourself a gushing review. No one has to see it. It's an inspirational exercise. Be in love with your story and your writing. Go into detail. What are the best parts of this wonderful novel you're about to write?

• **Jacket Copy.** Along the same lines, write your own book jacket copy. Read a few covers from other novels, then compose your own. What is it about your novel that will entice a potential reader to choose your story? This exercise can be useful when it comes to writing a query letter later on. If it is clear to you whom the story is about, what the main problem is, and where the story takes place, you're in good shape to start writing. In addition, if you understand what kind of book you're writing to the extent that you can write your own jacket copy, you'll have an easier time writing your outline.

As part of this exercise, create quotes from rave reviews and famous authors. Feel free to quote your own rave review from the preceding exercise.

• **Bio.** Compose your own author biography. Look at other books to see how much or how little is said. Write two versions—a short version (a sentence or two to be printed under your photograph) and a long version (one paragraph) to be used in your marketing materials once your book has sold.

• **Shelf Space.** Go to your local bookstore and find the area where your book will be shelved someday. Smell, feel, and browse the books there. Get a tactile sense of your novel's future home.

• **Visualization.** Before you start writing, close your eyes and picture your book's success. Use any image that feels inspiring. Maybe you picture the box arriving with your book inside. Or a display in a bookstore window. Maybe you picture your checkbook with five figures. Getting a call from your agent. Reading a positive review to your grandmother over the phone. Ordering lobster in a four-star restaurant instead of waiting on the table. Sending a signed copy of the book to your tenth-grade English teacher. Whatever form success comes in, hold it for a moment in your mind before you start to write.

INSPIRATION FOR LIFE

Inspiration for life means things you do for the person who is writing this novel (you need to take good care of yourself). You shouldn't only feel excited about what you are writing and the career you hope it brings you. You should also feel inspired about yourself and life. Writing a novel is a long process and can be stressful. To survive it in good health and happiness, you need to be kind to yourself.

- Play basketball, do yoga, go dancing (some kind of physical activity).
- Participate in favorite hobbies (follow your bliss).
- Drink plenty of water (helps both sides of your brain!).
- Spend time with people who make you feel good (who give you energy and don't drain you).
- Laugh a lot.
- Write and recite positive affirmations.

One good affirmation comes from a book by Florence Scovel Shinn called *The Game of Life and How to Play It.* "What God has done for others, God does now for me and more." Before I sold my first novel I would say this affirmation twenty times each day, looking at the cover of one of my favorite novels each time I repeated the words. By looking at these novels I was honoring their success, and by saying the affirmation I was reminding myself that I, too, would be granted this same success. So I would tip my proverbial hat to the cover of *Gone With the Wind*, to the cover of *Ragtime*, to the cover of *Jane Eyre*, and remind myself that, just as these successful writers were gifted with publication, I would be, too.

YOUR WRITING ENVIRONMENT

Setting up a working environment might sound like food for the left brain, but it's actually something you do for the right brain. Anything to make the technical end more manageable helps free your creative mind to create. You want to make your work space work so your momentum won't be interrupted.

Make sure the surface you write on (desk, table, TV tray) is stable and the right height for your chair. Make sure your chair is supportive; you don't want to quit writing for the day because you have a backache. Make sure the things you need (paper and pen, computer, glasses, tissues, reference books, coffee cup) are all easy to reach.

If you don't have everything you need at hand, you'll be tempted to get up whenever you hesitate about the next word to write. For example, if every time you stop to think about the next sentence you pick up your coffee mug, take a sip, get up from your writing area, and put the cup in the microwave for thirty seconds, *get an electric mug warmer* and keep it right next to your computer.

Make sure you not only make your writing area convenient, but effective. Just because you put everything in reach doesn't mean the space will work for you. Try it out. Maybe you'll discover the window glare is too much for your laptop screen. Move the desk or lower the blinds. Don't let anything be a hindrance—take care of the details in advance.

Make sure your writing space is yours. Can you use it whenever you need to? Does it feel good? (And here I don't mean is it warm and fuzzy—I mean, when you sit in it, does it feel like home to you?) This will be the place you go to climb into your story. When you step into it you need to feel welcome.

Now that the space is prepared, prepare the time. Some simple little rituals can get you in the writing mode faster and differentiate writing time from the rest of your day. You want your writing space to be sacred space and your writing time to be sacred time. You might light a candle while you work on your novel, putting out the flame when you finish for the day. At various stages in my life I have defined my writing time by putting on a lucky sweater or wearing a certain ring. Whatever you like to do to set this time apart from the rest of your day, do it without shame. It's no sillier than weeding a garden. It helps.

One very useful tip is to put a timer on while you write. I know this sounds like a left-brain thing, but it's all for the right brain. You want your creative brain to write at a full run for as long as it can. If you know you have to leave for work at 8:40 A.M. and you start writing at 7:45 A.M., your writing will slow down at about 8:30 A.M. and you'll start checking the clock. You'll keep checking it every two minutes and your writing will suffer. Put on a timer that you can't see or hear until it rings. (The stove or microwave timer will work if you're close enough to the kitchen, or use your wristwatch timer, even a bedside alarm clock.) If you know you have to stop writing at a certain time (for work, a date, to cook dinner), give yourself every one of those minutes you have on the timer, then forget about it until you hear the alarm go off. Once you get immersed in your story, forty-five minutes can seem like hours of freedom. Sacred time is funny that way.

Another effective tool is the novel soundtrack. Listen to music that brings up key emotions and moods from your story. Movie scores are good sources, but you can use anything—opera, jazz, bagpipes, electronic music, Gregorian chants, Polynesian drums, symphonies, ballets, folk songs, harp music, Irish tin whistles, even whale songs. You might want to stay away from too many songs with lyrics—outside words might interfere with your own words. Record these pieces of music together on one cassette or CD, or directly onto your computer. Name it after the novel (write the name on the cassette label, CD, or computer file) and play this soundtrack while you write. (But don't give it to anyone, sell it, or charge money to play it for anyone—that would be illegal.)

Another thing you can do to make your writing time sacred is to turn off your phone or let the machine pick up. Not everyone has this luxury. If you have small children or your job requires you to be on call, this won't work for you. But if you can detach from your phone for an hour or two, do it.

Some of you will not need to do any of the things listed above. Some of you can write anywhere (in a coffee shop, on a bus, during a lecture) and anytime (for ten minutes while waiting under the dryer at the hair salon, for five minutes in line at the post office, for thirty seconds while stuck in traffic)—the most important thing is that you write as well as you can.

PROTECTING THE CREATIVE PROCESS

You might be one of those writers who can tell everyone you know about the novel you are starting to write and then go and write it. Or you might be one of those writers who never tells anyone (not your spouse, mother, best friend, priest) about your idea. For some people, giving away the story verbally relieves some of the built-up passion required to write it down. If you feel comfortable telling people about your novel in advance, more power to you, but be aware that you might be affected by their responses. If they give you too much praise, will you feel the weight of trying to live up to their expectations? Will this energize your writing or give you writer's block? If the response is reserved or negative, will you doubt the value of your story? Will a cool response diminish your own love for the idea? If you think the work might be damaged by poor reactions and if you can live without the instant gratification of advertising your novel before it is written, protect the process of writing your book by keeping it to yourself. You can tell everyone you are writing a novel, even tell them how many pages you wrote last week, but keep the magic of the story to yourself and don't spring it on them until the writing is finished. You only have one chance to make a first impression.

If you feel you need guidance during the writing process, you might want to join a critique group. This is a group of writers who share and give each other feedback on works-in-progress. They are often geared toward writers of the same genre—science fiction, romance, fantasy, mystery. You can find groups through the Internet, bookstore bulletin boards, writers' associations, and colleges. But be careful—not all critique groups are helpful. If you join one and the members destroy the writing and tear down the author, rather than give constructive criticism and nurture the author, find a better group. Your critique group should inspire you to improve, not depress you into dropping your project. Listening to good advice is essential, but protect yourself and protect your process.

STATE OF MIND

Your state of mind will affect your writing. Here are some tips on how to hop over the most common stumbling blocks of attitude.

• **Own the job.** Once you've started your novel, if a friend or family member tells people you are a writer, agree with him. Do not negate the statement by saying you've never been published, that you've just started, that you don't have an agent, or that you're not any good yet. If you keep telling people you're not really a writer, your subconscious will start believing it. This is the job you've always wanted. You *are* a writer.

• **Love your story with an open heart.** You should be passionate about your novel without being closed-minded. You need to love your story and at the same time be open to advice about improving it. If you are too fixated on the writing exactly the way it is, you will suffocate it. Let it breathe.

• **Always write your best.** If you hear a little voice inside your head say, "Mediocre is good enough. Look at all those mediocre writers out there who get books published. You could write that stuff with half your brain tied behind your back!" *Do not listen to it!* That's not the little angel on your shoulder, it's the little devil. Never listen to anyone or anything that tells you not to bother doing your best. You can't improve as a writer if you don't give it your all at each level of learning. That doesn't mean kick yourself when you don't write a perfect scene. Nothing's ever perfect. Your writing just needs to be your best. If you settle for a half-assed job, you'll start to think that's all you need to do and all you can do. Do not settle. Your emotional state will be healthier if you write your best every day. (And if your first draft isn't great, relax. You can always rewrite it!)

• **Don't take things the wrong way.** Emphasize the positive and de-emphasize the negative. Things that go wrong are just little tests to see if you'll give up. Your best friend isn't crazy about chapter one. Your laptop has to go to the shop. You can't find your research notes. Everything will be all right. Don't let it get to you. When things go right, celebrate them. These are the true rewards of writing. Give more power to the good news and no power to the bad.

- **Don't judge others too harshly.** It's good to be discriminating (especially when choosing what you read or write) but don't overdo it. Analyzing what's flawed in a piece of writing so you can avoid making the same mistake is fine, but spending hours complaining about various books and authors is not. Too much negativity will eventually rub off on you. You'll feel irritated and uneasy. When you hear yourself nagging about your least favorite novels or writers, switch gears and talk about your favorites.

- **Don't judge yourself too harshly.** The same goes for bitching about yourself. Don't do it. You don't want to imprint your subconscious with insults. You can be kind to yourself because you're always doing your best.

- **Don't worry.** Worrying about things you have no control over (literary trends, the speed of the U.S. mail, how agents respond to query letters) wastes energy and increases stress. Unless it's a problem you can do something about (writing, rewriting, research), don't fret about it. Again, giving something negative too much attention empowers it. Relax and keep writing.

PROCRASTINATION

There are two kinds of procrastination: the good kind that works for you and the bad kind that works against you.

The good kind of procrastination is the kind that cautions you to wait until your story is ready to be written. Not everyone has this mechanism. If there's a story you want to write and every time you sit down to start page 1 or try to work on the outline, something just doesn't feel right and you can't move forward, don't panic. It might be that the idea has to cook in your head a little longer before it's ready to be made into a novel, like bread that has to rise before it's baked.

But if you keep putting off writing that outline or starting that research or sitting down to that first page of chapter one because you have to watch a rerun of *Friends* or read the sports page or clean your oven, it's probably the bad kind of procrastination. Most often this negative procrastination is brought on by the fear that your writing won't be good enough, a kind of writer's block. Don't use the word *block*, though—let's say *stuckness*.

If you keep procrastinating or feel stuck, stop and look inside. If your instinct tells you that your story is still cooking, give yourself some time. If your instinct tells you that you can't start yet because you're going to fail, push through the hesitation and just begin writing. Write anything. No one has to see it. You can fix it later or even toss it. If you can't seem to start with chapter one, try starting with your favorite scene from the middle, or use a warm-up exercise to break the ice. The best remedy for the fear of writing is writing.

RECOMMENDED READING

Zen in the Art of Writing, by Ray Bradbury. A combination of anecdotes and advice from one of science fiction's most passionate authors, *Zen* is deeply inspiring in the "idea gathering" stage of writing.

The Making of a Bestseller, by Brian Hill and Dee Power. While you fantasize your own rave review, you can hear about writing and selling bestsellers in the fifty interviews included in this book.

Writing Down the Bones, by Natalie Goldberg. This book offers unique instruction on writing as a natural act.

Page After Page: Discover the Confidence & Passion You Need to Start Writing & Keep Writing (No Matter What!), by Heather Sellers. If you start to feel stuck, here is an inspiring book that can help you get motivated again.

CHAPTER TWO:

beginning to write

OUTLINING YOUR STORY

Not every novelist uses an outline. However, maybe one in a million beginning writers sits down and writes a perfectly structured book without one. There are methods, like the ones described below, that you can use to make the outlining process less intimidating.

WHAT KIND OF BOOK ARE YOU OUTLINING?

If you want to sell this book, you should know who your potential readers are. Is it mystery? Horror? Erotica? Below is a brief list of genres and what the categories mean. If you don't already know where your story falls, go to the bookstore or library and browse the shelves. Read a page each of ten fantasy novels and see if you still think you're writing fantasy. Find your favorite author and see in which section he is shelved, if you don't already know. Below are some of the most popular genres and their definitions.

> **Armchair Mystery.** Same as a general mystery novel but not as gritty. Sometimes called *cozy*. Less sex, less graphic violence, and milder language.

Chick-Lit. Contemporary stories for women; although often centered on love and sex, are not traditional romances.

Children's. Novels for children tend to be for readers seven to twelve years old.

Erotica. Fiction centering on explicit sex.

Fantasy. Set in a world other than our own. Magic, wizards, witches, spells, and fantastic beasts are often involved. Sometimes the author draws from ancient religions or philosophies.

Historical Romance. A noncontemporary romance. Can range from prehistory to early twentieth century.

Horror. Whether supernatural (vampires, ghosts) or real (psycho-killers, sadists) the antagonist terrorizes the other characters. Involves one or all of: blood, guts, torture devices, psychological terrorism, sweat, tears, and other bodily fluids.

Legal Thriller. Like a suspense novel, only the plot centers on a trial.

Literary. The writing itself is viewed as more sophisticated than commercial fiction. Themes are given more weight than plot. If you win the Pulitzer Prize for Fiction, you write literature.

Mainstream. Fiction that has crossed out of a genre into popular readership. If an author of thrillers becomes so popular that everyone in the airport is reading her latest book, she has crossed out of suspense and is now a mainstream or commercial novelist. Perhaps last year her books were only in the suspense aisle at your local bookstore, but now she's on the big table when you first walk in. She might even have a cardboard stand just for her new novel.

Military Thriller. Action, adventure, suspense set in world of military life.

Mystery. Centers on the solving of a murder or some other crime.

Romance. Centers on the relationship between two people who eventually fall in love. The sexual content ranges from the equivalent of a G movie rating to an X. Usually employs female point of view (POV).

Science Fiction. Set in the future and in a reality of the author's creation. Always includes technology. Often includes other species, planets, weapons, vehicles, philosophies, and rituals.

Suspense. Drama centering on a dark threat (biological, homicidal, political) and keeping us in suspense until the last page.

Western. Adventures set in the American West, usually not contemporary.

Young Adult. Written for readers approximately grades seven through twelve.

The reason you might want to familiarize yourself with your genre before you start writing is to understand the length, number of chapters, POV, etc., your potential readers expect. You don't have to deliver what they're used to or comfortable with, but most book purchasers know what they want. They don't walk up to the cashier and say, "Surprise me."

CARDING THE STORY

In chapter one you read about listening for your idea and writing down notes about what you heard. Here is where those notes come into play. Take out that notebook of scribbling or that file folder filled with little scraps of paper. Take a package of 3 × 5 cards and copy each idea onto a card. Some will be broad: *Mary finds proof and destroys it.* Others will be very specific: *John sees a thread caught on the windshield and slips it into the envelope with Dave's letter while Beth isn't looking.* Even though some cards will have only a detail written on them, not a full-blown scene, we're still going to call these *scene cards.* Copy all the ideas down. Don't judge them yet.

If an idea is too long for a card, name it something that represents the whole and keep the longer version (the notebook page or slip of paper) for later when you write the actual scene. For now call it something brief like: *John takes thread.*

Once you have all your notes on scene cards, count them. If you have only twenty or so, you will be able to lay them out with no trouble. If you have a plethora of cards (more than fifty, let's say), sort them chronologically into three piles before you lay them out: (1) things that happen near the beginning of the story, (2) things that happen near the end of the story, and (3) things that happen somewhere in between. If you're not sure what pile to put the cards in, don't fret. Put them anywhere. The fun of making scene cards is that you can keep rearranging the pieces until the puzzle looks good. Here are some examples of the seeds of ideas that grew into famous stories:

- Toni Morrison came up with the idea for *Paradise* while researching ex-slaves who left plantations and started all-black communities after the Civil War.

- Elmore Leonard created the character of Karen Sisco, from *Out of Sight*, after seeing a photograph of a beautiful woman armed with a 9mm handgun and an enormous shotgun.

- Linda Bingham came up with the idea for the novel *Born on the Island* after losing a house to Hurricane Alicia in 1983.

As I started writing the novel *A Certain Slant of Light*, I wondered what it would be like to be a ghost and to be seen by a human being for the first time after having been invisible for over a century. This idea lead to a question—if someone can see her, how is he doing it? Why can only one person see her? Next I thought, perhaps the young man who can see her is like her, akin to her. Maybe he's a ghost, only he's walking around in a human body. This lead to the idea that, having this peculiar thing in common, the two would probably be very drawn to one another—perhaps would even fall in love. But what can they do? He's in flesh and she's a spirit. This led to the idea that they should find her a body. Now I had two ghosts hiding in bodies. What could make this situation worse? The homes of these two borrowed bodies should be so different from each other that a union would be nearly impossible.

Around this point, as I was getting to know these two troubled families, another idea came to me—the ghosts should realize at some point that they must give back the bodies. And this lead to another problem: How to lure back the souls that had abandoned the bodies? The two teens left their flesh behind because they were unhappy. What could call them back? And the next idea sprang from the last—what would it feel like if the male ghost was able to give back the boy's body before the female ghost could give back hers?

It is in this way—through a series of questions and possible answers—that one simple idea grew into a novel.

No matter how simple your idea, look at it for a while. Ask questions while jotting down notes—where might this story happen? Who might be affected? What year is it? What does the main character want? What does he fear? What could go wrong? What would be even worse? Soon you will have enough notes to start filling in scene cards.

ORGANIZING THE CARDS

If you ended up with only twenty to thirty cards you can use a kitchen table, but if you have three stacks of cards, find an open place on the floor or the dining room table. (A bed, even a king size, is not recommended. The first time you lean on the mattress to reach a card in the far corner, and they all slide together, you'll find out why.) Lay out the scene cards in order. Make your best guess. Nothing's permanent here. This is the easiest stage of the process in which to shift things around. So feel free.

Once you have them laid down in what you think might be the correct chronological order, read them through and see what you think. Remember, we're not done yet. This arrangement does not mean you have to write your story in chronological order. This is just a way of sorting the plot points.

It's possible that at this point you'll feel confused. Your cards won't read well. They might not even sound like they're from the same story. In this case, your novel might not be ready to be carded yet. Using the story of *Romeo and Juliet* by William Shakespeare, notice how an idea goes from vague to ready to outline.

NOT ENOUGH SCENES TO OUTLINE

- two families are feuding
- Boy and Girl from each fall in love
- secret wedding to Boy
- some kind of cool swordplay
- Boy has a friend who teases him

READY TO OUTLINE

- two families are feuding
- Boy and Girl from each fall in love
- Girl's folks pick fiancé for her
- secret wedding to Boy
- families brawl
- Boy's pal killed by Girl's cousin
- Boy kills Girl's cousin
- wedding night in hiding
- Boy banished
- Girl's other wedding set up
- Girl pretends to be dead to avoid it
- Boy believes her dead, kills self
- Girl finds Boy dead, kills self
- families step back from feuding

FILLING IN THE GAPS

Not every scene from the finished play is carded in the longer list above, but there is enough to start with. The rest can be filled in. The shorter list is not ready to be an outline yet. If your scene cards are this sparse in number and content, don't panic. Go back to listening for ideas. If the story is meant to be a novel, more scenes will come to you.

To fill in the gaps in your outline, think about what makes great storytelling. You have someone with a problem. You have a setting in time and space. (What year? What part of the world?) You have something working against this person.

What makes us love reading something? You'll hear more about plot and structure in chapter four, but for now think of it this way: Readers need three things to keep them turning the pages—believability, heart, and tension.

In the case of *Romeo and Juliet*, little details help to fill in the gaps in the scenes from the above list, paving the way for a successful outline. For example:

- When one of Girl's cousins kills Boy's best friend, it should start innocently so the violence is more of a shock. (Shakespeare fleshed out this scene so Mercutio, who is not even blood to Romeo's family, teases Juliet's cousin into a sword fight. It is Romeo's attempt to break up the fight that inadvertently causes the fatal wound.)

- The Boy and Girl should each have a confidant, but one of these should betray them to make it more heartbreaking. (In the play, Romeo has the faithful Friar, and Juliet the nurse who betrays her by changing sides and urging the girl to marry the wrong man.)

- There should be a hope that the Boy and Girl will end up happily together that gets dashed at the last minute by a twist of fate. (Shakespeare has the Friar's message of the "fake death" miss Romeo, who left as soon as he heard of Juliet's funeral from someone else.)

All three of these added scene cards provide heart or intimacy (we feel for the characters), believability (actions have realistic motivations), and tension (the brass ring is just out of reach).

Of course, fine storytelling is more complicated, but for the outline stage of your novel, you want to cover the basics: suspend disbelief, make the readers care about someone, and make them want something that might not happen or make them dread something that might.

SETUPS AND PAYOFFS

If there is a scene card near the end of your story that needs to be set up or explained, make sure there's a scene card earlier that takes care of this. For example, if at the end of your story your bookworm accountant defuses a bomb, you'd better have a scene card earlier in the outline that explains why he has this skill. If you want to play a card like that, you'd better set it up. And a half-assed setup won't help much. You can't just slip in a scene where the main character says, "My favorite hobby? Why, I enjoy a good bomb defusing!" If you can't make it believable and interesting, have someone else cut the wires. Or have the bomb go off.

If there is a scene near the beginning that needs to be followed through, look for the scene card near the end that is your payoff. If you write a scene early on that endears the main character to us because she is looking for her lost dog, you'd better find a place later in the story to include the dog again. Did she find him? Did she give up? Is he dead? Where's the payoff? There needs to be a reason we were introduced to the idea of that dog near the beginning, or it needs to be cut.

NONCHRONOLOGICAL OUTLINES

Now, if you like, you can mix up the scene cards and look at them in a different order to see how it feels, but number them on the back chronologically so it will be easy to put them back in order if you want. It's possible you might like telling the story out of order. Often a story starts at the most significant point of action, and the background gets filled in afterwards. Sometimes a character tells us about her childhood or how she met her husband or what her son was like when he was little by looking back at a significant moment.

Sometimes we have two sets of time we visit alternately. In Stephen King's *The Green Mile*, the story goes back and forth between the protagonist's days as a prison guard and his present life in a retirement home. It's fine to rearrange your scene cards to create a nonchronological outline, but have a good reason for doing it. Don't do it just to be different or artsy. Look for the right form for your particular story. (Obviously, if your plot is about nonlinear time, like *Slaughterhouse-Five*, by Kurt Vonnegut, or *The Time Traveler's Wife*, by Audrey Niffenegger, you will not leave your cards in chronological order.) Pause and ponder: What order will be the most satisfying for your book?

CHAPTER BREAKS

Novels have all different styles of chapter breaks. Some have dozens of short chapters, some have a few huge chapters (often called parts or books), and some have no chapters at all. The chapter break should be placed strategically. If, while constructing your outline, the thought of separating your plot into chapters confuses you or saps your energy, don't make chapter break decisions yet. Write a first draft of the whole novel, then come back to this section to place your chapter breaks with intention during your rewrite. But if, as you think about your story, the discussion of chapter breaks stimulates your imagination, construct your outline with chapter breaks included.

Take a look at your favorite novels. How did the author break up the story? The most important thing is that at the end of each chapter the reader should be craving the next chapter. Make the reader want to turn the next page. An old-fashioned cliffhanger is not required (though they still work), but tension of some kind is essential. End not where the action lulls but where it is the most dynamic. Give the reader new information right before you cut him off. The following are examples of strategic chapter breaks.

BRIDGET JONES'S DIARY, BY HELEN FIELDING
14 CHAPTERS, 271 PAGES

At the end of chapter "April" Bridget hints that she might be pregnant and then titles the next chapter "Mother-to-Be"—again, we have no self-control. We must read on. It's especially easy to keep reading Fielding's novel because the diary entries are often short. Just one more, we tell ourselves. It's addictive.

LULLABY, **BY CHUCK PALAHNIUK**
44 CHAPTERS, 260 PAGES

Chapter six: The hero tries a killer poem out on his unsuspecting boss. If it works, the man will be dead before daybreak. Instead of ending the chapter with news of the death, Palahniuk stops right after the hero decides not to try to explain the experiment to his employer.

"We both need some rest, Duncan," I say, "Maybe we can talk about it in the morning."

Of course we can't wait—we have to start chapter seven.

THE PRINCESS BRIDE, **BY WILLIAM GOLDMAN**
8 CHAPTERS, 399 PAGES

Chapter five: We know one of the characters has spent his whole life trying to track down an anonymous nobleman with six fingers on his right hand. At the end of chapter five another character notices that the man who is about to torture him to death has an extra finger on one hand! It doesn't matter that chapter five was one hundred pages long, or that chapter six is fifty-nine pages long; we have to turn the page.

CLIFFHANGERS

Cliffhanger is a term coined from its own best example—if you want to make sure the reader is enthralled, when you have your hero chasing the villain toward a cliff and you want to change scenes (or chapters), have the hero fall off that cliff and leave him dangling there while you show us what's going on back at the ranch. Cliffhangers can be psychological as well as physical. Perhaps your hero has just found out her true love is already married, but the chapter ends before we hear (feel) her reaction. A cliffhanger means something huge is at stake, and we are made to wait for the outcome at the most suspenseful point in the action. You can see why cliffhangers are good chapter closers.

To pinpoint your cliffhangers (or to create some), look at your story lines. Where are the moments when an action and reaction might be separated? As a basic, albeit corny, example, let's say a car flips over and your hero tumbles out alive. The separation point would be, of course, between the flip and the tumbling out alive. Let's say your hero goes to answer the door and instead of her ally being on the welcome mat, it's the villain, who comes in and attacks her. The separation goes between seeing it is the villain and having him enter. Perhaps your hero has been tracking a murderer with a certain nickname and, as he's listening to a voice mail from his girlfriend, he overhears someone in the background call her this name—now he realizes his sweetheart is the killer. You might separate the chapters between hearing the nickname and his reaction—it drives readers crazy (in a good way) when they think they know of a danger before the hero does. This all goes along with the idea of ending each chapter with new information.

Make that new information so important to the reader that he will slap the page open to the next chapter and read on. Even at two in the morning on a weeknight with a head cold.

WRITING DOWN YOUR OUTLINE

Now copy the scene cards on paper, leaving about two lines blank between each entry. Use one page for each chapter. Go through the outline again in this format and fill in the blank lines with new ideas that come to you as you read the outline aloud to yourself. New scenes for expanding your story will continue to bubble up in your mind. For a first novel, having one page of longhand notes per chapter should be the right amount of planning.

Now you have a page called "chapter one" that will help launch you into your novel, but first you have to decide who will tell this tale.

POINT OF VIEW

The point of view (POV) is from whose eyes we see the story. You can certainly have multiple POVs, but let's start with a single POV. Whose perspective are we taking? Through which glasses are we filtering the story? Most of the time, your main character, your hero, your protagonist, will be chosen for POV. For instance, it is Scarlett's, not Melly's, POV in Margaret Mitchell's *Gone With the Wind* because it is more fun to be Scarlett than Melly. In Alice Sebold's *The Lovely Bones,* the POV is that of the murdered girl, not of the girl's father or the homicide detective—if the story wasn't told by the victim, it would be just another murder mystery instead of a trip to the other side of death. John Knowles's *A Separate Peace* is told from Gene's POV instead of Finny's because it's more heartbreaking to be the one who shook the tree than the one who fell from it.

There are cases when the central character is not the POV character. In F. Scott Fitzgerald's *The Great Gatsby*, it is not Jay Gatsby but his neighbor Nick Carraway who provides the POV. Gatsby is out of touch with reality in such a way that the story needs a normal perspective to provide insight and empathy. Though Atticus Finch is the central character in Harper Lee's *To Kill a Mockingbird*, his daughter, Scout, narrates the story that he himself would be too humble to tell. The narrative voice of a woman looking back at her father, filtering the story through her memories of childhood, provides the perfect POV.

Think about your own story. Which POV will be the most effective? Whose take on reality do we need? In whose heart will we feel most alive? You should never tell a story like J.K. Rowling's *Harry Potter and the Sorcerer's Stone* from the Dursleys' POV—they are not central enough and they're depressing to be with. If you were brilliant you might be able to tell *Romeo and Juliet* from the Friar's POV, or *Hamlet* from the ghost's POV, and make it work, but most stories are best told through the character who has the most to lose, who has the biggest adventure, who will save the day.

When you know who your POV person will be, you still have to decide what "person" or tense to use: first, third, or second. (I put second last because it is not recommended.)

First-Person Past: I walked into a bar with a chicken on my head.

Third-Person Past: She walked into a bar with a chicken on her head.

Second-Person Past: You walked into a bar with a chicken on your head. (See? Not recommended.)

There is also:

First-Person Present: I walk into a bar with a chicken on my head.

Third-Person Present: She walks into a bar with a chicken on her head.

Second-Person Present: You walk into a bar with a chicken on your head. (Don't do it.)

Future tense? *I will walk into a bar. She will walk into a bar. You will walk into a bar.* Don't even think about it.

First and third, past or present, are the most common POV choices. Try them for a scene or two—see how they feel with your story and characters. Present tense might add a certain urgency to the action, but it might not match the tone of your story. Past tense is more common than present tense and is a natural way to repeat a story: *In the beginning there was the Word.* Try it for a scene. How does it feel? First person can be effective for making the reader bond with the narrator and his emotions and thoughts, but it is limiting in that only things the first-person narrator can see and hear may be included in the action. Experiment with this one as well—does it create problems for your story line? Take a look at a few examples:

THIRD-PERSON PAST

He broke out the window with a Rockette-worthy kick.

—*Runaway Heart*, by Stephen J. Cannell

FIRST-PERSON PAST

The summer my father bought the bear, none of us was born.

—*The Hotel New Hampshire*, by John Irving

THIRD-PERSON PRESENT

They shoot the white girl first.

—*Paradise*, by Toni Morrison

FIRST-PERSON PRESENT

I'm just about to ask for a little clarification on the peeing thing when her cell phone rings.

—*The Nanny Diaries*, by Emma McLaughlin and Nicola Kraus

You might have noticed from the examples that first person is more intimate, but not every protagonist makes a good first-person narrator. Scrooge would not have been able to tell us his story first person given the attitude he carried for the first half of his story.

TYPES OF THIRD PERSON

Third person can be effective for observing characters from the outside and reflecting on their behavior, but when you choose this POV you must decide which kind of third person you will use: omniscient third person, inner limited, or outer limited.

1. Omniscient Third Person (or Unlimited)

With omniscient third person, the storyteller can look into the hearts and minds of anyone and everyone in the novel. Omniscient is tricky because having the godlike power to experience the plot through any number of characters, at any moment in time, can lead to a lack of focus. We might not feel as strongly for the protagonist if we are constantly being dragged out of his feelings to dart into the heads of his cab driver, his neighbor, and even his dog.

If you do decide to write your first novel in third omniscient, stick to one character's head per scene unless you're writing a confrontation between enemies or lovers. If you want to use omniscient only because you want to show the villain hiding the pill bottle under the candy machine when he's by himself, while the rest of the book works better told only through the eyes of the hero, find some other way to get that candy machine into the story. Use omniscient consistently, or not at all. E.L. Doctorow's *Ragtime* uses omniscient third. Notice how these versions of greeting a morning, the first from Mother's point of view, the second from Father's, have very different tones.

> **Mother:** Ah, what a summer it was! Each morning Mother opened the white curtained glass doors of her room and stood looking at the sun as it rose above the sea.

> **Father:** Now every morning Father rose and tasted his mortal being. He wondered if his dislike of Coalhouse Walker, which had been instantaneous, was based not on the man's color but on his being engaged in an act of courtship, a suspenseful enterprise that suggested the best of life was yet to come.

2. Inner Limited

Grammatically written in third person, inner limited is similar to first person in that the storyteller is looking at life through only one character's heart and mind. As you tell the story from one character's experience you can use the vocabulary and thought patterns of that person or you can use a contrasting style. Not all protagonists make good narrators. If you think it will make your novel better, you can write about a king with the language of a peasant or tell the story of a coal miner using the voice of a philosopher. In a scene with two characters, you can certainly let us know how both are feeling by way of gestures and words, but only one person's thoughts and feelings can be tapped into through narration.

In this scene from James Joyce's *The Dead*, a man and his wife have a conversation about her first sweetheart, but only the husband's inner thoughts and feelings are revealed.

> "And what did he die of so young, Gretta? Consumption, was it?"
> "I think he died of me," she answered.
> A vague terror seized Gabriel at this answer, as if, at that hour when he had hoped to triumph, some impalpable and vindictive being was coming against him, gathering forces against him in its vague world.

3. Outer Limited

With outer limited, the storyteller gives us only what can be seen and heard, not what the characters are thinking. If you are smart, you can make this style work for you. Choose the perfect situations and setting, the precise gestures and dialogue to touch your reader. Be careful, though. If used incorrectly, this style lacks the emotion needed to keep readers involved. If readers can only see and hear what the characters say and do, the way a camera films a scene in a movie, be sure the heart of your story is on your sleeve. The following passage is presented first in third-person inner limited and then in outer limited:

INNER LIMITED

"I gave her up," said Dee, never releasing the photograph.

His chest cramped as if his ribs were breaking on the left side. He tried to focus on the image. She was telling him that he had once had a daughter and that he had missed her completely. Dee was only giving him a tiny glimpse of her, this amazing being with blue eyes, a little creature that he would never smell or lift from a crib or hear speak his name.

OUTER LIMITED

"I gave her up," said Dee, holding out a photograph toward him.

He caught a glimpse of a little face with blue eyes, four teeth, and a dimple in her right cheek. He held out his right hand toward the picture, his left hand clutched his heart. But Dee never released her grip on the photograph. She simply waved it past him, letting the glossy surface brush his trembling fingers, and then tucked it away again in her purse.

Remember, outer limited is what you might hear and see on stage during a play. Third-person omniscient is more common than either inner limited or outer limited.

MULTIPLE NARRATORS

A novel can have many narrators. In a first novel, I don't recommend this approach. Multiple narrators are hard to manage effectively, but here are some tips followed by some examples of multiple narrators that worked.

1. If you decide to use multiple narrators, choose them well. There should be a reason you decide to have both the man and his father narrate your story. They should contribute different insights, different information, or at least a different understanding of the same information. If you are writing a romantic comedy, you might want to let both your lovers be narrators. If you are writing a thriller, you might want to let both your detective and your killer be narrators. Perhaps even your victim. But ask yourself this question first—is your novel truly made better by it?

2. If you decide to use multiple narrators, don't choose too many. Two or three, perhaps even half a dozen, if that's how many members there are in the rock band, or nuns in the lifeboat. But all twelve jurors are probably too many.

3. Define where one narrator ends and another comes in. Use separate chapters, a different type font, or another device, like three asterisks in the center of the page.

4. Give your narrators unique voices. If your multiple narrators all sound the same, write your story in third omniscient instead. The only reason to have multiple narrators is because there is contrast between the ways in which they tell the story. You can have them all in first person, or all in third limited—any POV you'd like—or you can have one written in this style and one in that style. The important thing is to make sure they sound like themselves and they serve your story well.

Multiple narrators worked well for William Faulkner when he wrote his brilliant novel *As I Lay Dying*. The chapters alternate—narrated by the family members and acquaintances of a woman named Addie. Depending on which narrator is speaking, Addie is either dying or dead. One chapter is even narrated by Addie herself. The chapter headings indicate who is telling the story. Notice how distinct the voices are from one another:

> **Addie:** … that we had had to use one another by words like spiders dangling by their mouths from a beam, swinging and twisting and never touching,

and that only through the blows of the switch could my blood and their blood flow as one stream.

Cash, oldest son: But there wasn't no use in that. "There ain't no use in that," I said. "We can wait till she is underground." A fellow that's going to spend the rest of his life locked up, he ought to be let to have what pleasure he can before he goes.

Vardaman, youngest son: When they get finished they are going to put her in it and then for a long time I couldn't say it. I saw the dark stand up and go whirling away and I said "Are you going to nail her up in it, Cash? Cash? Cash?" I got shut up in the crib the new door was too heavy for me it went shut I couldn't breathe because the rat was breathing up all the air. I said "Are you going to nail it shut, Cash? Nail it? *Nail* it?"

Multiple narrators also worked well in Barbara Kingsolver's *The Poisonwood Bible*. The wife and daughters of a missionary preacher take turns, in alternating chapters, describing their life in Africa. Their narrations are so personal and distinct that it's like reading different diaries:

Orleana, the mother: And so it came to pass that we stepped down there on a plane we believed unformed, where only darkness moved on the face of the waters. Now you laugh, day and night, as you gnaw at my bones.

Ruth May, youngest daughter: The women are all Mama Something, even if they don't have children. Like Mama Tataba, our cooking lady. Rachel calls her Mama Tater Tots. But she won't cook those. I wish she would.

Adah, middle daughter, lame on one side: Walk to Learn. I and Path. Long one is Congo. Congo is one long path and I learn to walk. This is the name of my story, forward and backward.

GENRE AND POV

Best-selling authors in certain genres might use certain POV styles more often than others—lots of detective stories and romances are written in first person, lots of literary novels in third. Look at your favorite novels within the genre you have chosen. What POV do you run across most often? I find there is quite a variety out there. The following is a list of classic and best-selling novels in a range of genres.

MYSTERY

- *Black Alley,* by Mickey Spillane: first person/past tense
- *Incident at Badamya,* by Dorothy Gilman: third-person omniscient/ past tense

FANTASY/SCIENCE FICTION

- *Saucer,* by Stephen Coonts: third-person omniscient/past tense
- *What Dreams May Come,* by Richard Matheson: first person/past tense

ROMANCE

- *Up Island,* by Anne Rivers Siddons: first person/past tense
- *Gone With the Wind,* by Margaret Mitchell: third-person limited/ past tense

CHICK-LIT

- *He's Got to Go,* by Sheila O'Flanagan: third-person omniscient/ past tense
- *Bridget Jones's Diary,* by Helen Fielding: first person/past tense

HORROR

- *Rosemary's Baby,* by Ira Levin: third-person limited/past tense
- *The Dead Zone,* by Stephen King: third-person omniscient/past tense
- *Lullaby,* by Chuck Palahniuk: first person/present tense

WESTERN

- *Lonesome Dove,* by Larry McMurtry: third-person omniscient/ past tense
- *Sackett's Land,* by Louis L'Amour: first person/past tense

POPULAR FICTION

- *A Time to Kill*, by John Grisham: third-person omniscient/past tense

- *The Wedding*, by Nicholas Sparks: first person/past tense

LITERARY

- *The Catcher in the Rye*, by J.D. Salinger: first person/past tense

- *The Master Butchers Singing Club*, by Louise Erdrich: third-person omniscient/past tense

CHILDREN'S AND YOUNG ADULT

- *Harry Potter and the Sorcerer's Stone*, by J.K. Rowling: third-person omniscient/past tense

- *Shadow Spinner*, by Susan Fletcher: first person/past tense

Write your story the best way you can—one narrator or ten—using your gut. Just because a recent best-selling mystery was written in first person or your favorite romance was written in third person doesn't mean you need to go against your instinct for entertaining storytelling.

VOICE

When people talk about an author's voice, they're not talking about who you chose for POV or whether you decided on first or third person. Your voice is the way you write—the sound of your prose—and what makes your writing unique. Here are some examples of varied voices:

> Anyway. Here's how not to plan a career: a) split up with girlfriend; b) junk college; c) go to work in a record shop; d) stay in record shops for rest of life. You see those pictures of people in Pompeii and you think, how weird: One quick game of dice after your tea and you're frozen, and that's how people remember you for the next few thousand years.
>
> —*High Fidelity*, by Nick Hornby

In the desert the tools of survival are underground—troglodyte caves, water sleeping within a buried plant, weapons, a plane.

—*The English Patient*, by Michael Ondaatje

Orbiting this at a distance of roughly ninety-eight million miles is an utterly insignificant little blue-green planet whose ape-descended life forms are so amazingly primitive that they still think digital watches are a pretty neat idea.

—*The Hitchhiker's Guide to the Galaxy*, by Douglas Adams

It is not my own memory, but later you will understand how I know these things. You would call it not memory so much as a dream of the past, something in the blood, something recalled from him, it may be, while he still bore me in his body.

—*The Crystal Cave*, by Mary Stewart

I've already got one surefire contemporary audition monologue (Mozart in *Amadeus*, a prankish man-boy I was born to play), but I need to come up with a classical one, too. So I've bought myself a brand-new *Complete Works of Shakespeare*—a really nice one, with a velvet cover and gold leaf on the ends of the pages—and I'm going to spend my entire summer reading it. Plus work on my tan.

—*How I Paid for College*, by Marc Acito

I am not a smart man, particularly, but one day, at long last, I stumbled from the dark woods of my own, and my family's, and my country's past, holding in my hands these truths: that love grows from the rich loam of forgiveness; that mongrels make good dogs; that the evidence of God exists in the roundness of things.

—*I Know This Much Is True*, by Wally Lamb

In his dream the year seemed to be happening all at one time, all the seasons blending together. Apple trees hanging heavy with fruit but yet unaccountably blossoming, ice rimming the spring, okra plants blooming yellow and maroon, maple leaves red as October, corn tops tasseling, a stuffed chair pulled up to the glowing parlor hearth, pumpkins shining in the fields …

—*Cold Mountain*, by Charles Frazier

EMBRACE YOUR OWN STYLE

When Michelangelo was just beginning his career, he tried to age one of his sculptures, a reclining cupid, in the hope of fooling a buyer into believing it was an older statue and worth more money. Think about it. Making a piece of art look like it was not a Michelangelo in order to increase its value. If you feel tempted to imitate a current best-selling author, remember that you may be tomorrow's star. Claim your own voice. Be yourself.

Find Your Voice: Exercises

If you are new to writing, it might take a while to get into your groove and find your voice. Try one of the following exercises.

• **Paraphrased Passages.** Open a book that you perceive as having a very different voice from your own. Choose a paragraph and rewrite it with the same meaning, but in your own words. Try to make it as distinctly your own as you can. Notice what was the most changed.

• **Character Chat.** Take your protagonist, or antagonist, and imagine her in a setting, or staring at an object, that is in high contrast to her usual world. A preschool teacher describing a prison yard. A brain surgeon describing a Native American dance. A billionaire describing the flavor of SPAM Luncheon Meat. A homeless child describing an opera performance. If you try several of these "chats" you'll start to notice that one kind of perspective on life feels more right than the others. Why is that?

• **Many Moods.** Take a single page of any novel and rewrite it three ways—as if everything about the story infuriated you, as if it was breaking your heart, and as if it scared the hell out of you. Do the same with any one page of a novel and rewrite it twice, once as formally as you can and once as informally as you can. Now look at these pages you've created. Which one seems the most natural?

Maybe all of these exercises frustrate you. Great! Take out a fresh piece of paper and start writing about it.

If after trying these exercises you still feel unsettled about your voice, don't worry. Your most important job is to tell the best story you can in the best way you can. Stop thinking about voice for a while—let it go until you've written a few chapters and feel more confident. If you write while feeling self-conscious about your voice, your voice will sound self-conscious. Relax—your voice will come.

Annie Dillard, in her book *The Writing Life*, describes her struggle to chop kindling. She was hacking away at a chunk of wood on her chopping block, making tiny splinters fly yet making no headway, until she had a dream in which she realized she should aim her axe not at the piece of wood but at the chopping block underneath it. Suddenly her axe could make contact with the block, and the wood in the way split in two.

When you find yourself overwhelmed by concepts—POV, tense, structure—think about the heart of your novel, the reason you wanted to write this story in the first place. That's what you're aiming at.

RECOMMENDED READING

The Writer's Journey, by Christopher Vogler. Based on the teachings of Joseph Campbell, this book applies the mythic structure to the art of storytelling.

Novelist's Essential Guide to Creating Plot, by J. Madison Davis. As you think up new scene cards to beef up your outline, you can look to Davis's book for tips on maximizing intensity, solving problems, and creating subplots that work.

Mastering Point of View, by Sherri Szeman. This book shows you how to use POV to reveal or obscure your character's motivations, how to remain tasteful in violent or erotic scenes, and how to handle multiple POVs without being overwhelmed.

CHAPTER THREE:

the bones of your story

STRUCTURE AND PLOT

Plot is what happens in your story, and structure is the shape of that plot. Your outline is a map of the plot and structure you've worked out so far. Now we'll look at what makes a great plot and which story structures work the best. No one hires an architect who doesn't have a blueprint. Your outline is your blueprint—we need to make sure it's sound before you put a lot of work into building your novel from it.

When you're just getting started, you need to give your right brain a chance to play in the orchards of creativity. That's why it's best to listen to your ideas and scene card your outline before considering structure. Then, your left brain gets a chance to do its favorite dance.

There's no secret recipe for a good plot. Brilliance can be born of anything from a twelve-layered mystery to one old man in a boat trying to catch a fish. It's all in the telling. But make sure your plot has the elements of great storytelling: believability, heart, and tension. (We'll address believability in chapter six when we discuss detail, and we'll address heart in chapter five when we discuss character. We'll discuss tension here after a short introduction to structure.)

What kind of structure makes a great story? Here are some examples of story designs that work:

Rags to Riches. A character (Cinderella, Rocky) starts at the bottom and, through many adventures that show off his pluckiness, ends up on top. This structure works because everyone can relate to being at the bottom and everyone hopes to find happiness. All feels right with the world when the good guy (or gal) gets rewarded.

Boy Meets Girl. Two people meet, we want them to end up together, they are separated by something, and through many adventures they get back together for a happy ending. Romance novels usually have this structure. Fred and Ginger movies do, too. But the ending does not *have* to be happy, as in *Cold Mountain*, by Charles Frazier, or the relationship between Catherine and Heathcliff in *Wuthering Heights*, by Emily Brontë. Whether or not the fates were aligned, this structure works as long as the love was real. Readers want to believe in true love.

Coming of Age. The protagonist grows up and discovers a strength from within. This can be a literal coming of age, when a character goes from childhood to adulthood, as in *Jacob Have I Loved*, by Katherine Paterson, or *The Red Badge of Courage*, by Stephen Crane, or it can be an emotional coming of age, where a character has to transform emotionally or spiritually into the person he is meant to be. In Steve Martin's *The Pleasure of My Company*, the obsessive-compulsive hero has to battle his own mind to become a functioning adult.

Fall of the Corrupt. A bad person is brought down from a seat of power to the feet of justice: *The Caine Mutiny*, by Herman Wouk, for example.

The Making of a Hero. The protagonist starts in humble powerlessness, is at first reluctant or doubtful, then rises to save the day: for example, *The Dead Zone*, by Stephen King, or *Harry Potter and the Sorcerer's Stone*, by J.K. Rowling.

There's No Place Like Home. The protagonist longs to throw off her past and strives to get the goodies while the getting is good, only to discover that greed has a price and the original situation is ultimately the better deal. *The Wonderful Wizard of Oz*, by L. Frank Baum, is a classic example. Faust-based tales are also examples—*The Devil and Daniel Webster*, by Stephen Vincent Benet; *The Year the Yankees Lost the Pennant*, by Douglass Wallop; *The Firm*, by John Grisham.

Salvation. Someone struggles to open the damaged heart of another, the way Heidi warms her grandfather's heart. (This one doesn't work well without a happy ending.) It can also work with someone saving not just one heart but a whole community, as in *Chocolat*, by Joanne Harris.

Another way of looking at types of story structures is through the concepts of Man vs. Man, Man vs. Nature, Man vs. Society, and Man vs. Self.

Man vs. Man. The protagonist is fighting a person or persons—your hero is battling the villain who wants to steal his land, romance his sweetheart, ruin his reputation.

Man vs. Nature. The protagonist is fighting some literal force of nature—your hero is determined to get back to her family and has to fight a raging blizzard to do so.

Man vs. Society. The protagonist is fighting a group of people with a certain mind-set or code—your hero is trying to set up a college for young men and women of color in 1950s Alabama, to the disapproval of the Klan.

Man vs. Self. The two halves of the protagonist's personality are fighting—your hero wants to keep everyone happy and at the same time needs to break free. Will she stay in her loveless marriage for the children's sake, or run off with the traveling salesman?

Your story does not have to easily fall into any of the above categories, but it needs to do what they all do—deliver. Readers want to care about the characters and what will happen next. And when readers pick up your book, they make a deal with you. If they buy your book and it's a romance, they expect to fall in love. If it's a thriller, they expect to be thrilled. No matter what kind of story you choose to write, when it's done it needs to hold up its end of the bargain.

ARE YOU WRITING A SUBCULTURE STORY?

Sterling Watson, whose first novel, *Weep No More My Brother*, was about prison life, believes that many first novels are subculture books. A young protagonist is shockingly thrown into a strange, new world with its own rules, language, hierarchy of characters, goals, prizes, rites of passage, and themes. Watson believes the subculture must be implied, rather than explained, so the reader is thrown into this new world in the same shocking fashion as the protagonist. Some examples include:

- *The Great Gatsby*, by F. Scott Fitzgerald: the rich
- *A Separate Peace*, by John Knowles: prep school
- *The Godfather*, by Mario Puzo: the Mafia
- *The Secret History*, by Donna Tartt: elite colleges
- *Hell's Angels*, by Hunter S. Thompson: motorcycle gangs

USING THE THREE-ACT STRUCTURE

To get a fix on the shape of your story, divide your plot into three acts.

Act I. You create a problem for your characters and bring them to a turning point.

Act II. You complicate the story with tension and deepen the characters, holding out hope but throwing wrenches into the works, then end with another turning point.

Act III. You make the situation even harder to overcome, build to a climax, and deliver the resolution. The story can either end happily or unhappily.

Here are some examples of stories broken into three acts.

THE THREE BEARS

Act I. A family of bears has a problem with the temperature of their breakfast food. They go for a walk. While they are out, a little girl shows up at the house and (here's a turning point in your plot) she's *hungry*.

Act II. Goldilocks tries the various bowls of food, the chairs, and the beds. She's cuddled down for a nap upstairs when the bears come home and (here's the next turning point in your plot) they don't know she's upstairs, and she doesn't know they're downstairs.

Act III. The bears discover, one by one, that their furniture and vittles have been tampered with. They climb the stairs and find a human child in the smallest bed. Goldilocks wakes (the climax) and runs away screaming. The resolution, though not perfect, at least leaves the bears with a house free of humans and with most of their furniture intact. (We also assume Goldilocks has learned a lesson and will no longer break into strangers' houses, steal food, or destroy chairs.)

STAR WARS

Act I. There is trouble afoot, a hero is needed, Princess Leia calls for help, Luke Skywalker meets the wise mentor Obi-Wan but refuses the call to act. The turning point comes when Luke's aunt and uncle are killed and he leaves home ready to accept his role as hero.

Act II. Obi-Wan and Luke find allies in Han Solo and Chewbacca, they face danger as they rescue Princess Leia, Obi-Wan's death is a sacrifice for the cause. The turning point comes when Han quits and Luke goes on without him.

Act III. The final battle and the return of Han. The climax occurs when the Death Star is blown up.

your first novel

Act I. The concept of the DNA experiments is introduced and the major players brought in. The turning point is *Oh my God!* there are real dinosaurs walking around.

Act II. Conflict is created between the scientists who are curious about dinosaurs but have a respectful fear of nature and the business people who are greedy and foolish. The humans are placed in the dinosaur world. The turning point is when the humans discover that the fences are down and the dinosaurs are hunting them—it's life or death now.

Act III. Dinosaurs munch on some people and miss others—a chain of action cliffhangers. The climax occurs when the humans escape.

Look for the three-act structure in your own story. Where are your turning points? Where does the plot thicken? Where is the beginning of the end? If you can't find the dramatic peaks, look back at your scene cards and find the best spots to raise the stakes. You don't want a flat story line. Give your plot shape.

DENOUEMENT

Denouement is the way a story winds down after the climax. This is when the story lines resolve. You don't start rolling the end credits on *Star Wars* as soon as the Death Star explodes. You don't bring down the curtain as Juliet stabs herself. You don't end *To Kill a Mockingbird* with the discovery of Bob Ewell's dead body. There needs to be an unraveling and a debriefing. A brief debriefing—you don't want to go on too long. Go back and read the ends of your favorite novels. Try and feel where the climax ends and denouement begins. Now think about the climax of your own novel. How will you resolve your story lines? As readers we need a little decompression time, especially if the book is crammed with action or full of psychological suspense.

There are certain circumstances in which denouement is not recommended. If you are ending your novel with a kind of surprise, it might be more effective to leave your readers in shock. On the last page of *Rebecca*, Daphne du Maurier catches us off guard by closing with a powerfully understated description of the great manor house at Manderley burning down. It is so short we are left breathless, especially because the rest of the details in the story, down to what was served for tea, were described at length.

Denouement may also be excluded if the suddenness of the ending is meant to make the reader think—"How can it end there? We never found out who killed the dog. *Or did we?*" If upon reflection the reader realizes the clues were there all along—the fact that the bicycle was gone means the butler must have done it—denouement is excluded in favor of an abrupt ending that encourages the readers to tie off the loose ends themselves.

TENSION

Tension, that combination of conflict and suspense, is indispensable—it's what makes a reader buy your book after flipping it open and reading only one page. It's what makes a reader stay up all night racing through your book.

Make sure there is always something we're waiting for (suspense) and there's trouble at every turn (conflict). There always has to be fear, the possibility that we will lose something we want badly. When the reader is worried about what might happen in the next scene, he will not be able to put the book down. Here are some examples of common conflicts as applied to the classic structures we looked at earlier in this chapter.

> **Rags to Riches.** The antagonist or a group tries to block the protagonist from success. Cinderella is blocked by her evil stepmother and stepsisters.
>
> **Boy Meets Girl.** The antagonist (or something like self-doubt or social norms) stands between the two lovers. In *Pride and Prejudice*, by Jane Austen, as you can imagine, pride and prejudice stand in the way of the future Mr. and Mrs. Darcy.

Coming of Age. The protagonist (the person evolving) fights the transformation out of self-doubt, or an antagonist (or group) refuses to acknowledge the evolution. In *The Pleasure of My Company*, the reclusive protagonist literally has to learn to step off a curb before he can find true love.

Fall of the Corrupt. We want the person in power to get his just desserts, but he fights and weasels out of justice's grip many times before the end. In Charles Dickens's *Nicholas Nickleby*, it's the destructive acts of Ralph Nickleby, everything from sexual harassment to child abuse, that make his eventual financial and emotional breakdown so powerful.

The Making of a Hero. The chosen one is at first reluctant. The enemy is strong and almost destroys the hero. In *Harry Potter and the Sorcerer's Stone*, Harry starts out by insisting that he can't possibly be a wizard and is nearly defeated by "he-who-must-not-be-named" before winning the battle (though not the war).

There's No Place Like Home. People and circumstances make the wrong decision look right to the protagonist, but soon the false happiness starts to fall apart. In *The Year the Yankees Lost the Pennant*, the devil, the other woman, the team, and baseball fans across America all lull Joe into a false state of well-being while the reader knows that by selling his soul he's made a mistake that he'll have to pay for.

Salvation. The hard heart, or cold community, refuses for a long time to be healed by the protagonist. Until nearly the end of *Chocolat*, religious tradition resists the invitation to the proverbial party.

STAKES

To heighten tension, raise your stakes. When Scarlett took Melly out of Atlanta, they weren't just fleeing from the war; the whole city was in flames. In Arthur Golden's *Memoirs of a Geisha*, failing to win the Chairman as her patron would not only mean Sayuri would never have true love, it might also mean failure as a geisha and a life of poverty and shame. Harry Potter wasn't just defending himself at the climax of *Harry Potter and the Sorcerer's Stone*; he was protecting the entire world from evil. What is at risk in your story? How can you heighten the drama by raising those stakes?

Is your hero about to lose his girlfriend? Maybe it should be his wife. Maybe she's carrying their first child. Is the hero risking her reputation? Could she also have her sanity on the line? If the villain wins, what will be lost? Will a trial go wrong and an innocent be imprisoned? Executed? Will a child be given to the wrong parent? Does that parent mistreat the child? How could the situation be worse?

On a grand scale, our gut instincts tell us that if Robin Hood had not felled the Sheriff of Nottingham, if Richard the Lionheart had not returned to the throne, not only would England have fallen, but all the world would have suffered, too. In *Star Wars*, if the Jedi had not won, long, long ago in a galaxy far, far away, would we even exist to hear about it?

On a more personal scale, our gut instincts tell us that if Bridget Jones does not end up with Mark Darcy, true love does not exist. We know that if Atticus Finch does not turn the other cheek when Bob Ewell spits in his face, there is no hope for the nobility of humankind. A story doesn't have to involve a nuclear bomb to make us feel there is a lot at stake.

How does Harper Lee make us feel all our hopes are balanced on one man's shoulders? Why do we feel Mr. Rochester is the only man for Jane Eyre? We'll be heartbroken if Bridget doesn't get Mark Darcy because Bridget would be. We have almost become her by the end of the book. Small stakes become huge stakes when we've developed an intimacy with the characters.

That being said, don't be fooled—it isn't just small stakes that need character intimacy. Maybe you're writing about huge stakes. The hugest—the universe will explode if the hero doesn't make it to the red button in time. We still need to feel for, feel with, the hero, or we won't believe in or worry about his universe. (We'll talk more about making characters accessible in chapter six.) Raising the stakes only works if the characters care about the outcome and we care about the characters.

Just a reminder—tension is an essential element in any novel. No matter if your genre is comedy, romance, or thriller—tension is required. You might be dealing with a different style of tension in a mystery than in a chick-lit romp, but it's still tension. There must always be something we long for and haven't received yet, something we fear we'll never receive. Or something we greatly dread that is just around the corner, something we're worried about. There should be conflict at every turn, tension on every page, new information at the end of every chapter, no matter what genre you have chosen.

DOWNTIME

The term *downtime*, when referring to computers or machines, means a disruption in service caused by a malfunction. But writers use downtime on purpose to balance the tension—downtime is in contrast to action. Look at the most successful thrillers. A scene of wild action will often be followed by a quiet conversation, a love scene, narrative reflection, a subplot with a subtle clue, a scene of family life, even a dream. Your novel should take the reader on a thrill ride, whether you're writing a thriller, a comedy, or a romance. You need a varying rhythm. Fast and slow. Hot and cold. Bright and shadowed. If your action novel moves at breakneck speed for four hundred pages without variation, by page 200 your readers will start going numb—they'll get immune to the tension—and they'll close the book for relief. If your romance is titillating on every page, it will eventually become a turnoff. If your comedy has no dark moment, it won't seem real enough to make us laugh. Subplots are good ways to vary your story rhythm, and we'll get to those shortly.

THEME

I could tell you that theme is the concept that the novel illustrates, and I could give examples—"War is not glorious but ugly" is the theme of Hemingway's *A Farewell to Arms*, "Censorship is evil" is the theme of Ray Bradbury's *Fahrenheit 451*—but it would not make those novels any more enjoyable nor would it help you write a better novel.

Theme is such an inherent part of a good novel that it's hard—and inappropriate—to pull it out and examine it separately. The best advice is to not approach your novel through theme. Only one out of a thousand writers says, "I think I'll write a book on such-and-such a theme! Now what should my characters and plot be?" Barbara Kingsolver might be able to do this, but a first-time novelist creating a story this way would probably come off sounding preachy, fake, stilted, lifeless, and unreadable. Remember, your job is to write the best story you can in the best way you know how. The themes you will address in the novels you write will be themes that are part of you. They will come out naturally in the stories you fall in love with, the stories you write with care.

The one piece of advice I will give about theme is that when your theme appears to you somewhere down the line, honor it with subtle layers of detail and meaning while you rewrite your book. Don't plaster it all over every page in huge letters or (have mercy) name your novel after it. *Be gentle.*

You'll discover your theme by exploring your outline, getting to know your characters, and researching your setting. You'll learn how to weave theme subtly into your pages by looking at what your characters are struggling with on the inside and outside. In John Steinbeck's *Of Mice and Men*, there is a theme running through the book—the dual sides of a man, the stoic survivor and the impulsive child. On the surface, George and Lennie could not be less alike, but symbolically they are one. This theme, the dance between the adult and the child, comes through in both George's outer and inner lives. In the outer realm George is constantly having to remind his friend of things—Lennie keeps forgetting what he's supposed to say and not say, do and not do—George tries to manage his companion's behavior so people will give them work but also leave them be. The inner struggle is more difficult—George finds himself angry at Lennie for being his opposite, he has to choose when to unleash Lennie's physical power for their own protection, and he ultimately needs to sever the bond between them before they are both destroyed.

Think about the key tension in your story. How can you illustrate those dynamics through your characters' inner and outer struggles?

SUBPLOTS

A subplot is a smaller plotline that runs through your story, supporting your main plot and intertwining with it. If your outline is short, you might add a subplot, maybe even more than one. But don't add too many. And don't ever put in a subplot that is not vital to your novel. Not even if it's really cool. If it's really cool, cut it out and put it in a file folder called "Cool Subplots" and save it for a story that needs it.

The rule is, if you can cut out a subplot and your main plot doesn't fall apart, the subplot must go. Never put anything in your novel that's not essential to your story. A subplot has to add something. And that something can't just be more pages or characters. Some beginning writers will argue that a certain scene in which nothing vital happens is there because it helps you get to know the characters better. Still not good enough. Combine character painting with vital plot pieces.

- **A subplot that doesn't work:** If you took the story of Robin Hood and added a romance between Little John and one of Maid Marian's servants, no matter how sweet or sexy, it would not belong because it's not necessary.

- **A subplot that works:** In Harper Lee's *To Kill a Mockingbird*, the subplot in which a poor man is gradually paying off his legal fees to Atticus in bags of hickory nuts is essential because it is Scout's mentioning of this debt that disbands the lynch mob outside the jailhouse, saving Tom Robinson's life.

SUBPLOT AND THEME

The theme I mentioned from *Of Mice and Men*—the dance between the controlled and emotionless self and the loving but destructive self—is perfectly woven through two subplots. First, Lennie is attracted to little, soft things—his dead mouse, his puppy, a pretty girl—and George is constantly trying to keep him from harming these fragile things. Second is the dream of raising rabbits, a fantasy the two of them have created in which they save up enough money to buy a farm. This dream would give them a home, peace, warmth, plenty of food, privacy, security, and little soft furries for Lennie to pet—it seems like the only place on earth in which the Child and the Man could be safe together. For George it is just a daydream, something to calm Lennie and cheer them both, but to Lennie the rabbit farm is more real than any boarding house they've slept in or road they've walked. These subplots weave together when, just as they think they might be able to actually purchase a farm and make their dreams real, Lennie, while petting the soft hair of the foreman's wife, panics when she screams and accidentally kills her. Their dreams are over.

EXPOSITION

Sometimes it is necessary for information to be conveyed to the reader or to a character in the story. This is called *exposition*. But it is also absolutely necessary that the information be passed along in a natural way. That would be good exposition. If the exposition sticks out, if it slows down the action, or if, when your character speaks this information in dialogue, it sounds out of character, that's bad exposition—cut it out.

The beginning of a story is often a place where readers need some exposition—you need to lay out the main characters, setting, and central problem. Here are the openings of some successful novels. Notice how much we learn in only a few lines.

> At first, Officer Jim Chee had felt foolish sitting on the roof of the house of some total stranger. But that uneasiness had soon faded. Now this vantage point on the roof had come to seem one of Cowboy Dashee's rare good ideas. Chee could see almost everywhere from here. The drummers directly beneath the tips of his freshly shined boots, the column of masked dancers just entering the plaza to his left, the crowd of spectators jammed along the walls of the buildings, the sales booths lining the narrow streets beyond, he looked down on all of it.
>
> —*Sacred Clowns*, by Tony Hillerman

We learned: The protagonist is apparently a Native American police officer; a ceremony or celebration is taking place, including outside observers; and some kind of trouble might be anticipated if our hero is staked out where he can see everything.

> 124 was spiteful. Full of a baby's venom. The women in the house knew it and so did the children. For years each put up with the spite in his own way, but by 1873 Sethe and her daughter Denver were its only victims. The grandmother, Baby Suggs, was dead, and the sons, Howard and Buglar, had run away by the time they were thirteen years old—as soon as merely looking in a mirror shattered it (that was the signal for Buglar); as soon as two tiny hand prints appeared in the cake (that was it for Howard).
>
> —*Beloved*, by Toni Morrison

We learned: The house at 124 has been haunted for years by a spiteful entity, one likened to a baby, and three of the five family members are now gone—two driven out by violent and frightening episodes. What other writers might have taken twenty pages to explain, Morrison powerfully describes for us in less than a hundred words.

> The old ram stands looking down over the rockslides, stupidly triumphant. I blink. I stare in horror. "Scat!" I hiss. "Go back to your cave, go back to your cowshed—whatever." He cocks his head like an elderly, slow-witted king, considers the angles, decides to ignore me. I stamp. I hammer the ground with my fists. I hurl a skull-size stone at him. He will not budge. I shake my two hairy fists at the sky and I let out a howl so unspeakable that the water at my feet turns sudden ice and even I myself am left uneasy.
>
> —*Grendel*, by John Gardner

We learned: The protagonist is not human but has hairy hands and the strength to throw small boulders, and he emits a scream that freezes water instantly. He apparently lives in a time of kings, for he knows what they look like. The fact that he is bothered by the visiting goat gives us the impression he is used to solitude. The fact that he is scared by the goat even though he is so strong gives the impression that he is young.

Remember to show, not tell, the reader what he needs to know. If the reader needs to know that a character is smart, show her doing something smart—figuring out a code or riddle, solving a problem, catching someone in a lie. Don't have someone say to someone else, "Gee, that Jane sure is smart."

If you want to let the reader know that Joe is a doctor, show him writing a prescription, seeing a patient, cleaning his instruments. Don't have someone say, "Hey, Joe! You're a doctor. What do you think?" No one really tells someone else things they both already know.

If you need to communicate that it's winter, show us cold weather or Christmas decorations. Snow, fire in the hearth, coats, and hats.

If your protagonist's family is poor, show us shoes worn thin, only potatoes for dinner, broken windows taped up.

Exposition can be narrative as the above examples or set in dialogue like the following passage from the first page of Anne Rice's *Interview With the Vampire*.

> "But how much tape do you have with you?" asked the vampire, turning now so the boy could see his profile. "Enough for the story of a life?"
>
> "Sure, if it's a good life. Sometimes I interview as many as three or four people a night if I'm lucky. But it has to be a good story. That's only fair, isn't it?"
>
> "Admirably fair," the vampire answered.

Whenever you can, show rather than tell us what we need to know. In some cases telling the reader certain information might be part of your narrative style, or part of a character's personality, but never tell us things you could show us just to save yourself time. Let us find out what we need to know naturally.

BACKSTORY

Some exposition is just the present facts—we're in a meat factory, it's 1955, it's 33°, it's Valentine's Day. Some exposition is about the past—background information—which is called *backstory*. If the style of your narration is enhanced by giving the reader backstory up front, as in the opening of *Chocolat*, go ahead and start with it. But if you find your story is slowed down by walking the reader through something like the main character's childhood or most damaging trauma, save the backstory. Bring it out later in bits and pieces to add suspense. Carefully withheld backstory can be a powerful tool for tension. Backstory, like general exposition, can be conveyed through narrative or through dialogue.

When you decide to reveal a glimpse of your protagonist's past, place it strategically. The timing of the revelation should tell us something about the character. If she's a runaway, afraid that she's killed her abusive father, give her a trigger. Something makes her think of her past—a sight, sound, smell, taste, a cue for her bad memories to flare up. Perhaps he played a recording of *Aida* while he was beating her. Now opera brings back memories of his fists. The trigger could also be emotional. Whenever she feels trapped, or feels angry, or is thrown off guard, she remembers feeling afraid of his voice.

Try to include exposition and backstory in the most natural way you can. Sometimes you can sneak it into dialogue if your character is meeting someone new, but be careful you aren't forcing characters to say things they wouldn't say naturally. Also, be warned that withholding certain information can work against you. If you are telling your story with a first-person narrator, don't wait until the last page to say, "What they didn't realize was that I myself was the serial killer!" That's cheating. (And it's already been done.)

Here's an example of backstory revealed through dialogue from Toni Morrison's *Beloved*: Both the fact that Sethe, the second speaker in the example below, was scarred in a near fatal beating, and the fact that she is now able to talk about her life as a slave with such calm, show the reader a great deal about her past and who she has become.

> "What tree on your back? Is something growing on your back? I don't see nothing growing on your back."
>
> "It's there all the same."
>
> "Who told you that?"
>
> "Whitegirl. That's what she called it. I've never seen it and never will. But that's what she said it looked like. A chokecherry tree. Trunk, branches, and even leaves. Tiny little chokecherry leaves. But that was eighteen years ago. Could have cherries too now for all I know."

Get inside your protagonist's head—when and how would he reflect on his backstory? Does he have a trigger that brings up a certain memory? How does his past come back to him? In flashes at inconvenient moments, in a continuing conversation with the ghost of his brother, as hallucinations, as nightmares? List all the important pieces of backstory and search for the most powerful way to interweave them.

RECOMMENDED READING

Conflict, Action & Suspense, by William Noble. As you define your moments, try this book for tips on conflict, suspense, and mood.

How to Grow a Novel, by Sol Stein. Among other things, this brilliant book outlines how to capture your audience, how to use conflict to heighten drama, and how to give the reader an experience that is different from, and better than, everyday life.

Story Structure Architect, by Dr. Victoria Lynn Schmidt. This book on story structure includes unusual topics such as "complication motifs" and how to avoid getting bogged down in the middle of your book.

Plotting and Writing Suspense Fiction, by Patricia Highsmith. This fascinating book, by the author of *The Talented Mr. Ripley*, is full of detailed advice on creating tension in plot and character.

Plot and Structure, by James Scott Bell. This book offers advice on such topics as what to do when your plot is off track, achieving believability, and the LOCK system (Lead, Objective, Confrontation, Knockout).

CHAPTER FOUR:

fleshing out your story

CHARACTERS

Your characters, the people through whom you tell your story, are what make your novel worth reading. Your characters need to make the reader feel love, hate, fear, empathy, joy. The characters have to be accessible. If they aren't—if the reader cannot relate to them, if they are unlikable, if they are boring—your novel will fail, no matter how nicely you string together words and no matter how intricate your plot.

Before you create wonderful characters, let's review the terminology. Your protagonist is your hero or main character. Your antagonist is your protagonist's opposition. Often the antagonist is a villain, but not always. In Barbara Kingsolver's *Prodigal Summer*, Garnett discovers that his antagonist, Nannie Rawley, is actually an ally. In Shakespeare's *The Taming of the Shrew*, Petruchio's antagonist, Kate, becomes his true love.

Your protagonist or hero should be a character your readers will connect with, someone they can cheer for, worry about, and love. Someone they wish they were. Someone that seems enough like them to make them forget they are reading a story and feel like they are living one.

(I don't use the word heroine for a female hero because to me the term sounds like an ingenue, a sweet young thing, a romantic maiden who is rescued, the pretty woman who stands at the elbow of the male protagonist. A hero, on the other hand, sounds like a brave, powerful, central character who drives the plot. So I will refer to all main characters as protagonists or heroes, regardless of gender.)

Your protagonist might be an antihero—a protagonist who is not heroic in the traditional sense. One example of an antihero is the narrator from Patricia Highsmith's novel *The Talented Mr. Ripley*. Tom is a sociopath and yet, experiencing the story through his mind, we're invested in what happens to him.

Your villain, or antagonist, should be a character your readers will fear or want to deck with a good uppercut. Someone that they believe is powerful enough to be dangerous. Your hero needs a good villain to make the story stronger. Balance your villain and hero so the fight your reader paid to see will be worth every penny.

You can have more than one protagonist or antagonist, of course. In *Marathon Man*, by William Goldman, the story is told, at least at first, through two main heroes, Levy and Scylla—the separation of these two story lines and their dramatic fusion is very powerful.

In E.L. Doctorow's *Ragtime*, there are at least ten main characters: a black pianist, his sweetheart, the white woman who takes the girl and her baby under her wing, the woman's old-fashioned husband, the woman's fireworks-expert brother, a model who has been sculpted in the nude, her husband (who is on trial for murder), a bigoted police officer, a wise police commissioner, and an immigrant artist. Each of their stories is so gripping that any one of these characters could have generated an entire novel.

But if you are new to writing, it's simpler to limit the cast of your story to one hero, one central antagonist, and a few vivid secondary characters. Types of secondary characters include:

The Love Interest: the sweetheart for the protagonist

The Sidekick: a comrade for the protagonist

The Secondary Antagonist: the second-string villain

The Wrong Love/Antagonist: the person the protagonist should not get together with, sometimes an antagonist and sometimes not (For example, if the Wrong Love is a sweet person who is simply not the right match for the protagonist, he is not an antagonist. If the Wrong Love is lying to the protagonist, has only his own interests at heart, or has murdered the true Love Interest, he is an antagonist.)

The Ally: a friend or moral refuge

The Mentor: a teacher or moral guide

Here is a short list of well-known stories and some of their characters:

BRIDGET JONES'S DIARY

Protagonist: Bridget Jones
Love Interest: Mark Darcy
Wrong Love: Daniel Cleaver

THE WONDERFUL WIZARD OF OZ

Protagonist: Dorothy
Antagonist: Wicked Witch of the West
Sidekicks: Toto, Scarecrow, Tin Man, Cowardly Lion
Ally: Glinda

DOCTOR ZHIVAGO

Protagonist: Yuri Zhivago
Antagonist: Victor Komarovsky
Love Interest: Lara

CINDERELLA

Protagonist: Cinderella
Love Interest: prince
Antagonist: stepmother
Mentor: fairy godmother
Secondary Antagonists: stepsisters

THE ADVENTURES OF ROBIN HOOD

> **Protagonist:** Robin
> **Antagonist:** Sheriff of Nottingham
> **Love Interest:** Maid Marian
> **Sidekicks:** Little John, Friar Tuck
> **Secondary Antagonist:** Prince John

Know who the most important person in your novel is and choose your point of view (POV) with care. (See chapter three for more on POV.) Remember that in most cases your hero is the person who has the most at stake in the story, who is the most active in it, the most central to it. Usually it is the protagonist who will give you your best POV.

When you listened for your idea at the beginning of this book, you might have discovered your characters right away. If not—if your idea came as a plot or a setting—you will need to create characters who fit your idea. If you choose to pattern your main characters after real people, don't be too literal—unless, of course, you're writing about famous people. When Caleb Carr includes the character of Teddy Roosevelt in *The Alienist*, he wants to be as accurate as possible.

If you want to create characters from people you've known—your third-grade piano teacher as your villain and your favorite uncle as your hero—fictionalize them. Harper Lee might have used her own childhood as a foundation for the novel *To Kill a Mockingbird*, but Atticus is not literally her own father. The same is true for novelist Pat Conroy—the families in *The Great Santini* and *The Prince of Tides* are not identical, yet both have emotional material derived from his own past.

Combining characters can help free you from fixating on any one real person's specific actions or words. If you feel drawn to use real people as models, try creating a character who is a cross between two or three of them—a hero who is a cross between your track-star brother, your deaf cousin, and the guitar player you idolized in high school will probably end up richer than any one of those alone. This might help with villains, as well—imagine the antagonist standing in your hero's way as a cross between your dreaded gym coach, your best friend's flirtatious stepmother, and Caligula.

The most important thing about your characters is that they engage the reader. The protagonist needs to open your reader's heart. The antagonist needs to frighten or infuriate him. And the reader has to care what happens to these characters or he'll stop reading. Here are some examples of great heroes:

- Sir Percy Blakeney from *The Scarlet Pimpernel*, by Baroness Orczy
- Merlin from *The Cyrstal Cave*, by Mary Stewart
- Jane Eyre from *Jane Eyre*, by Charlotte Brontë
- Frodo Baggins from The Lord of the Rings trilogy, by J.R.R. Tolkien
- Mr. Chipping from *Goodbye, Mr. Chips*, by James Hilton

Now for some great villains:

- Bill Sikes from *Oliver Twist*, by Charles Dickens
- Nurse Ratched from *One Flew Over the Cuckoo's Nest*, by Ken Kesey
- Mr. Hyde from *Dr. Jekyll and Mr. Hyde*, by Robert Louis Stevenson
- Hannibal Lecter from *The Silence of the Lambs*, by Thomas Harris
- Greg Stillson from *The Dead Zone*, by Stephen King

INGREDIENTS FOR A GREAT CHARACTER

If you are not patterning your characters after real people, you can start from scratch. Choose the sex, age, occupation, ethnicity, and social seat that would work best for your idea. For example, it might be more interesting if the doctor in your hospital drama were a low-income Egyptian woman instead of an upper-middle-class white male. It might be interesting if the nun in your convent murder mystery were seventy instead of twenty-five. Look at what the plot requires of your characters, then experiment with other aspects to see what might spice up your story. Should the hero's father be blind? Should the antagonist's son be a lawyer? Should the homeless murder victim be from a wealthy family? Should the sidekick's spouse be male or female?

Some characters are complex, some are simple. If you are new to writing, and you're starting from scratch, first pick the basic elements of your character and dress him up with a few extras. Every important character should come loaded with at least one large piece of baggage, one small carry-on, and one surprise in his pocket.

The big bag is the character's main drive—this is what makes him who he is. For instance, Indiana Jones's big bag is his quest to uncover history—in the case of his first story, the Ark of the Covenant. The carry-on bag is another important issue or characteristic that adds tension to the first. The carry-on for Indy is his love for Marion. The surprise in the pocket is some fact or characteristic that is in such contrast to the main baggage that it alters our perception of the character or deepens our understanding of him. For Indy this is his fear of snakes. The fact that a hero who travels the globe, risking his life at every turn, has a phobia that is shared by the rest of us makes him suddenly human and endearing. Here is a list of the big bags, carry-ons, and pocket contents of a few famous characters:

ATTICUS FINCH, HERO FROM *TO KILL A MOCKINGBIRD*

Big Bag: fighting injustice as a peacemaker
Carry-On: raising children on his own
Surprise: he's an ace marksman

NARRATOR, PROTAGONIST FROM *REBECCA*

Big Bag: in love with Max but jealous of Rebecca
Carry-On: wants to fit into world at Manderley
Surprise: can actually stand up to Mrs. Danvers

MISTER, ANTAGONIST FROM *THE COLOR PURPLE*

Big Bag: abusive to Celie
Carry-On: in love with Shug
Surprise: by the end becomes Celie's sewing buddy

When you choose a character, and put together his luggage, think of it this way; the big bag drives the story, the carry-on makes the story trickier or more difficult, and the pocket contents add dimension. Indiana Jones goes searching for the Ark, which creates the foundation for the whole plot; he loves Marion, which creates the foundation for important scenes and turning points; and he's afraid of snakes, which creates the foundation for a couple of great moments.

Describing a character is a delicate process. Don't generalize as if your hero had a cardboard sign duct-taped to his chest reading "Heartbroken" or "Running From the Law." Describe him as if you were spying on him unawares, focusing your telescope on one drop of sweat on his temple, one trigger finger held still in his pocket, or one tear at a time.

CONFLICT AND CHARACTERS

We talked about conflict in chapter three. As you create characters, remember that conflict and tension keep the story moving. There needs to be conflict in your protagonist's path and conflict in your protagonist's soul. If your protagonist is a lawyer and the key piece of evidence to prove his client innocent is thrown out, that's conflict in his path. If he finds out that the witness he's about to put on the stand might be lying and he can't decide whether or not to proceed, that's a conflict in his soul.

MOTIVATION

The reader must believe your protagonist's motivations, so after you've created a character, review her motivations carefully. Why does the protagonist go back to that cemetery? Why does she call the villain? Why does she refuse to read her father's letter? How does she react to the situations and other characters? Knowing her as you do, or should, is that realistic?

An otherwise great story can be ruined if the reader thinks your hero or villain is acting out of character. If your plot requires your characters to make large leaps in behavior, set up the actions in a convincing way. Even little actions need clear motivation. Why does the villain come to her door? Why didn't he know where the key was—couldn't he have just asked the housekeeper? Why did he tell the hero his real name?

If you need your protagonist to show up early at her daughter's school to make the plot work, set it up. She has to come to her daughter's school before the killer has left the gym? Find her an excuse to make it a reasonable action. Perhaps she is required to turn in her daughter's vaccination card. Imbed the setup in an earlier conversation and surround it with other plot pieces. During a scene where the husband and wife are arguing, have the school call about the vaccination card. During a scene where the sidekick is arriving at the door unannounced, have the mother searching her files for the card. By the time she shows up at the school before the bell rings and turns the card in to the office, it will seem normal.

CHARACTERS AND EXPOSITION

Details in characterization—dialogue, habits, clothes, body language—can be extremely useful in exposition. When you need to know something about the setting, plot, or backstory, use a character. Instead of someone telling us we're in a hospital hallway, have the character wearing a white lab coat and pulling a stethoscope off her neck when she answers the phone. Instead of telling us George's family is blue collar, show the father peeling off his stained coveralls and washing the black grease off his face and hands when he comes home from work.

The more you understand about your characters, the more natural it will be to write exposition. One exercise to get to know your characters better is to interview them. Write down questions your protagonist (or antagonist) is meant to answer, then fill in the responses. But don't ask questions as elementary as *What's your favorite color? What's your favorite food?* unless those facts are connected to the plot. Ask things like, *What is your greatest fear? What makes you angry? If you could change one thing in your past, what would that be?*

Here are some questions you might want to use when interviewing your characters:

- What is your earliest memory?
- What do you like best about yourself?
- When was the last time you cried?
- Have you ever come close to dying?
- Do you believe you are a good spouse?

- Do you believe you are a good parent?
- What's the last nightmare you recall having?
- Have you ever had your heart broken?
- Have you ever broken another's heart?
- Have you ever stolen?
- What was the last lie you told?
- What makes you laugh?
- What do you read?
- Have you ever physically harmed another person?
- Have you ever saved someone's life?
- Do you believe in God?
- Do you pray?
- Do you have any superstitions?
- What languages do you speak?
- What sort of education did you receive?
- How well do you sleep?
- What was the last song you sang?
- When was the last time you danced?

THE "SHOW, DON'T TELL" OF WRITING CHARACTERS

Let your characters reveal themselves to the reader with actions rather than secondhand statements. A character will be flat and forgettable if we learn about her personality traits by being told in narrative summary or by having secondary characters define the protagonist in dialogue. You don't need to say someone is obsessed with computer games if you show him ignoring the ringing phone while he plays. You don't need to tell us someone is sexually timid if you show us the way she moves her legs away from the young man who sits down beside her in the subway. We'll know that someone is angry, without being told, if we see him slam the cupboard door so hard it bounces back into the wall.

A successful character "show" is found in Charles Dickens's *A Christmas Carol*. The first time Bob Crachit is free of Mr. Scrooge's presence, we don't need to be told what kind of spirit he has—the character demonstrates it perfectly.

> The office was closed in a twinkling, and the clerk, with the long ends of his white comforter dangling below his waist (for he boasted no greatcoat), went down a slide on Cornhill, at the end of a lane of boys, twenty times, in honor of it being Christmas Eve, and then ran home to Camden Town, as hard as he could pelt, to play at blindman's bluff.

An exception to this "show, don't tell" rule is when a character makes a statement that sums up a theme or that particular character's personal philosophy. In some ways this is a "tell" rather than "show" moment, but if handled well it can be very effective. But be careful—it's easy to cross the line—if you go too far you can end up sounding trite. A minor character can make a theme statement—it's not reserved for heroes only. Even a villain can be the messenger. As Donald Maass points out in *Writing the Breakout Novel*:

> If a [character's] conviction can be passionately and lyrically conveyed … in a way that is both natural to the situation and understated in its poetry, the passage can become a powerful defining statement, the protagonist's declaration of purpose.

In Stephen King's *The Green Mile*, the black prisoner, who is accused of murder but seems to possess the power to heal, makes a very simple statement that sums up his life purpose after he invites the protagonist to join him in his cell for a few minutes.

> "What do you want, John Coffey?"
> "Just to help."

At the opening of Carson McCullers's *The Member of the Wedding*, we learn that twelve-year-old Frankie is an outsider.

> This was the summer when for a long time she had not been a member. She belonged to no club and was a member of nothing in the world. Frankie had become an unjoined person who hung around in doorways, and she was afraid.

The following statement of purpose is delivered after Frankie is accused of being jealous of her brother's impending marriage. In a feverish rant, she declares her intention to go off with the bride and groom on their honeymoon and live with them, never to return home. It sums up her suffering.

> "We will have thousands of friends, thousands and thousands and thousands of friends. We will belong to so many clubs that we can't even keep track of all of them. We will be members of the whole world."

One character can also give the reader a sense of a whole group of characters. There's an example of this in the short-lived but beautifully written HBO series *Carnivàle*. In an episode titled "Pick a Number," written by Ronald D. Moore, the snake dancer, Ruthie, speaks for the group at the funeral of Dora May, one of the company's performers, who has been murdered. The informality in Ruthie's words perfectly illustrates the unexpected relationship this group of characters has with heaven. She doesn't beg or make excuses—she prays with the intimacy of someone addressing an equal, because God is one of their own.

> Lord, I knew this girl. Her name was Dora May Dreyfuss. She was like kin to me and everyone standing here. You knew her, Lord. You know she had a hard life. Some of what she done you may not approve of. Some of what she done you may call sin. But she was a good girl, Lord. And we loved her. And we want you to welcome her into your arms. And we know you will.

CHARACTER AND PLOT

If you are creating characters from scratch—not basing them on real people—think on this: What do your main character and your plot have in common? You're at the early stages here, the easiest time to mold your hero. Your protagonist's mind and heart need to be interwoven throughout the story. The hero and plot either mirror each other or contrast with each other. Somehow they must fit.

MIRRORING HERO AND PLOT

- A farm is dying and will be sold. The hero is a farmer who is old and dying.

- A marriage has become a façade and is crashing and burning. The hero is a playwright who has become cliché, and her plays are bombing.
- A kingdom is facing a battle it will probably not win because it has broken a treaty with the neighboring realm. The hero king is losing his grip on his sanity because he has broken a vow to his queen.

CONTRASTING HERO AND PLOT

- A town is succumbing to the control of conservative politics. The hero is a liberal who opens a New Age shop in town.
- A woman is killed, supposedly by a ghost. The hero is her brother, who investigates the death but does not believe in the supernatural.
- A plane makes an emergency landing in a swamp, where it is disabled and starting to sink. The hero is an obsessive-compulsive accountant who can't swim.

Look at your storyline and your protagonist's main desire or fear. Whether they mirror or contrast with each other, list how the two can work together or against one another to heighten tension.

RECOMMENDED READING

Writing the Breakout Novel, by Donald Maass. Here's a great book for learning how to develop your protagonist into an unforgettable character.

The Writer's Guide to Character Traits, by Dr. Linda N. Edelstein. This book offers an intriguing list of personality types from the mild to the wild, including specific behaviors and their corresponding influences.

The Writer's Guide to Writing Your Screenplay, by Cynthia Whitcomb. Although this book is about screenwriting, it is great for novelists, especially the section on character evolution.

CHAPTER FIVE:

making your story vivid

DIALOGUE

Once you have characters, they will start having conversations. *Dialogue* is the term for this verbal communication. It sounds simple, but dialogue needs to be well written and in balance with the story in order to work well. Too much or too little dialogue can damage your novel. At a writers conference I once attended, an editor on a literary panel confessed that she and her colleagues had a practice of flipping through the pages of manuscripts in their slush piles to look for the white space on the page made by dialogue. If there was too much white page, or not enough, they wouldn't even bother to read the first sentence of the novel before rejecting it.

What, then, is the perfect amount of dialogue? Different genres might have more or less conversation—a first-person detective story might have very little, a third-person comic romp might have quite a bit—but in general it comes down to two factors: having the right balance of narrative vs. scene, and distilling conversations.

SCENE VS. SUMMARY

In your storytelling some pieces of the plot will be scenes, the little dramas that you invite the reader into, and some pieces will be summary or reflection. When you let the reader into the room to watch a pair of lovers argue and then step back to tell us that afterward they slept in separate rooms and both tossed and turned until dawn, you have followed a scene with summary. When you let the reader into the courtroom for the protagonist's statement on the witness stand and follow it with half a page comparing the justice system to the fall of the Roman Empire, you have followed a scene with reflection. In the former you're giving the reader a shortened version of action, and in the latter you're stepping out of the action and making a philosophical, poetic, or psychological observation. In both cases, passages with dialogue alternate with passages that have none.

As an example, look at the simple tale of Cinderella. Meeting the prince at the ball requires a scene with dialogue, but getting Cinderella back to her cottage after midnight can be summarized. In *Gone With the Wind*, Margaret Mitchell writes the scene in which Scarlett tells Ashley that she loves him using nothing but dialogue, but the next two weeks, during which Scarlett prepares to marry Charles, she summarizes.

In *Lullaby*, Chuck Palahniuk goes from a dialogue scene in which a realtor is trying to sell a haunted house over the phone, to a reflective passage lamenting the limitations of linear time on storytelling. And in Daphne du Maurier's *Rebecca*, dialogue in which the protagonist's employer informs her of Rebecca's death is followed by reflection on first love.

> "An appalling tragedy," she was saying, "the papers were full of it of course. They say he never talks about it, never mentions her name. She was drowned you know, in a bay near Manderley …"
>
> I am glad it cannot happen twice, the fever of first love. For it is a fever, and a burden, too, whatever the poets may say.

If you find that your tendency is to write lots of dialogue, review your plot and summarize some less dynamic scenes, or pull back from an important scene and let the narrator reflect. If you find you are summarizing most of the plot with no dialogue, find important story points and make scenes out of them. Let the reader in for an intimate look.

DISTILLING CONVERSATIONS

Some people think that great dialogue must be a chain of clever remarks, an unending witty banter. Others think that great dialogue must be patterned after everyday speech, and you'd better get on a city bus and start recording everyday people's conversations word for word. But the truth is, great dialogue is a combination of the two. It has to sound natural but also be more potent than everyday language. What you need to do is listen for the natural voice of your characters, decide what they need to communicate, and distill these two elements into a concise conversation.

What does your character sound like? Is he a man of few words or is he verbose? Does your hero mask her meaning in polite flattery or is she straightforward? Is your villain formal or casual? Is the sidekick an optimist or a pessimist? Nervous? Stoic? If your main character has a very specific speech problem—for instance, if he puts together words in a very unusual way as one who is suffering from Alzheimer's—you'll need to do specific research, but otherwise you will probably be able to determine your characters' voices easily. You created them. Get out some paper and let them talk to you. Practice writing a diary entry from each main character's point of view to make sure you can hear them in your head.

From when and where do your characters come? Is your protagonist a 1920s baseball player from New York? Is your villain a 1960s biker from Texas? One trick to developing an ear for your characters is to read novels and rent movies with the locations and time settings of your novel. (Be wary, though—some books and movies are more accurate than others.) You can also find period slang dictionaries that might help you make your characters sound genuine.

Once you know how your characters talk, sketch out what needs to be communicated in your scene and then *do not have them say it that way.* You want your characters to say something that means what you sketch out in the outline, but you don't want to just put quotation marks around those words and phrases. You have to distill the meaning and put it *in character* first.

TO KILL A MOCKINGBIRD, BY HARPER LEE
OUTLINE OF WHAT NEEDS TO BE SAID

Jem should reprimand his sister, Scout, for picking on a boy smaller than her because that goes against the school yard code. Scout should complain that the boy, Walter, might be smaller than her, but he's older and so should know better. She should complain to Jem that Walter got her in trouble that day with the new schoolteacher. Scout's furious with Walter because she feels it was his fault that she was embarrassed in front of the entire class. The teacher said Scout was "starting off on the wrong foot." All this humiliation was Walter's fault.

UNDISTILLED VERSION

"Stop it, Scout," Jem reprimanded me. "Don't pick on Walter. He's smaller than you. That's not how we do things in the school yard."

"He may be smaller than me, but he's older," I complained. "He should know better. Walter got me in trouble with the new teacher." I was furious. "He embarrassed me in front of the entire class. The teacher told me I was getting off on the wrong foot, and it's all Walter's fault."

DISTILLED/PUBLISHED VERSION

"You're bigger'n he is," [Jem] said.

"He's as old as you, nearly," I said. "He made me start off on the wrong foot."

THE PRINCESS BRIDE, BY WILLIAM GOLDMAN
OUTLINE OF WHAT NEEDS TO BE SAID

One of three kidnappers needs to get the prince's betrothed to stop her horse so they can capture her. She should agree to listen. The leader should make up some lie about who they are—something believable for two men and a giant. He should make them sound unthreatening and harmless, perhaps even in need of help themselves. He should sound reassuring. And once they've gotten close enough to lay hands on her, they should drop the pretense.

UNDISTILLED VERSION

"Stop your horse, please!" the Sicilian cried, blocking her way. "But don't be scared. We're just harmless circus performers."

They seemed unthreatening so she stopped.

"We're lost and we need help," he said. "Be reassured, we won't hurt you." He stepped close enough to grab her reins. "Aha! Now it's you who needs help!" he laughed.

DISTILLED/PUBLISHED VERSION

"A word?" the Sicilian said, raising his arms. His smile was more angelic than his face.

Buttercup halted. "Speak."

"We are but poor circus performers," the Sicilian explained. "It is dark and we are lost. We were told there was a village nearby that might enjoy our skills."

"You were misinformed," Buttercup told him. "There is no one, not for many miles."

"Then there will be no one to hear you scream," the Sicilian said, and he jumped with frightening agility toward her face.

SAYING "SAID"

When you write a play, teleplay, or movie script, you indicate who is speaking a line of dialogue by printing the character's name before the words, and it is clear to the audience who is speaking because the actors are seen and heard. But in a novel you need to make it clear for the reader who is saying what. The most common tool for this task is the word *said*.

"The cat's on fire," said Zoey.

Adam said, "Hand me that seltzer bottle."

To make your dialogue roll tripplingly off the tongue, you don't want to put in too many *said*s or too few. Putting *said* after every spoken line is too much, but if you don't include enough direction you might confuse the reader as to who is speaking.

If only two people are talking together, and there is little description of action in between, you can go for several rallies of dialogue without repeating who said what.

> "You're home early," said Yuri.
> "Am I?" said Belle.
> "Where's your coat?"
> "I must've left it at the office."
> "Dinner's not ready yet."
> "I'm too tired to eat anyway."

It's easy to keep track of who said what here partly because the dialogue goes in an ABABAB pattern, and partly because one person has just returned home and the content of her dialogue reaffirms this.

Here's a situation in which there are four characters present.

> The man and his bodyguard helped Claire and Denise out of the cab.
> "Where are we?" she said.
> He handed her the envelope and said, "You told us you lived here."

Because there are two males and two females, it's difficult to tell which *he* or *she* is speaking.

Here's an example in which the number of exchanges, especially when broken with action, confuses the identity of the speakers.

> "Take that back," he said.
> She smiled and said, "Fat chance."
> "Then I won't tell you my secret."
> "As if I cared."
> The food arrived, two lobsters and two bibs.
> "Why do we always come here?"
> "We?"

By now it's impossible to tell if the last line was *his* or *hers*. After the plates of food arrived, there should have been a *said* to get us back on track.

You can use other words for *said—replied, answered, called,* but don't use weird replacements. Unless you are writing humor, and you're good at it, do not have characters *chortle* or *bellow*. Never have them *opine* or *orate*. Unless you're as brilliant as P.G. Wodehouse, you'd be safer with a plain *said*.

Literal Substitutes

Screamed, cried, shouted, yelled, called, whispered, hissed, and *laughed* can work well if they are used literally. If a character screams a word, such as her child's name, because she sees him about to run in front of a car, it might work. But if a character is simply annoyed at another character and screams, "I told you before, I can do it myself!" it will probably come across as bad writing. Remember to be frugal with *said* substitutes. Don't overuse them or you'll slow down the story.

The Invisible Said

Another substitute for the word *said* is an action that implies who is speaking. For example:

> "Are you all right?"
>> Frank stood up and rubbed his head. "I'm not sure."

And:

> "Give me a hand." Greta balanced a birdcage on each palm. "Take the lovebirds, will you?"

Name-Calling

Do not keep forcing characters to call each other by their names every other line. It's unnecessary, unrealistic, and annoying—it smacks of inexperience.

> "Holly, I told you I'm not well."
>> "But Ian, it's Papa's birthday. You want to be left out of the will?"
>> "Please, Holly," he said, "I've got a fever. A hundred and one."
>> "I knew you were going to pull this again, Ian. I felt it all the way home."
>> "Come on, Holly. I'm not faking."

No matter the content, making characters say each other's names when they wouldn't do so naturally is bad writing.

ACCENTS AND DIALECT

Dialogue printed with a character's accent spelled phonetically, so the reader can painstakingly sound out every word, is a story-killer. It not only slows down the action, it irritates the reader. The reader wants to concentrate on your plot, not decode words like *govnuh* (cockney for governor) and *eesta wabbut* (baby talk for Easter Rabbit). Instead use syntax—word order—and semantics—word choice—to give color to the dialogue of a character who has an accent or speaks a dialect.

In these lines from Alice Walker's *The Color Purple*, it's easy to understand exactly how Celie's voice sounds by the words Walker uses and the ones she leaves out:

> Don't cry, Celie, Shug say. Don't cry. She start kissing the water as it come down side my face.

A certain formality gives the dialogue in Arthur Golden's *Memoirs of a Geisha* a sense of otherness and realism:

> "Certainly it is your robe," she said. "But you are the daughter of the okiya. What belongs to the okiya belongs to you, and the other way around as well."

We hear the accents of the Price girls, in Barbara Kingsolver's *The Poisonwood Bible*, through their syntax and semantics:

> **Ruth May:** Mama Mwanza almost got burnt plumb to death …
>
> **Rachel:** I didn't see there was any need for them to be so African about it.
>
> **Leah:** His tone implied that Mother failed to grasp our mission, and that her concern with Betty Crocker confederated her with the coin-jingling sinners who vexed Jesus till he pitched a fit and threw them out of church.

"I KNEW HE WAS GOING TO SAY THAT …"

Beware of clichés in your dialogue. If the reader thinks to herself, "I knew he was going to say that" too often, she will lose respect for your writing. Find a fresh way to get around the clichés, but make sure they fit the character and the situation. Steer clear of exchanges such as the following:

Villain: Is that a threat?
Hero: No, it's a promise.

Boss: You're fired.
Employee: You can't fire me! I quit!

Antagonist: I'm going to call the mayor!
Protagonist: You do that.

Here's an example, from Elmore Leonard's *Get Shorty*, of something we don't expect to hear:

Harry: You gonna get rough now, threaten me? I make good by tomorrow or get my legs broken?
Chili Palmer: Come on, Harry—Mesas? The worst they might do is get a judgment against you, uttering a bad check.

Here's another unexpected comeback, this time from William Goldman's *The Princess Bride*.

What we expect:

Inigo: I hate to have to kill you.
The Man in Black: Let the best man win!

What Goldman gives us:

Inigo: You seem a decent fellow. I hate to kill you.
The Man in Black: You seem a decent fellow. I hate to die.

SETTING

Choose interesting settings for your novel. That being said, know that any setting can be interesting if described in an interesting way. The trick is to choose settings that work well with your plot, characters, and theme. For example, one of the important bonding scenes in Lauren Mechling and Laura Moser's novel *The Rise and Fall of a 10ᵗʰ-Grade Social Climber* happens when several high school girls are crammed into one bathroom stall. In Barbara Kingsolver's *Prodigal Summer*, Deanna and Eddie make love inside a huge hollow log. In Chuck Palahniuk's *Lullaby*, two characters have a conversation while wandering through a maze of towering antique furniture, and later have sex levitating near a chandelier that's in the ceiling of an empty house.

The ordinary setting of a mobile home is described in an extraordinary way by Dean Koontz in *One Door Away From Heaven*:

> Acoustic ceiling tiles crawled with water stains from a long-ago leak, all vaguely resembling large insects. Sunlight had bleached the drapes into shades no doubt familiar to chronic depressives from their dreams.

Settings can be literally matched or symbolically matched to the story.

Premise: a woman trapped in a bad marriage
Literal Setting: the home they share
Symbolic Setting: she works in a pet store full of cages

Premise: a trucker can't find his long-lost son
Literal Setting: his rig and the motels where he stops
Symbolic Setting: roads that are "closed" or dead-ends

SETTING AND PLOT

The setting has to work with your plot, of course. You can't have a trial in a legal thriller happen in a Laundromat. But, in the same way that the character and the plot either mirror or contrast with each other, the settings and plot need to be somehow complementary.

- **A setting that mirrors the plot:** A doctor is going blind and he lives in Alaska, where night can last for months.

- **A setting that contrasts with the plot:** A woman who has amnesia works in a scrapbooking store crammed with ways to celebrate and display your memories.

SETTING AND CHARACTERS

The same is true for the way your characters and your setting match. They should either mirror each other or contrast with each other.

- **A setting that mirrors the character:** Your protagonist is a kid at heart but going nowhere with his life—always going in circles, and he works at a miniature race car course.

- **A setting that contrasts with the character:** Your protagonist is homeless but lives in the vast gardens of a billionaire's estate.

SETTING AND THEME

The theme must also be enhanced by the setting.

- **A setting that mirrors the theme:** The theme is that humans must protect the environment, and the setting is a recycling company.

- **A setting that contrasts with the theme:** The theme is that true beauty comes from within, and the setting is a cosmetics store.

THE LONG AND SHORT OF DESCRIPTION

Some writers will take lots of words to describe a setting, and some will paint the picture of our surroundings with very few brushstrokes. Either style can work for you. Match the length of your descriptions to the tone and style of your storytelling—who is telling the story? How would your narrator describe the setting?

Here's an example of concise description from John Steinbeck's *Of Mice and Men*. At 36 words, it's one of two paragraphs describing the edge of a lake.

> They made their beds on the sand, and as the blaze dropped from the fire the sphere of light grew smaller; the curling branches disappeared and only a faint glimmer showed where the tree trunks were.

Now here's an example of lengthy description from Stephen King's *Bag of Bones*. It's 110 words in length and only one of a half-dozen paragraphs describing one house.

> Beyond the house, the lake glimmers in the afterglow of sunset. The driveway, I see, is carpeted with brown pine needles and littered with fallen branches.

The bushes which grow on either side of it have run wild, reaching out to one another like lovers across the narrow gap which separates them. If you brought a car down here, the branches would scrape and squeal unpleasantly against its sides. Below, I see, there's moss growing on the logs of the main house, and three large sunflowers with faces like searchlights have grown up through the boards of the little driveway-side stoop. The overall feeling is not neglect, exactly, but forgotteness.

If your protagonist is a woman of few words and her story a hard-boiled detective mystery, the descriptions will probably work best if written concisely and with wit. If your protagonist is a poet and his story a sweeping historical saga, the descriptions will probably work best if written in rich and insightful detail, like you were painting portraits of the events and characters. If you aren't sure what length of description best fits your novel, try writing the same scene twice, once with short descriptions and once with long. Your preference will surface.

RECOMMENDED READING

Steering the Craft, by Ursula K. Le Guin. This entire book is very helpful, but you might especially find chapters three through five useful (sentence length, syntax, adjectives, adverbs, subjects) while describing your settings.

The Writer's Guide to Places, by Don Prues and Jack Heffron. If you don't have the time or money to visit every city in your story, try this reference book—it includes not only the local food, climate, and landmarks but also the most loved and hated aspects of, and the most shameful bits of history from, dozens of potential settings.

CHAPTER SIX:

being unforgettable

DETAIL

It's the little things that make your writing come alive. The more vividly you paint the picture of your story, the more powerfully you'll affect your reader.

PROJECTING REALISM

Details can make your novel more real. If you can give the impression that your story actually happened, the readers' investment will be deeper and they will keep turning the pages. Notice how the two examples below are made real with a few vivid details.

NOT THIS

She looks from the crypt to the speakers where music comes down from the ceiling.

BUT THIS

She looks from Crypt Number 678 to up at the ceiling where the music comes down from the little speakers next to the painted-on clouds and angels.

—*Survivor*, by Chuck Palahniuk

NOT THIS

But Rafael Gordon carried a knife in his sleeve, and he always had a chain in his pocket.

BUT THIS

But Rafael Gordon carried a cork-hafted black iron fishing knife in his sleeve, and he always had a few feet of tempered steel chain in his pocket.

—*White Butterfly*, by Walter Mosley

PROJECTING TRUTH

Details can also push your prose past realism into truth. If the details with which you dress your story are chosen with care, they can resonate subconsciously with your readers—your novel will not only ring true to their left brains, it will ring of truth in their right brains.

> The Santa Anas blew in hot from the desert, shriveling the last of the spring grass into whiskers of pale straw.

In the first line from Janet Fitch's *White Oleander*, the author doesn't just tell us that the weather turned hot, she goes into detail: The wind has killed the grass. But the detail isn't simply accurate, it's allegorical—she chose the word *whiskers* carefully: The innocent blades of green have not only been blasted to death by the shift in the winds, they have become the sensitive feelers of cats—like abandoned daughters, cats scare easily, keep to themselves, watch the world mutely, and are left to fend for themselves in the margins of life. This is, of course, what *White Oleander* is about.

In Stephen King's *The Body*, a boy who has been physically abused by a father whose image he protects with a series of lies cannot sleep one night and watches the moon off-center in a pane of glass as he struggles with the mystery of this relationship. It is not just including what the boy is staring at that makes the detail meaningful; it is the way King matches the detail to the mood of the scene. That child will never be able to make his father love him any more than he can move the moon in the sky to fit into the center of that window.

IRRELEVANCY

The trick is to avoid irrelevant detail. You don't want to slow down your story with details that don't matter. I use *White Oleander* as an example again because Fitch is a master with detail. Notice how in these two versions of the same passage, in which Astrid goes through the garbage of the fascinating woman next door, the choice of details makes all the difference.

THE WRONG DETAILS

I found a broken comb under a mound of coffee grounds, an old stocking with a wadded-up tissue stuck to it, a soap box torn and empty, various bottles, old cigar butts, the ones thick as your thumb, not the slim as pencil kind, lolling at the bottom of the can, their burnt ends gray and papery, their chewed ends wet and dark.

THE REAL THING

I found a wide-toothed, tortoiseshell comb from Kent of London, good as new except for a single broken tooth, and a soap box, Crabtree & Evelyn's Elderflower. She drank Myers's Rum, used extra-virgin olive oil in a tall bottle. One of her boyfriends smoked cigars. I found an impossibly soft stocking, the garter kind, cloud taupe, laddered, and an empty flagon of Ma Griffe perfume, its label decorated with a scribble of black lines on white. It smelled of whispery black organdy dresses, of spotted green orchids and the Bois de Boulogne after rain, where my mother and I once walked for hours.

EXERCISE YOUR ORIGINALITY

What is different about your story? It might be your unusual voice, your quirky characters, your intricate plot, or your brilliantly mapped settings. Or all of the above. But something about your work needs to be like no one else's. Use these exercises to discover what is unique about your novel. Be aware of what sets you apart from the crowd. Later, this will be important when you compose your query letter and synopsis.

• **The Original Plot.** Write down the premise of your story (the basic idea) and then think of several other novels (or plays or movies) that have a similar premise. Now make a list of all the things that are different about your story. After you've made the list, order the items in that list with the most significant at the top. Now look at that list. These are the things that set your book apart and make it original. For example:

YOUR PREMISE
- Hero faces off with Evil to better the world.

OTHER STORIES WITH SIMILAR PREMISES
- Lord of the Rings trilogy
- Harry Potter series
- *The Exorcist*

DIFFERENCES
- uses first-person present tense
- takes place in Tulsa, Oklahoma
- the hero is in a wheelchair
- it takes place in the late 1970s
- the hero is a murderer released from prison
- the Evil is in the form of a television psychologist

REORDERING OF DIFFERENCES
- the hero is a wheelchair-bound released murderer
- the Evil is a TV shrink
- 1977 Tulsa
- first-person present tense

Looking over the last list should make you feel confident that you've found a fresh take on a classic premise.

If the differences you list are not this clear, answer the following questions:

- What is my favorite moment in my story?
- What is the best thing about my hero?
- What is the most interesting thing about my villain?

- What is the best sentence or paragraph I've written so far?
- Where in the story is the deepest sorrow, fear, or anger?

Here—what you love, what drew you to choose your story—is the core of your originality.

- **The Original Protagonist.** Answer the following questions for your protagonist:

    - Compared to other characters in fiction who have the same occupation, how does your protagonist do his job differently?
    - Compared to other characters with the same family makeup (married/single, parent/childless, big family/orphan), how does your protagonist handle his family relationships differently?
    - Compared to characters of the same sex, age, and ethnicity, how does your protagonist differ in attitude, behavior, appearance, or philosophy?
    - Compared to other characters facing the same plot problem, how does your protagonist handle it differently?
    - What is atypical about your protagonist's personal phobias, dreams, pet peeves, or turn-ons?
    - Compared to other characters with the same religious background, how does your protagonist express his beliefs?
    - In what way is your protagonist different from the typical character of his same gender and age when it comes to romantic and sexual interests?

- **The Original Villain.** Play the "what if" game with your villain. Make a list of circumstances under which an antagonist might do a protagonist wrong. Make note of how your villain would handle the situation. How is this reaction different than other villains' reactions?

    - What if your hero is broke and your villain has money?
    - What if your hero is drowning and your villain can hear him calling for help?

- What if your hero is hanging from a cliff and your villain has a rope?
- What if the hero is freezing and your villain comes by in a heated car?
- What if your hero asks for advice and your villain knows what's about to happen to him?
- What if your hero is feeling emotionally broken and asks your villain for comfort?
- What if your hero is running from the police and your villain finds him hiding?

READING ORIGINALITY

To get inspired about creating your own original story and characters, read how these authors took the road less traveled:

Examples of Original Plots

- *Life of Pi*, by Yann Martel
- *Fluke*, by Christopher Moore
- *The Time Traveler's Wife*, by Audrey Niffenegger
- *The Lovely Bones*, by Alice Sebold

Examples of Original Protagonists

- autistic teenager from Mark Haddon's *The Curious Incident of the Dog in the Night-Time*
- the young beast Grendel from John Gardner's *Grendel*
- a little boy with a high purpose in John Irving's *A Prayer for Owen Meany*

Examples of Original Antagonists

- Annie Wilkes from *Misery*, by Stephen King
- competing geisha Hatsumomo from *Memoirs of a Geisha*, by Arthur Golden
- a handsome genius who believes himself an avatar of Vishnu in *Kalki*, by Gore Vidal

THE CONCEPT OF MOMENTS

To be remembered, you need to punctuate your story with unforgettable moments. A moment is a scene or a bit of action that is so powerful it is what people talk about when they find someone else who has also read your book.

There are five kinds of moments—the ones that bring us to tears, the ones that scare the hell out of us, the ones that turn us on, the ones that make us laugh out loud, and the ones that make us cheer.

1. Opening Hearts. These moments are the ones that are touching, either through sorrow or joy. Reunion scenes, deaths, births, and confessions can all be heartbreakers.

In Louisa May Alcott's *Little Women*, Beth, on her deathbed, says this to Jo: "Love is the only thing we carry with us when we go." In *My Daniel*, by Pam Conrad, a girl is hurried out to the edge of a field where her father lifts her in his arms to witness the "matted brown sadness" of a lone buffalo, and she feels "the sudden trembling of her father's ribs" as he mourns.

2. Instilling Fear. These are moments that frighten us, whether with a shock or a skin-crawling tension.

In Stephen King's *Bag of Bones*, a widower watches the shadow of a shrouded ghost woman in his bedroom doorway raise her arms to him and sing: "It ain't nuthin' but a barn dance, Sugar!" These are the moments I refer to as "That can't be good" moments. In *The Exorcist*, by William Peter Blatty, a possessed child turns her head completely backwards and says, in the voice of the man she has murdered, "Do you know what she did?"

3. Raising the Temperature. These are moments that arouse us. From G to X, no matter the orientation, romantic or not, these are the erotic hot spots in a story.

In Barbara Kingsolver's *Prodigal Summer*, an animal protector and a hunter discover each other in the woods:

His hands moved to her chest and began to part the layers of clothing that all seemed to open from a place above her heart.

4. Getting a Laugh. These are the moments that make us burst out laughing so loudly that we are forced to read them aloud to other people because the source of our laughter is an irritating mystery to them.

In Douglas Adams's *The Hitchhiker's Guide to the Galaxy*, a newly created whale tries to develop the language for its experience as it falls through space toward its death:

> What's this thing suddenly coming toward me very fast? Very, very fast. So big and flat and round, it needs a big wide-sounding name like … ow … ound … round … ground! That's it! That's a good name—ground! I wonder if it will be friends with me?

5. Winning Victories. These are the moments that make books worth reading. The hero wins the race, the villain is caught, the war is won, the unjustly imprisoned woman is set free. We've waited patiently for these victories, and we celebrate them with the characters.

In *The Princess Bride*, by William Goldman, Inigo finally kills the six-fingered man who murdered his father: The count's "eyes bulged wide, full of horror and pain. It was glorious. If you like that kind of thing. Inigo loved it." In John Grisham's *The Rainmaker*, the verdict goes in our hero's favor:

> There's a gasp from behind me, and a general stiffening around the defense table, but all else is quiet for a few seconds. The bomb lands, explodes and after a delay everyone does a quick search for mortal wounds.

The above examples appeared in their respective novels at different places. The four most common homes for big moments are (1) at the beginning, where Kingsolver placed the above sex scene; (2) at the defining moment, where King placed the above chiller; (3) at the dramatic climax, where Grisham placed his *Rainmaker* victory; and (4) at the very end.

1. **The Opener.** Opening with a moment will hook your reader into the book. When the curtain goes up in *Hamlet* there is a ghost sighting taking place. *The Scarlet Pimpernel*, by Baroness Orczy, opens with

a heroic rescue. Each of the three paragraphs on page one of John Grisham's *A Time to Kill* opens with a description of one of the three people involved in a rape.

> Billy Ray Cobb was the younger and smaller of the two rednecks.
>
> Willard was four years older and a dozen years slower.
>
> She was ten, and small for her age.

It's such a chilling moment, we can't look away—we are forced to read on.

2. **The Defining Moment.** Creating a powerful moment at a defining place in your book will deepen the effect of the change that has taken place. In *Rebecca*, by Daphne du Maurier, the protagonist finally stands up to her nemesis, at the beginning of act three:

> "I'm afraid it does not concern me very much what Mrs. de Winter used to do," I said. "I am Mrs. de Winter now, you know."

3. **The Climax.** Putting a moment at your climax is a great strategy. It means you didn't deliver the expected scene—you went a step beyond and made the climax blaze in your readers' minds. Voldemort is found inhabiting the back of a mild-mannered professor's head in *Harry Potter and the Sorcerer's Stone*.

4. **The Closer.** Having a moment on your very last page is impressive and effective. Not the easiest task, but very satisfying when it works. In Chuck Palahniuk's *Diary*, the whole purpose for the story is revealed at the very end. (Don't worry, I'm not going to spoil it for you.)

FINDING THE MOMENTS IN YOUR NOVEL

If you feel you haven't found your story's big moment yet, use these cues to help you discover what the moments should be and where they should go.

- Is there a fear your protagonist hasn't faced yet?

- Does your antagonist have a weakness that might turn her around?

- Is there an annoying character that needs to be told off?

- Is there a secret that needs exposing?

- Are there two secondary characters who haven't met but who would create a scene, if thrown together, that would effect the outcome of the plot?

- Is there a character who might surprise us with a quality we don't expect?

- Is there a bully who hasn't been felled?

- Is either your antagonist or your protagonist holding back an emotion—rage, despair, love, lust?

- Is there a monkey wrench you could throw into the plot that would heighten the tension by making it nearly impossible for the protagonist to live happily ever after, or survive at all?

- Is there a character who should die but you've been too fond of to kill off?

Look at the crosshairs of your story. The crosshairs of *Rebecca* focus on the moment the protagonist realizes Maxim never loved his first wife. In *White Oleander* it is when Astrid asks her mother to let her go. Hamlet is presented with an opportunity to kill his uncle, but hesitates. Harry Potter stands up to Voldemort. Helen Keller makes a connection between water and the word for it. Most moments stem from a certain action and reaction, a key choice a character must make. The heart of your story, the truest seed of emotion, what makes your novel worth reading, comes from and leads to your moment.

METAPHORS AND SIMILES

Two writing devices often used in description are metaphor—describing something by saying it is something else—and simile—describing something by saying it is similar to something else. *Her hands were two small birds* is a metaphor, and *Her hands were like two small birds* is a simile. You can use metaphors and similes to demonstrate your originality, but don't fall into a cliché—*His eyes were burning coals. Her lips were like cherries. War is hell. Love is like a thorny rose.*

Here are some famous writers making use of metaphors and similes:

METAPHORS

… her tears the strongest of aphrodisiacs.

—*Sleep, Pale Sister,* by Joanne Harris

The floor was winter to his skin as he knelt there …

—*Atticus,* by Ron Hansen

… the backdrop of his life had changed completely …

—*The Unbearable Lightness of Being,* by Milan Kundera

She studied the back of the fat man's neck … a riot of hacked stiff hairs.

—*The Tortilla Curtain,* by T.C. Boyle

SIMILES

He held one arm up, like a statue in front of a courthouse.

—*The Mosquito Coast,* by Paul Theroux

… she rolled on like a car that had lost its brakes on a downhill slope.

—*The Florabama Ladies' Auxiliary & Sewing Circle,* by Lois Battle

… the dog, slick with blood, slithered madly in his grasp like a monstrous newborn.

—*The 25th Hour,* by David Benioff

I admire the beauty of scorpions. They look like black-ink hieroglyphs of themselves.

—*Under the Tuscan Sun,* by Frances Mayes

Metaphors and similes, like all description, should fit your point of view (POV) character and your voice. They are not required—use them only if it feels natural.

EXERCISES FOR MAINTAINING YOUR MOMENTUM

If, as you are writing the first draft of your novel, you get stuck or your inspiration feels parched, take a look at what you've written thus far and try doing one of the following writing exercises to revive yourself. Each of the exercises below builds on a skill discussed in earlier chapters, so you can look back if you need a quick refresher.

• **Stripping.** Take a page of what you've written so far (or a page of a published novel, if you haven't started yours yet) and remove all the adjectives and adverbs. Read it back. This may or may not have improved the page, but seeing something in a different light can be refreshing. For example:

> The emerald-colored topiary devotedly carved for thousands of years by too-careful monks strangely was no longer bound within recognizable animal forms, and during the dreary, long day weary nurses gently wheeled silent patients among the lost and long-forgotten shapes.

Removing six adjectives and three adverbs leaves us with the much superior version by Michael Ondaatje from *The English Patient*.

> The topiary carved for thousands of years by too-careful monks was no longer bound within recognizable animal forms, and during the day nurses wheeled patients among the lost shapes.

• **Redressing.** Take a page of your novel or someone else's and change every noun and verb to a different noun or verb. At first you'll probably start by replacing *child* with *kid* and *sidewalk* with *pavement* but soon you'll start getting creative. Remember, if you're using your own work, these are just warm-up exercises—don't keep any idea that isn't an actual improvement. Take a look at the following sentence.

> With a sound like an old branch breaking, a piece of the edge of the vase came off in his hand, and broke into two pointed pieces which fell into the water and went to the bottom in a swaying motion together, and lay there, not touching, moving in the broken light.

By changing eight verbs and nouns, and a few other words, we get Ian McEwan's superior version from his novel *Atonement*.

> With a sound like a dry twig snapping, a section of the lip of the vase came away in his hand, and split into two triangular pieces, which dropped into the water and tumbled to the bottom in a synchronous, seesawing motion, and lay there, several inches apart, writhing in the broken light.

• **Throwing Your Voice.** Take a page or scene from your novel and deliberately change the voice. If you are writing in a breezy, informal tone, try a brooding, pessimistic one. Again, these are just exercises. Playing at different styles is just another way of loosening yourself up to write. Here are some examples of different voices:

> It looks like the kind of hair that if you sniffed it, it would just smell too human to bear.
>
> —*Little Altars Everywhere*, by Rebecca Wells

> The very cream of Doric mausoleums, of gables and pergolas and boxwood gardens and dovecotes and some fragrance heavy and maddening on the evening air.
>
> —*The Caveman's Valentine*, by George Dawes Green

> First time I got the full sight of Shug Avery long black body with it black plum nipples, look like her mouth, I thought I had turned into a man.
>
> —*The Color Purple*, by Alice Walker

• **POV Switching.** Take a page or scene from your novel and tell the same story from someone else's viewpoint—see the action through someone else's eyes. Even if your story is about a man stranded alone on a tropical island, for this exercise rewrite the scene from the POV of the sand or a mango spider.

• **Mixing It Up.** Take a scene from your novel and try something completely different—write it in rhyme or in all one-syllable words or in the form of a letter. Or you could look at a famous piece of literature in a different way. How about Hamlet's soliloquy as a math problem?

Slings + arrows = fortune

Troubles > the sea

How about an English problem?

Life is to mortal coil as _____ is to shuffling?

Another good way to mix up your writing for a fresh perspective is to take a paragraph of your story and copy it down in backward sequence. Don't write the letters backward or the words backward, just put the last sentence first and the next to the last second, and so on.

• **Doubling Dialogue.** Take a section of dialogue and try to double or triple it in length. Just like stripping away adjectives and adverbs or redressing your nouns, doubling your dialogue may or may not improve your work. For instance:

> "Tell me more, Jacob. Say something comforting."
>
> "No, Ebenezer Scrooge, I am only allowed to say a little. And the message is not at all comforting."

By doubling the words, we have the much more charming and spookier version by Charles Dickens from *A Christmas Carol*.

> "Jacob!" [Scrooge] said imploringly. "Old Jacob Marley, tell me more! Speak comfort to me, Jacob!"
>
> "I have none to give," the Ghost replied. "It comes from other regions, Ebenezer Scrooge, and is conveyed by other ministers, to other kinds of men. Nor can I tell you what I would. A very little more is all permitted to me. …"

• **Doubling Description.** Take a page or paragraph of description and double it in length. Again, it's just an exercise. Try it.

> A holiday was declared, but fine foods were hard to come by.

By doubling the words, we get James Hilton's much more colorful version from *Goodbye, Mr. Chips*.

A whole holiday was decreed for the School, and the kitchen staff were implored to provide as cheerful a spread as wartime rationing permitted.

• **Whittling Down Dialogue.** Take a page of dialogue and cut the number of words. Can your characters say the same things in half the words? Look at the difference such a change can make:

> "Hey, I haven't seen you two around here before," Curley said. "You the new guys the old man was waitin' for?"
>
> "That's right. We just come in. I'm George. This here's Lennie."
>
> "What's the matter with him? Let the big guy talk."
>
> "Lennie here's kinda quiet. S'pose he don't want to talk?"
>
> "By Christ, he's gotta talk when he's spoke to. What the hell are you gettin' into it for? You lookin' for a fight?"
>
> "No one wants to fight. We travel together. Lennie's none too smart. I look out for him."
>
> "You look out for him? Oh, so it's that way."
>
> "Yeah, it's that way. We stick together."

With half the amount of dialogue, we're left with John Steinbeck's much more powerful version from *Of Mice and Men*.

> Curley stepped gingerly close to [Lennie]. "You the new guys the old man was waitin' for?"
>
> "We just come in," said George.
>
> "Let the big guy talk."
>
> Lennie twisted with embarrassment.
>
> George said, "S'pose he don't want to talk?"
>
> Curley lashed his body around. "By Christ, he's gotta talk when he's spoken to. What the hell are you gettin' into it for?"
>
> "We travel together," said George coldly.
>
> "Oh, so it's that way."
>
> George was tense, and motionless. "Yeah, it's that way."

• **Whittling Down Description.** Do the same with description. Choose your words so carefully that half the words have the same impact. They might even have more impact. Take a look at this example:

He seemed much thinner, his uniform jacket now hanging on his small frame, baggy at the shoulders. He looked nothing like his former self, once so robust and vibrating with energy. Now his face looked tired and pale, lined, dark shadows circling his eyes, his cheeks sunken in as if he were half-starved. He looked like a man nearing death, tired of living, weary of questions and decisions.

When you cut the number of words by half, you are left with the much more effective version by Jack Higgins from his novel *Bad Company*.

He seemed shrunken, the uniform jacket too large for him; the face seemed wasted, the eyes dark holes, no life there at all, his cheeks hollow, a man at the end of things.

• **Charging Up the Senses.** Take a page from your novel and rewrite it, adding or intensifying the senses of touch, sight, sound, smell, and taste. Or choose one sense only and concentrate on that one. Don't just tell us the air was smoky—show us exactly what it smelled like. Show us the feel of the wet mattress. Show us the taste of the dying man's lips. Show us exactly what the cry of a wounded doe sounds like in the quiet woods at dawn.

But what looks like an old blanket in a dark puddle on the shed floor is really a little girl, lying face up, one arm extended, her blond hair fallen across her face.

This is what some writers might ask us to see, but Stephen King and Peter Straub don't let us just glance at this scene. They force us to stop and stare. We are blessed, or cursed, with perfect vision in this excerpt from *Black House.*

As for the something that is not an old army-surplus blanket, beyond a swirl of dusty tracks and furrows, at the floor's far edge, its pale form lies flattened and face-up on the floor, its top half extending out of the dark pool. One arm stretches limply out into the grit; the other props upright against the wall. The fingers of both hands curl palmward. Blunt strawberry-blond hair flops back from the small face.

FOLLOW-THROUGH EXERCISES

The preceding exercises are good for getting unstuck or for stimulating your muse. Some writers have an unending flow of inspiration but have trouble completing long manuscripts (novels, plays, screenplays). For follow-through and completion help, try one of the following exercises.

• **Short Stories.** Short stories are not easier to write than novels, but they are shorter and usually take less time to compose. Many successful novelists—David Schickler (*Kissing in Manhattan*) and Janet Fitch (*White Oleander*), for instance—wrote and sold short fiction before their first novels were published. (Ann will discuss this approach in greater detail in chapter thirteen.) A short story is a challenge because all the meaning has to be communicated in only a few pages, but if you need a sense of completion to set you free, try short fiction.

• **Writing Courses.** Take a writing class (poetry, short story, playwriting, screenwriting) that will require you to finish and turn in one or more writing projects before the last session. Deadlines can be very useful.

• **The Three-Day Novel Writing Contest.** If you really want to challenge yourself, try this exercise. Participants sit down with only an outline and compose a novel (or novella) in seventy-two hours, starting at midnight on Friday and stopping Monday at midnight. The average length of contest manuscripts is one hundred pages. Once you have scaled this mountain, you know what you are capable of—you can write fast and produce over thirty pages a day under pressure. These are not the conditions that usually produce the best writing, but the experience gives the participant a unique sense of accomplishment. (To find out how to enter the actual contest, see the Web site for the International 3-Day Novel Contest at www.3daynovel.com. But you don't have to enter the contest to play the game. Just set aside any three-day weekend.)

Choose an idea that doesn't need research and is easy to track. Choose a voice that comes to you naturally and rolls off your imagination without a hitch. Write the outline in enough detail so you don't have to stop and figure out plot points, but don't write it in so much detail that you're tired of scenes before you get to them. It must all be fresh. If you're going to write forty pages a day you need to come to each scene chomping at the bit. Also, find a place to hide where you won't be interrupted by phone calls, television, pets, or visitors. Don't plan to do anything else during those seventy-two hours. Make sure you have everything you'll need (food, paper, ink, references, outline) so you won't be forced to stop for a shopping trip. Sleep some. Sixty hours of writing with a fresh brain is better than seventy-two hours of writing with a mush brain.

At the end of the weekend, you might not have a masterpiece, but you might have a draft you can rewrite and expand into a good novel. You might have a novella you can trim down into a good short story. Or you might not have anything worth keeping, but you'll still have had a great adventure.

THE ENDING

As you finish your first draft, slow down when you get to the last page or two. The words you use to end your story flavor the whole novel. This is your chance to shine your brightest. Bring together all the power and beauty of your storytelling as you say goodbye to your readers. Show them where they've been—remind them what it's all about—and save the best for last. Here are examples of great endings.

> Above, the sky was clear, growing pale towards sunrise. Still in the sky, high now and steady, hung the star. But while I watched it the pale sky grew brighter round it, flooding it with gold and soft fire, and then with a bursting wave of brilliant light, as up over the land where the herald star had hung, rose the young sun.
>
> —*The Crystal Cave*, by Mary Stewart

> It was a secret wanting, like a song I couldn't stop humming, or loving someone I could never have. No matter where I went, my compass pointed west. I would always know what time it was in California.
>
> —*White Oleander*, by Janet Fitch

By and by all trace is gone, and what is forgotten is not only the footprints but the water too and what is down there. The rest is weather. Not the breath of the disremembered or the unaccounted for, but wind in the eaves, or spring ice thawing too quickly. Just weather. Certainly no clamor for a kiss. Beloved.

—*Beloved*, by Toni Morrison

They all come from the same place and go back to a time when only the stones howled. Step-and-a-Half hummed in her sleep and sank deeper into her own tune, a junker's pile of tattered courting verse and hunter's wisdom and the utterances of itinerants or words that sprang from a bit of grass or a scrap of cloud or a prophetic pig's knuckle, in a world where butchers sing like angels.

—*The Master Butchers Singing Club*, by Louise Erdrich

Go back and read the last paragraphs of your favorite novel. What do those few sentences say about the whole story? Does a simple image point to a larger theme? Now think about your own work. What images, messages, or reflections will you use to echo the most powerful ideas in your story?

RECOMMENDED READING

Bird by Bird, by Anne Lamott. If you ever feel overwhelmed by the concept of writing a three-hundred-page novel, read the story that plays the title role in this charming book. Lamott's method of looking at a character through a one-inch frame is an excellent exercise for finding meaningful details. (And her take on professional jealousy is a hoot.)

Immediate Fiction, by Jerry Cleaver. As you create your best moments, this book can help you build to them by teaching you to wind up a ticking clock.

CHAPTER SEVEN:

the nuts and bolts

MECHANICS

Different people write in different ways. Some write from the first page and plow through to the last. Others write a scene from chapter five on Sunday and a scene from chapter two on Monday. Some rewrite each chapter several times before moving on to the next. Some write one hour a day, others six. Some produce five pages a day and some five sentences. But whether you write ten pages a day or one, at some point you will have a complete rough draft. Here's where the nuts and bolts come in.

You have now written a wonderful story, but it will not win you an agent, or sell to a publisher, if it is laced with technical errors. Your spelling, grammar, and punctuation need to be correct, even if you're only handing over your manuscript to a close friend or critique group member. Mistakes are not only distracting to your reader, they tell him you are an amateur and not ready to break in. The fact that your verb tense is wrong in one line might not seem very important compared to your huge, brilliant novel, but if the mistake shows up on page 1, you've ruined your reader's first impression of you.

GRAMMAR

Most word-processing programs have a grammar checker. This might not work perfectly for you every time, but look at the hints. Read Strunk and White's *The Elements of Style* to brush up your grammar. Mistakes will not only make you look bad, they might transform your story in ways you hadn't intended. For example, there's nothing wrong with writing a scene where your hero is summoned by the doorbell before he has a chance to get dressed in the morning, but if you say *He opened the door in his pajamas*, you've turned him into a flasher. If you're not writing science fiction or horror you'll want to avoid images like this: *That day a snake was discovered by a backpacker with two heads.* And your protagonist will be unintentionally menacing if you make this mistake: *She decided the dog was a threat to her little boy. He'd have to be put to sleep.*

SPELLING

Spell check is also part of most word-processing programs. Use it! Again, don't press the "replace" button without looking at what it suggests. I once wrote the name of a music store, the *Wherehouse*, and my computer offered to change it to *Whorehouse*. And always have a dictionary nearby when you write. *Isle* and *aisle* are very different, but if you use one for the other your computer will not highlight it as misspelled.

If you have a character name that, when typed incorrectly, is another word (like *Brian* misspelled as *Brain*, or *Dan* as *And*), look for the possible misspelling of these names carefully. Also, if you replace a character's name using the replace function, do a search for the new name through your manuscript.

PUNCTUATION

Again, your word processing program might help you out here, but *The Elements of Style* is still my favorite book on the subject. If you write *it's* (it is) when you mean *its* (possessive), you'll look like a beginner. If you have any doubt about a punctuation mark, look it up.

PARAGRAPHS

Look at books in your genre. How many lines are in the average paragraph? Don't use a paragraph break every other line, but don't write two-page paragraphs, either. Spread out your pages, a few at a time, and see how you have chosen to break up the text. If you need to combine paragraphs, or create new breaks, think about changes in action or thought that give your prose shape. If something is very important to remember, start a new paragraph with that point, or give it its own paragraph.

SO VERY SUDDENLY ...

Use the Find tool on your word-processing program to look for *very*, *suddenly*, and *so*. These are three commonly overused modifiers. Notice how the following passage is improved by deleting them.

WRONG

My slippers were so very thin: I could walk the matted floor as softly as a cat. Suddenly he glided up the gallery and up the stairs, and stopped in the very dark, low corridor of the fateful third story: I had followed and suddenly stood at his side.

RIGHT

My slippers were thin: I could walk the matted floor as softly as a cat. He glided up the gallery and up the stairs, and stopped in the dark, low corridor of the fateful third story: I had followed and stood at his side.

—*Jane Eyre*, by Charlotte Brontë

Without the words *so*, *very*, and *suddenly*, this passage is 10 percent tighter.

TENSE

If your tense is off, the word-processing program will usually catch it. Pay attention. You'd have to have a brilliantly artistic reason for breaking tense.

NOT THIS

He opens his coat and takes out a knife, then smiled.

BUT THIS

He opened his coat and took out a knife, then smiled.

OR THIS

He opens his coat and takes out a knife, then smiles.

SENTENCE STRUCTURE AND SHAPE

Part of the beauty of great prose is the rhythm of the words, the shape of the sentences and paragraphs. Your sentence lengths should vary. If you write too many short, or too many long, sentences in a row, adjust for variation. Don't be random. Read your work aloud and listen for the natural flow of your writing.

NOT AS GOOD

He noticed the ladder wasn't where he expected it to be. It was usually lying there. Now it was raised against one of the windows. It was a second-floor window. The window stood wide open. He passed the ladder. Looking back, he saw a man descend the ladder.

BETTER

He noticed that a ladder, which usually lay there, was raised against one of the windows, of the second floor, which was wide open. After passing, he looked back and saw a man descend the ladder.

—*A Study in Scarlet*, by Arthur Conan Doyle

NOT AS GOOD

And, of course, there were some more who were frankly jealous, and very few of them hated her, and only three of them were planning to murder her, but Buttercup, naturally, knew none of this.

BETTER

And, of course, there were some more who were frankly jealous. Very few of them hated her.

And only three of them were planning to murder her.

Buttercup, naturally, knew none of this.

—*The Princess Bride*, by William Goldman

FREQUENTLY MADE MISTAKES (FMMS)

Even if you are only handing your novel over to a friend or family member, it's best to take care of potential problems before you let *anyone* see your work. The following is a list of some of the most common errors found in the pages of first novels.

- **Technical Errors.** Blatant mistakes, like the ones described earlier in this chapter.

- **Who Cares?** A plot in which nothing important happens, or that is filled with characters we don't care about. (Review chapter four for tips on creating tension and chapter five for ways to create characters that get under the reader's skin.)

- **Déjà vu.** Common plots, cliché lines, stereotypical characters. If you're going to write the story of benign robots that turn against their creators, you'd better have a fresh take on the subject. Don't describe a cop as a loose cannon or as a guy who plays by his own rules. If you feel like you've heard it somewhere before, you have. (Review chapter six for tips on enhancing your originality.)

- **Mixed Points of View (POVs).** Worse than choosing a tricky POV (see chapter three) is being inconsistent with the one you choose. For example, here's a mix of first person and omniscient.

    > I walked up to the clerk and handed her my ticket. She looked at the small slip of paper, wondering how long it would be before her dinner break.

- **Misguided Presentation.** You want to make an impression on your reader, but let the novel speak for itself. Don't detract from the story with gimmicks. No fishing story manuscripts delivered in tackle boxes, no werewolf stories that look like they have claw marks on them, no medical thrillers with blood stains on the cover. In 99 percent of these cases, gimmicks hurt rather than help.

LENGTH

You're telling the best story you can think of in the best way you can—you should be free to use the exact number of words you feel is needed. Nonetheless, it's important to think about length and your potential audience. Look at the page counts of successful books in your genre. But good things come in packages of all sizes. Here are examples of some big sellers and their page counts:

- Bernhard Schlink's *The Reader*, 218
- Alice Walker's *The Color Purple*, 245
- Michael Ondaatje's *The English Patient*, 307
- Ian McEwan's *Atonement*, 351
- Olive Ann Burns's *Cold Sassy Tree*, 391
- Dan Brown's *The Da Vinci Code*, 454
- Barbara Kingsolver's *The Poisonwood Bible*, 546
- Elizabeth Kostova's *The Historian*, 642

Look at what your potential readers expect in terms of length—chick-lit comedies aren't one thousand pages long and historical romances are never under a hundred pages. If you find your novel is too long or too short, you can make additions or cuts as suggested in chapter eight. But, of course, there are always exceptions. Harry Potter books are now far longer than the average children's novel (number six was 652 pages). Richard Bach's *Jonathan Livingston Seagull* has sold millions of copies and is only ninety-two pages long. But try to come close to the length of book to which your target reader is accustomed.

THE FORMULA FOR WORD COUNTS

If you are reading guidelines from a particular publisher, and a word count range is requested, you'll need to know how many pages they're asking for. A romance publisher might ask for 65,000 to 100,000 words, a publisher of thrillers might ask for 80,000 to 110,000, a young adult imprint might ask for 35,000 to 75,000. A manuscript page of 25 lines, doubled spaced, in 12-point font, equals approximately 250 words. So there are four pages to each 1,000 words—a book of 75,000 words is 300 pages long. This does not mean that the published book will be 300—most published books are shorter because each published page holds more lines than your double-spaced manuscript page. The published version of your novel may have anywhere from 20 percent to 30 percent fewer pages.

RECOMMENDED READING

The First Five Pages, by Noah Lukeman. Lukeman has great advice on the topics of planting a good hook, avoiding melodrama, and finding focus.

Grammatically Correct, by Anne Stilman. This book demonstrates how incorrect usage can alter your meaning, how logical sentence structure can help the flow of your writing, and how the effects of the active and passive voices can slow your pace.

The Elephants of Style, by Bill Walsh. As you review your mechanics, try Walsh's book for a witty overview of the basics—everything from Great Moments in Obfuscation to Lies Your English Teacher Told You.

CHAPTER EIGHT:

repairs

SELF-EDITING

Chapters eight and nine deal with the revision process. And there are several kinds of rewriting to be done—checking for mistakes, adding, cutting, refining. Some writers complete an entire first draft before they do any revision; others rewrite each chapter before they start the next. Do what works best for you, but I recommend that when you finish a first draft of your first novel, you put the manuscript aside for a few days (a few weeks is better) to give yourself more perspective. After taking a break, some passages will impress you, and others will embarrass or depress you. Not to worry. Help is on the way.

FIXES

Before you rewrite your manuscript, it is helpful to read through it first with a careful eye, not to criticize your work but to fix it up so it will be as good as possible. As you read, mark things that bother you—things that seem off. Mark certain sentences with the word *fix* in the margin or by running a highlighter through a problem passage. It might be helpful to use the categories of *fixes* that I mark on my own rough drafts. It speeds up the reworking process when I find these words as hints written in the margins.

Awk: Awkward—something about the wording or the meaning is off. It needs to be thought through again.

More: More is needed—you realize that a passage was underwritten or something was not explained well enough. Perhaps there was even some piece of information left out.

No!: This is way off!—a passage might have seemed like a good idea at the time, but now you see that it is wrong and will have to be completely replaced.

Close: This part is almost there—the sentence, metaphor, paragraph, bit of dialogue is nearly right. It's not awkward, but it can be improved. You're not going to throw it out—you're just going to tweak it a little.

Circling: Circle words you know are not perfect. For instance, in the first draft you may find yourself inserting an occasional placebo word with the intention of replacing it with a better word later.

Move: This bit is in the wrong place—some scenes or pieces of narration are misplaced in the rough draft. Now that you're standing back and looking at the big picture you can mark those passages and find their right homes.

Check Fact: Sometimes in your rough draft you will write something you haven't researched yet. You guessed how many miles it was between Paris and Berlin, or who was President in 1958. Now you mark those lines so you can check the facts and make a correction if necessary.

Check Back: Cross-check specific names and descriptions for consistency. Make sure that the name of your character's home town or street or goldfish, doesn't change halfway through the book.

CUTTING AND ADDING

To perfect your story you need to cut out what is not essential and add whatever you need to for clarity and beauty. All adding and cutting should heighten the drama, or humor, of your novel.

REPETITION

Certain instances of repetition are good—sometimes we need to be reminded that Vince is Bruno's cousin, especially if we haven't heard from him in a hundred pages—but remove all unnecessary repetition: mistakes like having someone sit down again when you've already got him seated, using the same description twice, giving the same piece of backstory in chapter three that you gave in chapter two. Repeat only with the intention of reinforcing something vital, and only with finesse. Here are two examples of bad repetition and how they can be fixed.

BEFORE

> She unlocked and opened the door and he stepped through the doorway.
> "What's with the chain?" he asked when she had let him in. He watched her close the door softly, sliding the lock back in place.
> She said nothing. He had a bunch of daisies and a box from Bronzini.
> "What's the matter?" he said, handing her the flowers.
> She closed the door, rechaining it. "I'll tell you inside," she said as he gave her the daisies and a kiss.

AFTER REMOVING REPETITIONS

> "What's with the chain?" he asked when she had let him in.
> She said nothing, closing the door and rechaining it.
> "What's the matter?" He had a bunch of daisies and a box from Bronzini.
> "I'll tell you inside," she said as he gave her the daisies and a kiss.
>
> —*Rosemary's Baby*, by Ira Levin

BEFORE

> I sat down again and tried to keep the old conversation going. She was a lousy conversationalist. "Do you work every night?" I asked her—it sounded

sort of awful, after I'd said it. I sat there. She wasn't very talkative. She didn't sit down.

"Yeah." She was walking all around the room. She picked up the menu off the desk and read it.

I didn't get up—just watched her standing there. "What do you do during the day?"

AFTER REMOVING REPETITIONS

I sat down again and tried to keep the old conversation going. She was a lousy conversationalist. "Do you work every night?" I asked her—it sounded sort of awful, after I'd said it.

"Yeah." She was walking all around the room. She picked up the menu off the desk and read it.

"What do you do during the day?"

—*The Catcher in the Rye,* by J.D. Salinger

WHERE DOES THE STORY START?

Your story might seem to start with the beginning of your protagonist's life, but if the first relevant thing that happens to her is at age twelve, cut out the first twelve years. You might think that because your story begins on your hero's birthday you need to tell us about the whole day. You don't. Notice that Dickens's *A Christmas Carol* starts on Christmas Eve, but not in the morning, because things don't get cooking until after dark. If something in your character's past is important to your story, can it be saved and brought up later? Try to find the real beginning of the story. *Romeo and Juliet* starts with a street fight, *Gone With the Wind* starts with Scarlett finding out Ashley is engaged, *Interview With the Vampire* starts after the reporter has already begun to ask questions.

The Implied Openers

Some conversations and scenes can be trimmed at the front as well. When one character calls another up on the phone you don't have to start with hello. Let's assume they greeted each other.

DON'T START HERE

Jack was just about to leave for the pool hall when the phone rang. He caught it on the second ring.

"Yeah?"

"Is this Jack Knight?" came the voice on the other end.

"Yes."

"This is detective Laurence."

"What do you want?"

"I'm calling because we found your brother's body in Macy Park this morning."

START HERE

Before Jack could get out the door, the cop from Nick's party called with a piece of news that stopped him dead.

"We found your brother's body," the detective said, "in Macy Park this morning."

And when a character goes from one place to another you don't have to start with the car pulling up or the door opening. We know how people enter office buildings. Start the conversation or scene where it becomes important to us.

DON'T START HERE

It was eight in the morning and raining hard. She pulled up to the curb, parking her car in the crosswalk. Maybe she would get a ticket, but she didn't care. A handful of yuppies filed in and out of the Contec Building. Olive rode up to the seventh floor in a mirrored elevator, standing between a middle-aged man in an Armani suit and a teenaged delivery boy carrying a pastry box.

Patrick's office door was open and his receptionist was nowhere to be found. Olive strode in and slapped the newspaper down under her ex-husband's nose.

"What the hell is this?" she asked him.

START HERE

"What the hell is this?" Olive slapped the newspaper onto Patrick's desk.

THINGS YOUR READER ALREADY KNOWS

Look for places where you can cut words because you're telling or showing your reader something she gets already. For example:

> He would have to speak to her soon. He stood up at last from his bath, shivering, wet, in no doubt that a great change was coming over him. Without dressing, he walked naked through his study into the bedroom.

If you cut out three words you will have the passage Ian McEwan actually wrote in *Atonement*. Cut out the word *wet*—the reader already knows that a bath includes water. And cut the words *Without dressing*—if the character walks naked into the study, the reader will assume he didn't get dressed.

PADDING

Too many adjectives, adverbs, and extra words can muddle your dialogue.

BEFORE

> "You're not quitting, are you?" she asked coyly.
>
> "Well, maybe not. Maybe just one more."
>
> He playfully dropped one more shining dollar into the hungry machine and cheerfully pulled the still-warm handle, realizing ruefully this was exactly how profitable casinos made the majority of their money.

AFTER TIGHTENING

> "You're not quitting, are you?" she asked.
>
> "Well, maybe not. Maybe just one more."
>
> He dropped one more dollar into the machine and pulled the handle, realizing this was exactly how casinos made their money.
>
> —*Indian Killer*, by Sherman Alexie

BEFORE

> "You don't have enough for a whole script. You need more substance. You have the beginning of an idea that doesn't go anywhere …"
>
> "No, really, I've been developing it. I put in more characters. There's a girl in it now."

"Oh, yeah—and so what happens? Where's the action? What's the story?"

"You mean what's the theme? Theme is tricky. I'm still thinking about the visual fabric, as they say. I'm fleshing it out."

AFTER TIGHTENING

"You don't have a script. You have the beginning of an idea that doesn't go anywhere ..."

"I've added to it. There's a girl in it now."

"Yeah—and what happens? What's the story?"

"You mean what's the theme? I'm still thinking about the visual fabric, as they say."

——*Get Shorty*, by Elmore Leonard

CLARITY

You might need to add words to your text to make things more clear.

BEFORE

"Quin failed this math test," she said.

He looked past her. "Rats!"

AFTER CLARIFICATION

"Quin failed his math test," she said.

He looked past her at the mouth of the tunnel, which was filled now to overflowing with a swarm of filthy rodents. "Rats!"

If you describe actions too briefly, there might be some ambiguity about the physicality of the scene.

BEFORE

He put his arm around her waist.

"What do you think of my idea?" he asked.

"Don't make me laugh," she said.

AFTER CLARIFICATION

He put his arm around her waist.

"What do you think of my idea?" he asked.

"Don't make me laugh," she said, squirming delightfully under his fingers.

DEPTH

You might find you want to add words that enhance the resonance of your story. For instance:

> The social worker passed a wad of letters across the sticky table to me. Such potential for damage. I didn't even want to pick them up. I hated the sight of them, my mother's handwriting, the crabbed lines I could see through the blue airmail envelopes. She could get seven pages per stamp, and each thin sheet weighed more than the night.
>
> —*White Oleander*, by Janet Fitch

That last phrase isn't required for clarity, but it deepens the meaning. Unlike padding, these kinds of additions enhance the quality of the writing rather than diminish it.

RECOMMENDED READING

On Writing, by Stephen King. King not only tells the story of how he became a horror writer, he offers concrete advice in an accessible way. My favorite tip was about finding and cutting the extra words that weaken your writing.

Self-Editing for Fiction Writers, by Renni Browne and Dave King. Browne and King's book can help you with depth by covering more advanced topics such as sophistication, interior monologues, and proportion.

Webster's New World Roget's A–Z Thesaurus, by Charlton Laird. When struggling to find the right words, have a hefty thesaurus on hand. At more than nine hundred pages, this one is a good choice.

CHAPTER NINE:

making it shine

REWORKING

Reworking is the process of looking again at the story to make sure you're not missing an opportunity to be stunning. There are five things to look for at this stage of rewriting: beginnings and endings that match, varied locations, character arcs, glowing points, and finesse.

1. BEGINNINGS AND ENDINGS

After you've rewritten your rough draft by cutting, adding, and fixing things, review your first page and your last page, or first scene and last scene. A novel is like a symphony—it's long and complex, and it has themes. It takes us on a journey, and the best ones close with a memory of where we came from. It might not be in the same key or recall the exact melody line, but the last movements of great symphonies refer back to their opening measures. Something about your first page relates to your last page, whether your novel is a hundred pages long or a thousand. No flashback is needed. No repeated lines. But reflect on your opening as you rewrite your last page. Reflect on your last scene as you rewrite your first paragraph.

For some wonderful examples of openings and closings that are well matched, reread the first and last scenes of the following novels:

REBECCA, BY DAPHNE DU MAURIER

Opening: with a dream of the grand mansion Manderley as if it still existed but had gone to ruin

Closing: with the haunting image of the same house burning to the ground

THE WORLD ACCORDING TO GARP, BY JOHN IRVING

Opening: with the protagonist's mother

Closing: with the protagonist's daughter

THE TURN OF THE SCREW, BY HENRY JAMES

Opening: with the beginning of a story in which a child sees an apparition and wakes his mother, who sees it as well

Closing: with the end of a story where a governess sees an apparition and, in forcing a boy to see it as well, puts him to sleep forever

THE GREAT GATSBY, BY F. SCOTT FITZGERALD

Opening: with an eloquent argument for avoiding judgmental observations of one's fellow man

Closing: with an observation of Gatsby that is profoundly empathetic

CARRIE, BY STEPHEN KING

Opening: with an excerpt from a newspaper about an unexplained phenomenon, closely followed by the introduction of a girl with a power that explains the mystery—"What none of them knew, of course, was that Carrie White was telekinetic."

Closing: with an excerpt from a letter introducing a girl whose power to make marbles move by themselves is unexplained

DRACULA, **BY BRAM STOKER**

> **Opening:** with a journal entry that begins the odyssey into horror
>
> **Closing:** with a journal entry that points out that journal entries do not actually prove that the horror happened

PRODIGAL SUMMER, **BY BARBARA KINGSOLVER**

> **Opening:** with a hunter observing a woman who is the protector of coyotes
>
> **Closing:** with the same hunter observing a female coyote and letting her live

2. VARIED LOCATIONS

This is also the time to review your settings. List them as if your novel were a play or a movie. If you have too many scenes that take place in the bedroom or in the car, find other places for your characters to have the same conversations—waiting in a movie line in the rain, walking around a strange neighborhood in search of a lost dog. Settings should be striking whenever possible without being so odd that they distract from your story. Make a list of your settings and, if they've slipped into a rut, find more interesting environments.

3. CHARACTER ARCS

This is also the right time to make a list of what each of your main characters is experiencing in the novel—what emotions is each going through? Look at these character arcs separately. Each character has his own journey through your story. If you find one of your characters is either always hitting the same note (sad in every scene) or flip-flopping too much (too often, let's say, going from scared to angry) you might want to make adjustments. What would be an overall realistic or desired emotional journey for this character? Should she start with suspicion and build to anger, breaking into fear in the last chapter? Be true to your characters. The plot needs to work for them, not dictate fake behavior for them. This exercise will also let you know if you've spent too much time on one character and not enough on another.

4. GLOWING POINTS

Glowing points are those phrases, paragraphs, or scenes in your novel that you admire so much you can hardly get over yourself. Now think about why you love those bits. Imagine that those sections are true representations of your talent. Then rewrite your novel, lifting the rest of your writing to that level of excellence. Okay, I admit, it's easier said than done, but it can't hurt to try. At the very least, it gives you more practice and hopefully a few additional glowing points.

5. FINESSE

Finally, rewrite for finesse, looking for subtle changes that might make the novel more refined. Scan for things that don't look broken but might be enhanced by a fix. This flashback might be better in chapter nine instead of chapter seven. Rather than a dead cat in chapter eleven, it should be a dead dog, because that will remind the hero of the family dog she had to put to sleep years ago. In chapter five, why not have the lady across the hall fail at dialing 911—maybe her phone's out—so she has to scream down the fire escape like the antagonist's mother used to do? In the last chapter, the movie on cable that the snitch is watching shouldn't be an action movie—a sitcom or a children's cartoon would be quirkier. How about a *Will & Grace* rerun? Scan for those little things that might make your writing more memorable.

THE POET'S EAR

Whether the voice you have chosen for your novel is first or third person, whether your genre is literary or horror, whether your style is clipped or

Victorian, your novel can be improved by reviewing it with a poet's ear. I'm not suggesting you sprinkle in flowery or antiquated phrases. What you want to do is find just the right words to make your prose resonate. Your choice of verbs, the details you choose to describe, your metaphors and similes all make up your personal poetry, the quality in your voice that makes it stand out.

One way to improve the sound of your writing is to transform your clichés. If you find your pages full of worn-out phrases like "sweltering heat" or "pouring rain," look at the scene with new eyes. Would it be more telling for your protagonist to notice that it's so hot it feels like his eyes are cooking? Maybe your antagonist finds the rain so brutal it scours the paint off her car like acid. Catch a glimpse that is unusual but that rings true to your narrator. What is it that your character might focus on? Hailstones the size of babies' teeth?

Sometimes it's not that a cliché has been used, but that a bland phrase has crept in here or there. If you find yourself using the same words over and over—*he turned, she looked at him, he moved to the door, she walked away, they sat down across from her*—you might want to go over some of the sentences with a poet's ear. Sometimes a thesaurus helps to stimulate the imagination, but don't just look up synonyms for the overused words. Think about other phrases that would have the same function but would be more interesting. And decide whether the boring bit is even necessary.

In *Of Mice and Men*, Steinbeck could have written:

> Lennie grabbed Curley's fist in his big hand and crushed it.

He could have flipped through a thesaurus and tried:

> Lennie snatched Curley's fingers in his huge paw and pulverized them.

Instead Steinbeck wrote:

> Curley's fist was swinging when Lennie reached for it. The next minute Curley was flopping like a fish on the line, and his closed fist was lost in Lennie's big hand.

Sometimes the poet in you can improve a paragraph or page by refining the rhythm of the language, even the placement of the white space. When a scene ends before you know if your hero will murder his betrayer, the double space that lies between it and the next scene is a held breath. Read your scenes out loud. Does part of the page feel better than the rest? If the pattern of short to long sentences feels perfect in one area but awkward in another, go back and try to rework the awkward area with a poet's rhythm in mind.

Poets have the freedom to shape their words on the page. They put a single word on a line by itself when doing so will bring the desired emphasis. In *The Princess Bride*, when a gust of wind picks up half the contents of the royal dining hall, William Goldman places the line: "Particularly the hat of Princess Noreena" in its own paragraph because he wants to emphasize Prince Humperdinck's distaste for bald brides.

Poetry can and should be applied to all the senses—smells that conjure images from your hero's past, sounds that reflect your antagonist's loves or fears, qualities of light or tones of color that in their references bring significance to the telling of your story or project the plot's outcome. Little things make a big difference when the cumulative effect becomes part of your writing style.

But only bring into your language what feels brilliant to you. If someday a literature student were asked to write an exercise in *your* style, how would you want her to perceive your voice? That's the kind of texture you want to add. It's you, only more so. Enhance your brightest qualities as you polish your rough draft.

Remember that using a poet's ear does not mean adding adverbs and adjectives. Don't start piling on the descriptors to heighten the writing. Your story is your art, and your paint is language. The more adjectives you throw in, the more you will muddle your painting. It's not the number of words that makes your story vivid, it's the right words. And if the words are dog-eared, readign them would be like seeing the same picture page after page. Show the reader something new with each picture. Upend the rock and disturb what's under it, peek behind the curtain of the hearse, look at the fire through the fingers of a child.

Here are some dull descriptions and some successful writers' alternatives:

BORING

By the time John had got to the top of the stairs he was dead tired.

BETTER

By the time John had got to the top of the stairs his face was streaked in sweat and he was wheezing like a perished accordion.

—*The Stars' Tennis Balls*, by Stephen Fry

BORING

The congregation grew restless.

BETTER

Fans crackled, feet shuffled, tobacco-chewers were in agony.

—*To Kill a Mockingbird*, by Harper Lee

BORING

In New England summer comes on hard and fast.

BETTER

In New England spring really only comes for one priceless week and then the deejays drag out the Beach Boys golden oldies, the buzz of the cruising Honda is heard throughout the land, and summer comes down with a hot thud.

—*The Dead Zone*, by Stephen King

BORING

Sleeping all night on the bench made her muscles stiff.

BETTER

Nine, ten hours on this bench, a simple stretching exercise would have been orgasmic.

—*A Drink Before the War*, by Dennis Lehane

BORING

Marley's face had a ghostly glow.

BETTER

Marley's face … had a dismal light about it, like a bad lobster in a dark cellar.

—*A Christmas Carol*, by Charles Dickens

BORING

I was sick from starvation.

BETTER

My stomach ached, my period stopped. I rose above the sidewalks. I was smoke.

—*White Oleander*, by Janet Fitch

BORING

The Circus-Circus is twisted.

BETTER

The Circus-Circus is what the whole hep world would be doing on Saturday night if the Nazis had won the war.

—*Fear and Loathing in Las Vegas*, by Hunter S. Thompson

A MATTER OF WORD CHOICE

Here are examples of sentences tightened and improved by replacing a few ordinary words with one right word:

- They built a bridge across the narrow opening between the hills.
- They built a bridge across the gorge.

- For Eudora, love was difficult to find.
- For Eudora, love was elusive.

- Don't sully the reputation of my father.
- Don't denigrate my father.

- He was abstaining from sexual relations.
- He was celibate.

- She was accused of stealing personal property.
- She was accused of larceny.

- Norman was unable to cope with the demands of his social environment.
- Norman was maladjusted.

- Rita was doing a humorous, exaggerated imitation of her grandmother.
- Rita was doing a parody of her grandmother.

- He would not say all that he knew or felt.
- He was reticent.

- She wrote the note in a hurried and untidy manner on a napkin.
- She scrawled the note on a napkin.

- He repeated the story in exactly the same words.
- He repeated the story verbatim.

TITLES

Early on I asked you to make up a name for your novel idea. You may have been using that code name ever since. But now is the time to come up with a good title, one you'd be proud to type on your title page or put in your query letter. Authors pull titles from everywhere—song lyrics (*Proof Through the Night*, by K.P. Burke), children's rhymes (*Along Came a Spider*, by James Patterson), Shakespeare (*The Sound and the Fury*, by William Faulkner), mythology, legal terminology, you name it (pardon the pun). Oh, yes. And puns.

The first thing I recommend you do is write a list of all the words you can think of that are central to your book. If it were *A Christmas Carol*, the list might look like this:

miser	spirit	Christmas
childhood	regret	memories
choices	love	forgiveness
ghosts	party	second chances

sorrow	future	making amends
charity	prayers	tombstones
debts	chains	human kindness
hell	family	gifts

Don't judge the words you think of, just write them all down. One that isn't a good title idea might trigger you to think of one that's perfect. Out of that list you might eventually choose *A Christmas Carol* because it represents a little story with a promise of a moral ending. Your list can also include the names of characters, the names of locations, and any jargon that goes with a central field (law enforcement, medicine, sculpture, psychology). If nothing in your list jumps out at you right away, never fear. Save the list and look at it later—something might appear tomorrow or next month.

If you are in a critique group or a writers' support group, have the group do a brainstorming session with you. If the members haven't read your manuscript, tell them a little about it, as much as might be on the dust jacket. Then have them brainstorm titles. Don't judge. Just write everything down. Several of my friends have found good titles this way.

Many recent bestsellers have adjective-noun structures:

2nd Chance
The Da Vinci Code
The Bourne Legacy
Little Scarlet
Dark Destiny
Weekend Warriors
The Lovely Bones

And many have more unusual structures :

The Curious Incident of the Dog in the Night-Time
Sam's Letters to Jennifer
The Secret Life of Bees
Kiss Me While I Sleep

To get a feel for what kinds of titles sell in your genre, go to the largest bookstore near you and walk around in that section of shelves—see what titles made it. You probably won't find a literary novel titled *The Devil Wears Prada* or a chick-lit book called *Atonement,* but go and look! There might be surprises waiting.

The two most important things about the title of a novel are that it makes the reader lift the book off the shelf and that it is a true window into the story. My favorite titles are symbolic; they give a clue about the subject matter and a hint of the emotional atmosphere. I like titles that are little poems unto themselves. Some of my favorite titles are:

> *The Heart Is a Lonely Hunter*
> *The Poisonwood Bible*
> *The Catcher in the Rye*
> *To Kill a Mockingbird*
> *Of Mice and Men*

Other titles I love:

> *A Wrinkle in Time* (children's)
> *The Lion in Winter* (play)
> *Lonesome Dove* (Western)
> *Me Talk Pretty One Day* (memoir)
> *Out of the Silent Planet* (science fiction)

Make a list of the titles you love and think about what makes them great.

Two more important things to remember: Do not choose a title that sounds like something else if that something else would turn off your potential reader. *Balance Sheet* might be an erotic in-joke between your two brilliant and charming lovers, but if it sounds like a dull finance meeting, no one will buy it (unless there are naked people on the cover, but that's out of your hands). Also, when you come up with a good title, Google it. You want to make sure no recent book, movie, play, or TV show beat you to it. There is no copyright on titles, but you want to avoid confusion.

If you are writing mysteries or thrillers and plan to make a series, you might link the titles with a gimmick. Sue Grafton is using the alphabet (*A Is for Alibi, P Is for Peril*), Walter Mosley is going through the colors (*Devil in a Blue Dress, White Butterfly*), James Patterson is working his way through Mother Goose (*Jack and Jill, London Bridges*).

One last piece of advice: Whatever title you choose, even if it lands you a great agent, might still be changed at least once before your novel makes it to print. Be open-minded. Publishers and editors are professionals. They usually know what they're doing.

RECOMMENDED READING

The Writing Life, by Annie Dillard. Focusing on your book can be a lonely experience. Dillard finds insight instead of cabin fever as she isolates herself to work on her novel *The Living*.

Stein on Writing, by Sol Stein. Among other wonderful advice, Stein provides a powerful chapter on finding a meaning title for your book.

CHAPTER TEN:

preparing to be read

PREPARING THE MANUSCRIPT

When you've rewritten your novel—when you've gone through it over and over until you can no longer tell which parts need fixing—you should let someone close to you read it. Don't send it to an agent or editor yet. Choose someone you think will like the kind of book you've written, who will be honest but constructive, and who supports your dream of becoming published. This might be your spouse, your best friend, your child, your sibling. Whomever you choose, you will want to prepare the manuscript so it looks professional and is easy to read.

• **Spacing.** Always double-space your manuscript. There should be approximately twenty-five lines per page. Use twelve-point font and either Courier New or Times New Roman. Put a 1-inch margin on all sides.

• **Page Numbers.** If your friend accidentally drops the manuscript, it should be easy to put the pages back in the right order. Number them. The top right corner is common. Do not number the title page.

• **Title Page.** Your title page should have the name of the novel centered. Under the title, type the words "A novel by" followed by your name, also centered. Use a larger type font here. You are taking credit for and *owning* your novel. You want that pride to show on the title page. Even if your first reader is your own spouse, include your contact information (address and phone number) in a single-spaced block near the bottom of the page on the left.

• **Quality Paper.** Use white twenty-weight paper all from the same batch—don't print the first third of the novel on one brand of paper and the other two-thirds on a second brand. Be consistent. It will look more professional. If you go to a copy store, when you put in your order, make sure the original you give them is complete and in good condition. Whether you print out your own copy or have it photocopied, always count to make sure every page is in the right order before handing it over to your first reader.

• **Clear Copy.** Don't use carbon paper. If you work on a typewriter rather than a computer, it's all right to keep a carbon copy for yourself, but take the original to a photocopy shop. Also, if your typewriter or printer produces pages that are too light, change the ribbon or ink cartridge.

• **Clean Copy.** Make sure the copy you give your reader is clean—no torn pages, dog-eared corners, coffee cup rings, or ink scribbling in the margins.

• **Bound vs. Unbound.** For a friend or relative you might three-hole-punch your book, especially if it's more than three hundred pages, and put it in a three-ring binder. For agents and editor you'll leave the pages loose—most volunteer readers will be fine with loose pages, as well. But put the manuscript in a new, clean file folder with thick, soft rubber bands around the manuscript to make sure it won't slide around in transit.

• **Packaging.** You might be tempted to use a cute color of paper or pattern of envelope, but don't. Let the quality of your writing do the talking. If you feel you need gimmicks to make your novel appealing, you should rewrite it again and not show it to a reader yet.

• **Presentation.** When you give this professionally packaged manuscript to your first reader, don't toss it on the coffee table as if it doesn't matter. You might be feeling insecure, but don't present the novel that way—hand it over with confidence and gratitude. Be accommodating about how long it will take the reader to get back to you. Novels (especially first novels) aren't always fast reads. Don't forget to thank the reader.

RECEIVING NOTES

When the reader does get back to you with his opinion of your novel, accept the written or verbal comments graciously. If they're verbal, take notes. Resist the urge to argue. When he says he thinks it would be better if the protagonist were a painter instead of a sculptor, don't go into a rant about why you are right and he is wrong. Just say something mild—"That's an interesting idea"—and move on. When the reader is done, if he hasn't told you, ask what his favorite parts were. These are always nice to hear, and it's more fun to end on a positive note. Thank the reader. Take him out for pie. He might have been nervous about giving you notes—make sure he feels appreciated.

Think about these notes you have just received for a while—let them sit. You'll be tempted to ignore certain things and try to rewrite other things immediately, but don't. Sleep on it. Reread the notes in a few days and they will feel different. Remember not to take things the wrong way. Notes are a gift to you. Use them to do another rewrite.

If you truly don't agree with a certain note, don't fret. Move on. Use your gut, but watch out for ego. Again, this is where the two- or three-day break comes in handy. You'll be much more open-minded if you take a step back and address the notes when your feelings have stopped smarting.

STATE OF MIND REVISITED

As you finish the writing process and begin the submission process, remember that the best thing you can do for yourself, for your future agent, for your career, is to *write great*. Be patient and persistent. Know that the more turndowns you get, the closer you are to finding the right agent or publisher. Those who reject you today might kick themselves tomorrow. Persevere! Remember, there are lots of agents out there and lots of first novels published every year.

And look at it this way—millions of people say they want to write a novel and never do anything about it. Thousands buy books on writing and never read them. Thousands read the writing books but never get around to starting a novel. Thousands read the books, take seminars and workshops, start a novel, and then never finish it. *When you finish writing a draft of your book, you are already ahead of millions of other people.*

You know what boosts your self-esteem as a novelist even better than completing your first book? It's proving you have another one in you. Start your next project right away. This is your new life. You are a novelist.

Note: If you have read this far and still find you can't start writing, be not afraid. You're still a writer. Return to the listening stage. Don't stare at a blank computer screen or sit down with a blank piece of paper and suffer in stuckness. Go outside. Take a walk. Watch people in the park. Listen to the wind and feel the sun on your back. Play music in the dark. Pay attention to your dreams. Read. And always have a tablet and a pencil in your pocket. You are in the cave. Your idea is right there.

RECOMMENDED READING

The Career Novelist, by Donald Maass. There is a plethora of good advice here—some topics important at this stage might be "The Right Attitude for the Career Novelist" and "Envy."

The 3 A.M. Epiphany, by Brian Kiteley. As you take a break from your first novel and start your second, get your inspiration back on track. Kiteley's book is a refreshing read that uses uncommon exercises to challenge your preconceived ideas.

The Pocket Muse, by Monica Wood. Another good read while listening for your next idea is Wood's book of prompts and exercises.

PART TWO

---

publishing your
NOVEL

CHAPTER ELEVEN:

what a literary agent does—and why

When asked what I do for a living, the answer, "I'm a literary agent," draws as many puzzled looks as it does knowing nods. To the question "What does a literary agent do?" the simple answer is, "An agent helps a writer find a publisher for his book."

An agent has two primary duties: to oversee his clients' careers and to know as many people as possible in the business. Why does he need to know so many people?

Because, while anyone aspiring to write a book might know the names of different publishing houses, like Doubleday or Penguin, and might even have some idea of the kinds of books that come out under those imprints, the reality is that each publishing house is staffed by (among many other people) a cadre of editors, each of whom has different tastes and interests and publishes different kinds of books. The job of the agent is to know as much as possible about each editor, so that when, say, a book on rock climbing crosses his desk, he'll be able to come up with a list of editors who might find it interesting. The more he knows about them—not only their tastes but their career histories, their relationships with their colleagues and their bosses, their successes and failures and future ambitions—the better he'll be able to match them up with the right writers and books.

THE THREE-HOUR LUNCH AND YOUR CAREER

Since fiction doesn't fall as easily into specific subject headings as non-fiction, the job of knowing an editor's tastes is a little more complicated. Agents encounter editors in many ways, from e-mail and letters to meetings, parties, conferences, and lunches, and at each encounter they can learn something about the editor that they'll be able to put to future use.

Publishing people are famous—or notorious—for being the last ones to leave a restaurant—usually a nice one—at lunch. During the course of the two- or three-hour meal, the agent and the editor get to know one another. The agent might try to draw the editor out on a number of different levels. First, he might find out where the editor has worked before and how long she's been at her current position. This gives him a basic idea of her level of experience.

Then he might ask the editor about the books on her current list that she's most excited about publishing. Through the way she describes them, he can learn something about her taste, what fascinates her, what kind of writing or story grabs her, and how well she talks about the book. Because the editor is a book's primary advocate and champion within the publishing house, the agent wants to find out if she can communicate her enthusiasm—make him feel that the book she's describing is a book he must read. If she can do that, it follows that she'll be good at conveying her enthusiasm to the rest of the staff, like the sales representatives, the publicists, the marketing and advertising departments, the people who sell rights to book clubs and foreign publishers and, above all, to her boss—the person who must okay any financial offer the publisher makes.

The agent might try to move the conversation to more personal topics as well, such as where she lives, where she grew up and went to college, whether she's planning a vacation this year and where it will be, and whether she's married and has children. He wants to uncover any surprising nuggets of information that might lead to a match with a certain kind of book or a certain kind of author. He might want to find out if certain kinds of cultures fascinate her—does she love the South and fiction set in the South?—or if there are certain things she has an aversion to. For instance, if an editor has very young children, it's unlikely she'll be able to read a novel about a child in dire jeopardy with any degree of comfort.

MAKING THE APPROACH AND FOLLOWING THROUGH

Putting all these bits of knowledge together can lead to obvious matches, but sometimes it's just food for intuition. At one lunch, I decided to bring along a first novel I hadn't been able to sell after a few months of submissions. Set in Jerusalem, it was the story of an unmarried woman and her struggle to find not only the right man but the right relationship with God. My lunch date was someone I'd known for years, and I knew she had four children and was raising them in an observant Jewish home. Yet I also knew her tastes were more commercial than this novel.

At lunch, the editor handed me a copy of a book that was to be published that week and told me the story of how she'd bought it, and all the prepublication signs that seemed to be pointing to a big success. (It later became one of the year's biggest bestsellers.) I put the manuscript I'd brought off to the side of the table so she could see it, but I didn't mention it. Instead, we caught up with each other's lives until the coffee came. At that point, I told her that I'd brought a book that was probably not right for her list at all, but there was something about it that made me think of her. She agreed to take it with her and get back to me soon.

When I called the editor early the next week to follow up, she told me she'd liked the novel, but she thought it needed work. We embarked upon a forty-five minute discussion of the novel, its strengths and weaknesses, its potential audience, what the author was like, and whether she would be willing to revise. At the end of the conversation, the editor said, "Wow, that was like a reading-group discussion! I'm going to get a few other people to read the book and get back to you next week." Naturally I told her of the handful of other editors who still had the manuscript under consideration, and she promised to be quick.

Later that afternoon, the editor called again and got right down to business: "Listen, I don't want to wait. I want to buy the novel today. I talked to my boss about it and she said to go for it. Here's the offer. It's only good for today, so talk to the author and call me back." Even though the book needed editing, the editor was confident she'd be able to work with the author to get it into good shape. By the end of the day, my client, who had worked hard for several years and through many revisions on her first novel, had a publisher.

CHAMPIONING YOUR WORK OVER THE LONG HAUL

As you can see, many factors went into that sale—the relationship between agent and editor, the editor's proven ability to publish well, her professionalism, her ability to move quickly when she found something she wanted to publish. But none of those factors would have meant anything if the book hadn't been wonderful. The fact that I believed it to be a good book committed me to selling it and made it easy for me to keep trying to sell it even in the face of several rejections. What you will want to find in an agent for your first novel is a person who believes in your book, believes in you, and isn't swayed by the opinions of others.

Here's another example of combining commitment to a writer's work with knowledge of an editor's personal interests. I once invited an editor of children's and young adult books (neither of which I represented) to my house to watch a football game on television with me and my husband. Although this editor is one of publishing's true intellectuals, completely steeped in books and writing, literary criticism, and the history of publishing, he was also, I had discovered, a major Giants fan.

When he arrived, he told me he had a new job: He was going to start up an imprint to publish multicultural literary fiction for young adults. As it happened, I had in my office a novel about a young woman in Japan whose mother had committed suicide. The prose was incredibly poetic and beautiful, yet thirty adult-book editors had already turned the collection down because it was "too quiet." In the meantime, several chapters had been published in literary magazines, so at halftime, the editor read the one that had just come out in the *Kenyon Review*. When he finished, he said, "This is exactly what I'm looking for. Send me the manuscript." He bought the book within a couple of weeks, and when the book was published a year later, the *New York Times*, in a long and glowing review, called it "the kind of novel that comes along once in a generation." Titled *Shizuko's Daughter*, the book won numerous awards for young adult fiction and is still in print fifteen years later. It's been published around the world, most recently in China, and the author has since published four other books.

The author of that book, Kyoko Mori, had first approached me over the transom—meaning she hadn't been referred to me in any way but had simply sent a blind query letter to the agency where I worked at the time. Her letter was impressive, and I asked to see her manuscript. I read it right away and loved the book, but as a new agent I hadn't yet developed a long list of contacts or a full sense of a variety of editors' likes and dislikes. The book was beautiful, yes, but it *was* quiet, and for months I considered sending it back—but I simply couldn't get it out of my mind. The characters and their trials and tribulations, the vivid poetic images, and the exotic Japanese setting combined with the universal theme of a child grieving for her beloved parent came back to me again and again. Finally I decided that was the best test of whether I should choose to represent a book or not. I called the author and asked to represent her. Thankfully, she said yes.

While it took me an inordinately long time to respond to Kyoko's manuscript, the lesson I learned—that if you can't forget a book, it's worth taking on—has stayed with me, and it's one of the indicators most agents and editors use when making a decision about whether or not to publish a work of fiction. It's only through such an intense connection with a book that an agent will be able to keep going through (in this case) thirty rejections and get you both to the lucky thirty-first submission. If a book holds such fascination for an agent, he can truly believe it will hold an equal fascination for some editor somewhere, and certainly for readers. And because not every one of those thirty editors turned the book down flat—several of them, younger editors largely, wrote and said they'd tried to buy it but their bosses hadn't allowed them to offer for it—my belief in Kyoko's work held firm until I found someone to publish the novel I couldn't forget.

When you're looking for an agent, you'll want to find someone who believes in you and your work. For some, this will happen serendipitously. For others, many years, many revisions, many rejection letters, and many hours of despair will come along before they connect with an agent who can help them get published. Yet even getting an agent is no guarantee—I've heard too often of the agent who sends a manuscript out to six or seven editors, then drops it when there isn't a quick sale. On the other hand, you and an agent might agree at the start that that's what you want to do: If a small segment of the market speaks and says "no," you're both planning to move on. The important thing, after all the research you've done to confirm that the agent is credible—something we'll discuss in greater detail later in this book—is to listen to your instincts about whether the person is working well for you or not.

BUILDING YOUR CAREER

There are writers who are convinced that only the biggest advances are meaningful, but most first novelists just want to get their book published. In the first flush of excitement over a book, an agent will dream, just the way you do, that every publisher in town will want to publish it, there will be a big auction, and you'll become a millionaire overnight. That does happen. But not usually. And even when it does, it might not be the best thing for your budding career as a published writer.

While most agents are thrilled to make a big deal, most have also been burned by the big advance that overwhelmed the first book. Most agents I know are prouder to tell the story of the book that received many rejections before finding a publisher than they are to tell the story of the book that got the huge advance and disappeared without a trace. That's because we take on novelists in the hope and belief that we're going to work with them to build a writing career, and a huge advance for a first book can often create too much pressure on everyone, from the author to the bookseller, to find and grow the author's audience. For every big deal that results in a first novel hitting the best-seller list, there are at least ten such deals that don't have that happy result.

MAKING THE MATCH

In addition to trying to get a good advance for a first book, agents try to match the author up with an editor who is savvy enough to get in-house attention for her books. As noted, we get to know who those editors are by meeting them, but also by talking to other agents or tracking the editors' careers through trade publications and Web sites like *Publishers Weekly* (www.publishersweekly.com) and Publishers Marketplace (www.publishers marketplace.com). Editors often send out letters outlining the kinds of books they're working on and proposing a meeting to discuss future projects. Many agents keep some kind of a database of editors and their areas of interest so they can quickly develop a submission list for each new project. Through being selective and only submitting a book to an editor who's fairly certain to be interested, an agent can ensure that his submissions will get immediate attention from busy editors. We know that a quick answer is better than no answer at all for any writer, and it's one of the ways we try to keep our clients in good spirits so they can go on doing what they do best: writing new and better books.

TALKING YOU UP

Another career-building move that agents make on your behalf is talking about your work to contacts other than editors. Movie producers come to New York to meet agents and talk about the kinds of books they've made into movies and the kind of material they're looking for. Foreign publishers come by when they're in town to talk about their lists and to hear about ours. We also see each other at conventions (like BookExpo America [BEA] and Bouchercon World Mystery Convention) and book fairs (like the Frankfurt Book Fair, the London International Book Fair, and the Bologna Children's Book Fair). At these fairs and conventions, we schedule meetings every half hour starting at breakfast and often going on beyond dinner. These meetings, conventions, fairs, and parties can lead to immediate results—an unplanned convention-hallway meeting with, say, a Russian editor can lead immediately to a deal—or they can serve to expand our list of contacts as well as our knowledge of the publishing business, both here and abroad.

If you find an agent who constantly refreshes his pool of contacts and increases his knowledge of the industry in this way, you'll find someone who can:

- come up with new ideas for how to sell your book even many months after it's been rejected by what seems like every publisher in town
- get your name known by talking about you to as many industry and industry-related people as possible
- develop further outlets for your work after it is published, like foreign translations and film options
- help you build your career as a writer so that perhaps one day you can make a living

IT'S LIKE A MARRIAGE ...

Although I prefer to regard it as a business partnership, the author-agent relationship has often been likened to a marriage—but so have business partnerships. There's the glowy honeymoon period where you both believe that only good things lie ahead. Then reality sets in, when you come to

153

know the other person's strengths and weaknesses, the things he can be relied upon to do and the things you're going to have to get on his back about. As long as you both accept that you're each going to have to row to stay afloat and to get somewhere, you'll probably be okay.

Communication is as key to this partnership as it is to any other. It's important to remember that while you have only this book, this contract, this editor, this publication, an agent has many of the same. I don't want to imply that your agent will or should be too busy to talk to you. But given the many demands on his attention, it's no good sitting around waiting to hear from him and hoping he'll read your mind. You've got to ask, and you've got to learn how to ask in a way that makes him, and eventually your editor and publicist, want to return your calls.

Unlike a marriage, where the roles of the two partners grow and change, merge, and divide over time, the agent in this partnership has a certain number of clear-cut duties. Yet there are also things you shouldn't expect. Here are some things a literary agent does and doesn't do:

WHAT AN AGENT DOES

- attempts to sell your book to a reputable publishing house
- keeps up-to-date with editors' interests as well as their contact information
- negotiates the terms of your contracts with publishers
- works on commission

WHAT AN AGENT DOES *NOT* DO

- guarantee fame and riches
- sell every manuscript he agrees to represent
- write the publishers' contracts for them

WHAT AN AGENT CAN DO

- offer editorial guidance or suggestions for improving your book
- get it into the hands of editors
- secure an advance or sell your book at an auction

WHAT AN AGENT *CANNOT* DO

- rewrite it or make it perfect for you
- guarantee those editors will read every word
- guarantee anyone will come to an auction even when they've told the interested editors they're holding one

WHAT AN AGENT SHOULD DO

- return your calls and e-mails within a reasonable period of time once you've signed on together
- give you realistic expectations
- be as interested as you are in getting a good advance—the better you do, the better he'll do

WHAT AN AGENT SHOULD *NOT* DO

- refuse to tell you anything he's done (Even if he has taken no actions at all, he should tell you that.)
- promise you a fortune
- accept or turn down advances without consulting with you

KNOWING WHICH QUESTIONS TO ASK WHEN

An important aspect of an agent's job is to manage the relationship between his client and the publisher. After selling a client's book to a publishing house, especially the book of a first-time author, an agent will try to make the process go as smoothly as possible by guiding the author on how best to communicate with his publisher. When clients ask about publicity, I tell them, "I don't handle the publicity for your book, but I can tell you which questions to ask when." The author and I put our heads together over all sorts of details: Should he rewrite the jacket copy the editor sent for his approval? (Sometimes.) Does he have to accept every editorial change? (No.) Should he come to town to meet people from the publicity and marketing departments? (It's usually a good idea.) Should he ask whether or not the publisher will advertise the book? (Yes.) How much time should he spend on the author's questionnaire? (A lot.) Can he ask to see the press release before it's sent out? (Definitely.)

While an agent can and does ask many of these questions on the author's behalf, he also encourages the author to communicate directly with the editor as much as possible in the interest of relationship- and career-building. If the communications go well and continue to improve, the editor will be a better in-house champion of the author's book, which in turn will result in a better publication, which will lead to the publishing house wishing to buy the author's next book. And isn't that the whole point? If it isn't, it should be: If you're not eager to make a career of your writing, a publisher won't be eager to publish you. There's an enormous investment of time and money that goes into publishing one novel, and the only way to hope to recoup that investment is to build on the initial investment with the publication of more and, it is to be hoped, increasingly successful books.

FINALLY ... WHY?

Why do agents do what they do? Why aren't they editors or writers? Why not sell real estate or wine or cars instead of books?

I guess we all have our different reasons for being literary agents. But the really good agents I know love books, they love to discover new writers, they love to exercise their powers of persuasion, and they love the thrill that comes from landing a publisher for a client. They have something of an entrepreneurial spirit, disliking corporate life and enjoying the competitive marketplace with all its ups and downs. (No one really likes the downs, but experience tells you they're followed by ups.) They like the satisfaction that any successful working person has of getting better at what he does year after year. And they like the financial upside: that once they've worked with a writer to build his career, they continue to share in his success by receiving a commission on all the book sales, even on contracts they negotiated years before. Writers have given the world so much. Advocating on their behalf is not only the least we can do in return—it's the heart of an enormously satisfying career.

RECOMMENDED READING

Author and Agent: Eudora Welty and Diarmuid Russell, by Michael Kreyling. Eudora Welty's agent, the founder of Russell & Volkening, was a young man when he first wrote to a young Welty after he'd read her stories in magazines. Their career-long partnership—which, thankfully, was played out in their voluminous correspondence—is delineated in this illuminating book.

Shizuko's Daughter, by Kyoko Mori. This first novel was rejected by thirty publishing houses, yet it went on to win awards, find publishers around the world, remain in print in its paperback edition, and launch the author's career.

I also recommend two excellent and informative resources that are published yearly. Not just directories, each contains articles about what agents do, how to find them, and how to work with them. They are: *Guide to Literary Agents,* edited by Joanna Masterson, and *Jeff Herman's Guide to Book Publishers, Editors, & Literary Agents,* by Jeff Herman.

Finally, although I am not going to dwell on trying to get published without an agent, I would like to recommend *How to Be Your Own Literary Agent,* by Richard Curtis. Richard, former president of the Association of Authors' Representatives (AAR), is one of the best agents ever and an excellent writer as well. My only two caveats about serving as your own agent are (1) it's probably easier to get a work of nonfiction published without an agent, and (2) doing it on your own is a full-time job.

RECOMMENDED WEB SITES

Association of Authors' Representatives (www.aar-online.org). Here you'll find the names and addresses of every agent member of this trade organization. Because every agent accepted into the organization must prove that he has sold a certain number of books within a certain period of time and, when accepted, must sign a Canon of Ethics, I recommend you make every effort to sign with an agent who is a member. (In the interest of full disclosure, I must report that I'm not only a member, I'm the treasurer.)

BookAngst 101 (http://bookangst.blogspot.com). Written anonymously by a publishing professional who was recently unmasked as Editor Dan Conaway of Putnam, this by turns painful and hilarious blog is a must-read for any aspiring writer. Look particularly at these two posts: One tells about going through four agents before finding happiness with the fifth ("Misadventures in [Mis]representation" by Lauren Baratz-Logsted), and the other talks about a successful career with five books published that didn't start out with big advances ("Anatomy of a Career").

mediabistro.com (www.mediabistro.com). While this Web site covers all forms of media, two regular columns are of particular interest: "Pitching an Agent," which profiles both established and emerging literary agencies, and "Lunch at Michael's," an amusing feature that tracks who's lunching with whom at the midtown New York City restaurant Michael's, a hotbed of media biz power lunchers. In addition to book people, television, newspaper, and magazine personalities are named with the restaurant's seating chart.

CHAPTER TWELVE:

before you submit your manuscript

As any seasoned novelist will tell you, most first novels are not first novels. The real first novel is locked away in a drawer, never to see the light of day. (Until, of course, you're famous and dead, at which point someone will publish it.) The real first novel is the practice novel. It is the creative space where you, as a writer, learn your craft. How to write a novel, for starters. How to make characters that seem real. How to create drama and tension. How to write dialogue, move forward in time (the wonders of the four-line-space break!), how to give the reader enough without giving too much or too little. The real first novel might be the one you write after reading Laura's chapters on how to accomplish all these things, and more. It might not get published, but it won't be a wasted effort. It's an essential part of your learning process on the road to becoming a published writer.

I'm not saying that *every* first novel is a practice novel. But a lot of them are. And you're only shooting yourself in the foot if you think you'd better rush this half-baked version off to agents and editors now, just because you've finished it and you spent a lot of time on it. Everyone knows you're writing your first novel, and wants to know not only when it will be published but who's going to make a movie of it. You can't disappoint everyone and embarrass yourself all at once by just putting it in a drawer, can you?

You can. Don't look at it as a total loss, but please: Put it in a drawer. Put it away for at least six weeks, if not two months or a year. And start writing something else. While not every first novel is a practice novel and not every first novel gets put in a drawer, too many novice writers rush the practice version off to agents and editors the minute they've finished it. After spending a great deal of time on it, and telling everyone they're writing their first novel, they're motivated to take it to the next level. Finishing it and putting it in a drawer is like admitting they've failed.

They haven't failed: They've begun their apprenticeship the way any craftsperson must. In *Literature and Revolution*, Leon Trotsky, of all people, wrote of literature, "Technique is noticed most markedly in the case of those who have not mastered it." When I read the first draft of a manuscript by someone who has never written fiction before or who has, perhaps, only been writing fiction for a year or two, I'm uncomfortably aware of every rough passage, every clumsy transition, every wooden phrase or cardboard character.

A majority of the submissions I receive each week describe first novels that are clearly not ready for publication. When someone writes (as a great many people do), "I quit my job a year ago to pursue my first love, writing fiction," I know that I'm being asked to read the first draft of a first-time writer's first novel. It doesn't matter to me whether the writer worked eight hours a day for a year on the manuscript or whether he calls this manuscript the third or fourth draft. I know that the writing will rarely display the level of craft required to make a really good book. But I also know that the writer wants to discover whether the book has any merits at all. He has been pretty alone with it for a year and, in spite of nice comments from his spouse and best friend, has finally hit a wall and hopes to get serious feedback from a publishing professional.

What I want to tell him is that he needs to learn to be the judge of his own work before asking anyone in publishing to read it. I know it doesn't seem easy when you're midway through the first draft of your first novel. Some days you think what you've written is good, and some days you think what you've written is bad. Some days you might be, as best-selling author Dennis Lehane has confessed to being from time to time, "terrified to put it down on paper." And it's after too many of those days that you start to feel you've entered the mirrored fun house at the circus and can't judge anything you've done in any objective fashion whatsoever.

Dennis once said to someone who expressed those fears, "Welcome to writing." I think the first important thing you can do is realize you've joined a sort of secret society of people who walk through the fun house daily, yet somehow emerge in the sunlight at the other end. I can even say with certainty that if you *never* feel uncertain about what you've written, it's probably not very good.

Kyoko Mori, the novelist and essayist discussed in chapter eleven, once said to me, "Any section that feels like a hot potato is the section the writer should concentrate on." Remember the tense fear and excitement with which you played the game of "hot potato" as a child? The main goal was to get rid of it the minute it touched your hands. And as adults, we know the sensation of trying to peel a just-boiled potato and dropping it repeatedly into the sink before it blisters our fingers. But on those dark days when you're actually afraid of your own work, it might be helpful to remember that the best and most flavorful potato salad is made with the hottest potatoes. Concentrate on those "hot potato" sections and see what you find there.

IN THEIR OWN WORDS: KATHLEEN GEORGE

Every published novelist has his share of false starts, unfinished manuscripts, and first novels that remain tucked away. Here's what Kathleen George, author of the suspense thrillers *Taken* and *Fallen*, has to say:

> I'd always heard a writer had to have five in the drawer before one got taken. I thought that was extreme, but I came to think maybe not. I had messed around without bringing to completion a couple of ideas. Then I got serious and wrote what I considered my first novel. And the thing is, I know I will go back to it some

day. It almost made it to publication, but I just wasn't ready to do something that big yet. It required an authority I didn't have then.

Next I tried to write to demand—usually a bad idea. But I'd had a comic story in *Mademoiselle* and everybody was asking me for a novel with that character in it. So I wrote that damn novel twelve or thirteen times—I mean really wrote and rewrote it—until one summer I admitted to myself that it isn't always possible to turn a short story into a novel, even if lots of people want you to, and even if you know all the pitfalls ahead of time and think you're smart enough to outsmart them.

Well, in that same summer, depressed and discouraged, I started a thriller—just a few notes, I told myself, just to entertain myself. That became *Taken*, my first novel. It took me for a ride. I had a good time writing. Something of my wish to entertain myself made its way to the page. When it was accepted, I was thrilled, of course, but a part of me thought, yes, I felt it, I felt that authority thing coming over me as I wrote. Part of my success with this manuscript was that I was practiced. Another part of the success probably came from the fact that I was detached, but playful. And another part of the reason I think—to be honest—that *Taken* sold was that I'd committed to a highly plotted story that operated on necessity and inevitability.

JUMPING THE GUN

By seeking professional feedback after finishing the first draft of a novel, you significantly reduce your novel's chances of ever being published. Agents and editors should not be your first readers. They are looking for polished manuscripts, not rough drafts. By its nature, any novel that hasn't been read by several other people is a rough draft, no matter how often it's been rewritten.

GOING BACK TO SQUARE ONE

What you should do is print your novel out and read it straight through, then put it away for six weeks. Then start something else—go back to Part

I of this book and follow some of Laura's suggested writing exercises, write a story, begin a new novel, write some essays. Many writers I know like to begin other projects in different genres when they're working on a novel. If you do this and refrain from rushing your first effort out, maybe the new project will be the published first novel while the one you finished first goes to live in a drawer somewhere.

BE A LUDDITE WHEN YOU EDIT

Before we get to a list of practical steps you can take to improve and evaluate your own work, I want you to promise that you will never, under any circumstances, rewrite your completed novel on the computer screen. I want you to promise that you will print out the manuscript, or print out what you have so far, and sit down with it and a pen or pencil to edit it. The computer is a wonderful thing for word processing. Although most writers I represent don't compose their work on computers, many people do, and they're grateful for the ease with which they can type, correct, and save their work.

But like the practitioners of any craft, most writers savor the tools of writing and have a deep interest in paper, notebooks, pens, pencils, erasers, typestyles or fonts, and ink. There is a famous photograph of John O'Hara at his writing desk, which prominently displays not only a manual typewriter but an enormous pot of rubber cement. In those typewriter days, writers had to physically wrestle with each page—feeding it into the typewriter, pounding on the keys, pulling the typed page out of the typewriter, adding a fresh sheet, and so on until they were ready to take the pages in hand and rework them. They attacked the raw material with pen or pencil, crossing out sentences and writing new ones, even cutting sentences or entire passages from one part and pasting them into another section. I've heard of writers who pinned the entire manuscript up on the wall as they worked and others who spread the whole thing out on the floor. Technology has helped writers enormously, but it hasn't figured out how to spread the pages of a novel out on the dining room table so you can see each of them whole. While you will of course edit, correct, and reword passages and move others around as you compose on the computer, the real work of rewriting requires something more.

TEN WAYS TO GO FROM GOOD TO GREAT

Here are ten exercises to prepare you for the day you will submit a novel to agents or publishers. You can do the following exercises whether you've already written a novel or are about to start writing one. The difference will be that if you haven't written the book yet, you'll spread these exercises out over the time it takes you to complete a novel. If you have written a book, you'll do these exercises in quicker succession—but they won't be any easier for being done faster.

You can start the first three exercises before your novel's six-week hibernation period is up, or even before you've written the novel. But you shouldn't attempt the others until you've stayed away from the manuscript, and then gone back and overhauled it. All of the exercises are things you should do well in advance of contacting an agent or a publisher.

1.   **If you haven't done so already, join or form a writers' group.** It doesn't matter where you live—there are other writers there. Sometimes I think there's not a soul in America who *isn't* writing a book. There may be some truth to this impression: A recent article in the *Economist* reported that, while reading declined dramatically from 1982 to 2002, "the number of people in America claiming to do 'creative writing' increased by 30 percent" in the same time period. So don't skip this step because you think you don't know any writers. Chances are the person at the dryer next to yours in the Laundromat is a writer. There are groups of writers who gather just to write, to generate fresh material, and others who gather to read works in progress. Try to find a group that meets once a week, and remember to be conscientious about others' work—you're all in this together.

2. **Sign up for a writing workshop.** This is a more formal gathering that's often led by a professional of some kind; there is frequently a fee charged for participation. You may be given assignments, and each week you'll be asked to read a few pieces of work and be prepared to discuss them in the group. I know of one well-run workshop in which each participant has to say one good thing and one critical thing about a piece of work, no one can repeat anything that's already been said, the writer can ask questions but not "defend" his choices, and the teacher leads a discussion after the comments. This is clearly a very well-organized workshop and bound to be helpful to anyone who enters it with serious intent, but these groups can be hit-or-miss. You'll have to shop around and talk to people who have been involved in some. Listen to their recommendations and warnings. Even in an extremely nurturing atmosphere, whether your work improves or not will depend on how well you can filter criticism and comment, discarding what's not helpful and using what is. If you find yourself in a workshop that's disorganized or that features an overly critical member, at the very least you'll get a tougher hide, which is essential for anyone who wants to get published. Ideally, you'll find one that makes you feel that lightbulbs are flicking on in your head at each session.

3. **Take a creative writing class.** These are everywhere—at nearby universities, at local schools, in people's homes, on the Internet. You'll be given writing assignments, which is a good way to generate new work and develop discipline. It's important that you pay careful attention to discussions of technique. A good creative writing class encourages you to read good literature with the aim of evaluating the writer's technique. In creative writing classes and good work-shops, you learn the common language of writing—its terms and major concerns—and that's an important part of your education as a writer.

After your novel is complete and has had its hibernation, take some of these steps:

4. **Read your novel aloud.** Yes, that's right, read the whole thing out loud. Stop and make a note whenever you hear anything that sounds awkward, pretentious, or dull. Notice the parts where you want to stop reading and ask yourself why. Do you think it's just because you're tired? Think again. Remember how difficult it is, even in a state of exhaustion, for you to put aside a gripping book? If you want to stop reading your own novel, and it's not three o'clock in the morning, what do you think your reader will want to do? After you've made notes throughout, revise.

5. **Now sit down with the manuscript and read it through with one thing in mind.** For instance, during the first read-through, concentrate on the dialogue. On another, focus on the time frame. On a third, practice turning every three sentences into one—or, as the Reverend Sydney Smith recommended in *A Memoir of the Reverend Sydney Smith 1771–1845*, by Lady Holland, "In composing, as a general rule, run your pen through every other word you have written; you have no idea what vigor it will give your style." These exercises build objectivity and discipline. Doing them will also enhance your mastery of the craft.

6. **Stage a reading of the manuscript in your living room.** In this scenario, you won't be doing any of the reading. Three or four or five friends, acquaintances, or family members will be doing it for you. You're going to sit in the corner and listen and make notes. Playwrights often give their work semi-public readings, in which actors sit at a table and read their parts and neither the director, playwright, nor audience make any comment at all unless (on the part of the audience) it is to express appreciation. In a private reading of your novel, you'll have to work out how you want the different readers to handle it, whether they rotate chapters or read the lines of different characters, with one person serving as narrator.

You should also decide ahead of time whether you want feedback from the readers and whether you'll read the entire manuscript in a marathon session or just the first eighty pages or so. Finally, it would be a good idea to offer refreshments to these very good friends of yours.

7. **Sign up to read your work at local venues.** Many towns have pubs or cafés that feature readings. Contact the manager and ask how to get on the list of readers. If your town or area doesn't have any readings, go to a local hangout—again, a pub or a café, a bookstore, or even a stationery store—and ask if you can create a reading series for them. At the reading, you'll read a chapter or part of a chapter from your book. In your brief introduction, don't go into great detail about what you're trying to accomplish with the book; just set up the scene so the listeners can follow it without wondering who the characters are. The purposes of giving a reading before trying to find a publisher for your work are (1) to practice reading in public, (2) to get used to the idea of readers hearing your work, and (3) to experience your work from a different angle so that afterward you're better able to look at it with fresh eyes when revising. I would even advise you to read the section you're most confused or worried about. Remember that all of these exercises are designed to give you feedback *before* approaching agents and editors and to help you develop some objectivity about your work. Without some kind of feedback, you might be tempted to dump the sections that worry or frighten you. But remember the hot potatoes.

As your manuscript becomes more refined as the result of each of these exercises—because after each one, you'll go to work revising—you're going to get closer to thinking about submitting your work for publication. Before you do:

8. **Hire a proofreader to read your manuscript and correct typos and other errors.** Does your town have a local newspaper? Does

that newspaper employ a proofreader? Chances are that person takes freelance work. Don't ask a relative to do this work unless that relative has actually worked as a proofreader or is the best speller you have ever met.

One don't:

9. **Don't hire a professional editor.** I know many good editors who, having been downsized by big publishing houses, work as freelance editors or ghostwriters. I recommend them for works of nonfiction, but I've never signed on a novelist who has come to me after working with a professional editor. Why? Because you have to grow to learn what your novel needs, and learn to do the work of revising and editing yourself. Someone who has worked with a professional editor displays an uncertainty in his abilities. Agents and editors need to see someone who has a great deal of belief not only in his work but in his ability, and a great deal of commitment to the work. Once we see that, we know we can work with the person. If we see someone who has written a novel and then, despairing of its ever being published, hires an editor to get it into shape, we are looking at someone whose goal is simply publication, not creation. As Gertrude Stein said, "You will write if you will write without thinking of the result in terms of a result, but think of the writing in terms of discovery."

Last but not least …

10. **After you've done some or all of the above, put your novel away for *another* six weeks or more.** Work on something else. Write another short story or essay if that's what you did before, or go back to the other novel you started or, if you haven't started one, start one now. Then take the first manuscript out and read it through again. Don't read it with the expectation that it will now be in perfect shape to send out. Read it with the expectation that you might have to go through steps four through eight all over again, and read it

with William Butler Yeats and Truman Capote looking over your shoulder: Yeats said, "Cast a cold eye," and Capote, "Good writing is rewriting."

This quote from Ursula K. Le Guin will inspire you to keep going in the face of uncertainty and loneliness, common places—like the mirrored fun house—for a writer to find himself.

> Writers have to get used to launching something beautiful and watching it crash and burn. They also have to learn when to let go of control, when the work takes off on its own and flies, farther than they ever planned or imagined, to places they didn't know they knew. All makers must leave room for the acts of the spirit. But they have to work hard and carefully, and wait patiently, to deserve them.

RECOMMENDED READING

The Hand of the Poet, by Rodney Phillips. This marvelous illustrated book shows the manuscript pages of well-known poets, from John Donne to Julia Alvarez, with their handwritten revisions.

The Calling, by Sterling Watson. Dennis Lehane calls this novel the best depiction of a writing workshop ever written.

The Happiness of Getting It Down Right: Letters of Frank O'Connor and William Maxwell, edited by Michael Steinman. This correspondence between the great Irish short story master and his editor at the *New Yorker* brings us into the minds of two artists and the process of writing, editing, revising and, well, getting it down right. Stanley Kauffmann's blurb on the back of the jacket says it perfectly: "Here is a marriage of true minds, between a superb author and a perfectly attuned editor (himself a fine writer). Anyone curious about the making of literature will be fascinated—and moved."

Poets & Writers. P&W is the dream publication for every aspiring writer. With regular features like "The Practical Writer" and "The Literary Life" as well as brilliant profiles of well-known and emerging writers, it's essential for inspiration, knowledge of the craft, and a sense of community in a lonely profession.

RECOMMENDED WEB SITES

ShawGuides to Writers Conferences & Workshops (http://writing.shaw guides.com). Hands down the best and most comprehensive listing of writers conferences throughout the world, not just the U.S. You can search by place, date, and genre. It's amazingly well organized and easy to use.

Poets & Writers, Inc. (www.pw.org). The Web site is every bit as good as the seminal magazine that launched it. In addition to access to the magazine's contents, it offers a message forum, links to resources for writers, an admirably brief and useful page called "Top Six Questions Writers Ask," and best of all, a directory of writers that you can access to form your own writing group.

CHAPTER THIRTEEN:

the first steps on the path to publication

I hope that you experience that day when, as Ursula K. Le Guin wrote, "the work takes off on its own and flies." But it won't do that until, as she also wrote, you've worked "hard and carefully, and wait[ed] patiently." As you can see from the previous chapters, you do have to alternate periods of hard, careful work with patient waiting—writing the book is one thing, but putting it away and waiting until it's ready to take you back is quite another. Another time you'll need to exercise patience is while waiting until you're ready to find the right agent or publisher for your work.

You're not going to sit down and wait for anyone to find you once your book is done, of course. If you were that kind of person, you wouldn't be reading this book. But now you're ready to start meeting people—other writers, good readers, people who know other people who might put out a helping hand on your journey to publication. And you're going to start regarding some of the writers and readers you already know in a different way. Whereas to this point you've needed support and feedback for your writing, now you need support for your belief that you are not only ready to be published but that you *will* be published.

MEETING OTHER WRITERS

When you're starting out as a writer of fiction, it's essential to find other writers who really like what you're doing in your writing. Those writers are your audience, in many cases they'll be your friends, and they're the people you should stay in touch with. If you've workshopped your novel, attended a writers conference, or gotten an M.F.A. in creative writing, you've met other writers. And they've met you and know something of your work.

WRITING GROUPS

Let's start with your writing group—you do have one, don't you? If you do, you've already begun to spend time with other writers. You might now need to assess the kinds of writers in your group. Have any been published at all? Have any had fiction published, whether short stories or novels? Have any landed an agent? If your answer to all these questions is no, you're going to need to widen your circle of writers.

There are almost certainly better or more successful or more well-connected writers in your town or community. If you've been immersing yourself in the writing life, you've undoubtedly heard of them and may even have met them. Now is the time to get to know them better.

How do you approach them? I don't need to tell you that you're not going to be pushy, arrogant, or rude. If you're quietly confident in your work, and believe that the writer you'd like to get to know better will truly respond to the kind of work you're doing, you'll find it easier to make the first contact. Be aware that if the writer you have in mind is quite successful and well known, he undoubtedly receives many requests for help of all kinds: *Will you blurb this novel? Will you speak at our library? Will you attend our conference? Will you write an article for my magazine? Will you give me some advice?* So until you, too, have achieved some level of success and recognition, that very successful writer may not be able to give you the attention you need right now.

Instead, look for another just-starting-out writer who may still have the time and inclination to form connections with other local writers. Tell him something of yourself in an e-mail or a note—something about you as a writer—how you've been in a writing group, you're sending out stories, you think your novel is ready—and invite him for coffee, a meal, or a drink. Ask if he would be available to meet for lunch on a particular day two or three weeks away, and put in your telephone number and e-mail address for reply.

It's helpful if you can reference a mutual friend or contact. For instance, you can telephone if you keep the conversation to "[Name] suggested we meet because we're both novelists, so I'm calling to see if you would be free for [lunch/coffee/a drink] on [a date two or more weeks away]." Be definite with the invitation. Don't say, "Maybe we could have coffee sometime," because those kinds of suggestions rarely result in anything. And while we're in the Emily Post portion of our program, may I also remind you that when you do meet, you must pick up the check. Don't sit there with a vacant look in your eyes when it comes. If you're deep in conversation, put your hand on it as soon as it arrives and slide it to your side of the table, keep talking, take your wallet out, and put your credit card or cash down. If the other person puts up an argument, just say "next time" and change the subject.

What you get from this meeting is up to you. If this writer, like you, feels ready to find a way to get his work published, or perhaps has already begun, I hope the two of you hit it off and travel some of the journey together. Maybe you'll join the other's writing group or he'll join yours. Perhaps you'll agree to get together once a month or so to read each other's writing. Maybe you'll become regular e-mail correspondents and share leads on editors and agents looking for fiction like yours. The point of this relationship is less writing support than networking, because by now you are both at the point where you need more of the latter than the former—even though you will never stop needing the former.

WRITERS CONFERENCES

Conferences are a terrific way to meet like-minded writers. A good conference is one that's organized into intensive workshop sessions or seminars by category of writing: popular fiction, literary nonfiction, memoir, literary fiction, poetry, etc. It will feature well-known writers who will conduct sessions during the day and give readings of their work in the evenings. You'll be given time to write, and to read portions of others' work, and there are generally a couple of evenings set aside for student readings. In addition, you will often be given the option of signing up for a one-on-one consultation about your work with a member of the writing faculty. Conferences are frequently held at colleges that are out of session, so the attendees can stay in the dorms. It's a Spartan existence that helps you concentrate exclusively on your writing. And it's the rare conference attendee who doesn't find another writer with whom to share work and ideas.

ONLINE WORKSHOPS

These are proliferating, and most people I've talked to who have participated in those offered by reputable entities like The New School (www.online.newschool.edu), Gotham Writers' Workshop (www.writingclasses.com), and Zoetrope Writing Workshops (http://zoetrope.writingclasses.com) have had very positive experiences. You'll read weekly lectures and receive weekly assignments. In addition, there will be a separate forum where students can meet and talk. From one of these online workshops, you might form a virtual friendship with another writer with whom you can swap ideas and leads or share your writing.

LOCAL HANGOUTS

I've said it before and I'll say it again: There are writers everywhere you look. If your town or neighborhood is lucky enough to have a good independent bookstore, the owner or manager probably knows just about every writer around. Get to know the plugged-in bookstore staff and see if they can lead you to other writers who might be good contacts. Attend readings by visiting writers and see who comes out of the woodwork. If the writer who's reading is someone whose work you admire, or someone who writes in the same genre, you will certainly find other writers like you in the audience. See if you can meet one at the reception or signing after the reading.

MAKING A NAME FOR YOURSELF

With your novel done, and with the idea of getting published ahead of you, what are you going to offer editors and agents besides your unpublished novel? Have you written any short stories or essays? Could a chapter of your novel stand alone as a story, or could it be adapted to stand alone? Now is the time to make a concerted effort to publish your short pieces. You will get more attention from agents and editors if you have some sort of publication history. Not only will they pay more attention to your query letter if you can cite publication or readings at reputable venues, it is possible that you'll be discovered this way. Many agents and editors read literary magazines in the hope of discovering new talent. I represent several writers whose work I first read in journals or magazines, and there are some famous examples: The authors of both *Under the Tuscan Sun* (Frances Mayes) and *Million Dollar Baby* (F.X. Toole) were discovered by agents after publishing work in little magazines.

LITERARY MAGAZINES

If you have a full-time job and you've been writing and rewriting your novel in a happy haze of hobbyism, now is the time to take a second job whose paycheck might not come in for a while. Your new job is basically to be your own secretary. Here's what you'll be expected to do:

- Ensure that all your stories or essays are in printable form: polished to perfection, free of errors and typos, and arranged in double-spaced type.

- Spend time at a library or good bookstore developing a list of journals or magazines that publish the kind of work you've done. Take a look at annual directories like *Writer's Market* and *Novel & Short Story Writer's Market*. Make sure the names of editors and the addresses of the publications are up-to-date. You might have to call them or look in several sources to accomplish this.

- Note as exactly as possible the submission guidelines for each and every journal. If one journal's guidelines state its editors only read in September and October, do not send them a story in May. If another's state they only publish epic poetry, do not send them an essay on the birth of your first child after reasoning that a seventy-two-hour labor could be considered "epic."

- Write a brief cover letter that can be easily adapted for each submission. The letter should have no more than one line about the piece you're submitting; two or three lines about who you are, who you've studied with, whether you have any publication credits or have received any recognition for your work by winning awards or contests; and no more than a line or two about "looking forward to hearing from you." Try to determine what the editor wants to hear by reading the journal's guidelines. Many editors of journals and "little magazines" have told me they believe authors who wish to be published in their journals should read an issue or more, and if you desire publication in literary magazines, you should support their shoestring efforts by subscribing to several each year, either the same ones or new ones with each subscription cycle.

- Assemble envelopes, stamps, labels, and stationery. Take your stories to the post office and determine what the postage will be when one is in an envelope with a self-addressed stamped envelope (SASE) and what it will be when it is in the SASE alone on its return journey. Write these rates down and don't put too little postage on the envelopes you send out or on the envelopes you enclose for the return of your material. Make sure, too, that the return envelopes are big enough to hold the material you want back; if you don't want it returned, make that clear in your cover letter. Journal editors have told me of the feats of origami they've performed in an attempt to return material in too-small SASEs.

- Start submitting your material. It's permissible (unless one journal's guidelines forbid it) to send a piece to several editors at once, but you must say that's what you're doing in your cover letter.

- When you get a story back, send it out to the next editor on your list *immediately*. No detours through the Slough of Despond allowed. However, if you're lucky enough to receive a letter with some remarks about the story's strengths and weaknesses or even some suggestions for revision, consider this information very carefully before submitting the piece elsewhere.

Don't be discouraged by the number of rejections you receive. F. Scott Fitzgerald wrote in his journal that he had 122 rejection slips pinned up on the wall of his apartment, yet he went on to publish many short stories and, of course, the brilliant novels for which he is still known.

Do be encouraged by the slightest sign of life in the responses, even if it is a lightly penciled "Try us again" on the form letter. Many, many writers regard a rejection as just a rejection. But very few of the form rejection letters sent out by journals and magazines bear those little penciled notations, so you should take them to heart if you get them.

OTHER FORMS OF PUBLICATION

Why not try to publish something in your local newspaper? You could approach the editor with an idea for a column, or get your foot in the door by writing an op-ed piece. A poet I know called me when Allen Ginsberg died and asked if I knew anyone who would publish his own brief poetic ode to Ginsberg. While he had in mind *Parade* magazine or the *New York Times*, I suggested he think locally. Sure enough, his hometown newspaper in Santa Cruz ran the piece the next day.

Do you read current fiction? Submit some reviews. Writing reviews of new books has several advantages: It keeps you abreast of what's being published, it forces you to examine the tools of craft employed by published writers and, by virtue of your byline, it might circulate your name in some small fashion among publishers, editors, agents, and other writers.

Don't limit your consideration to your local newspaper. Think about other kinds of publications, such as weekly city magazines focusing on entertainment and the arts, your bookstore's newsletter, your college's publication or

the first steps on the path to publication

Web site, or any publication put out by a professional organization of which you're a member. One or two overworked but dedicated and energetic people typically put together these kinds of publications, and they're always on the lookout for contributors.

Finally, there's the Internet, with any number of chat rooms, online journals, and blogs. Bearing in mind that "publication" on most of these sites doesn't count for much in the eyes of book editors and agents, it is another way, especially if you're selective about where and what you post, to circulate your name and to practice writing. Online publications that are meaningful include *Slate, Salon, About.com,* and the online versions of major news publications or organizations from the *New York Times* to *Newsweek* or CNN.

There are so many blogs on the Web nowadays that, if you are going to start one, I suggest you keep the subject very focused. Your blog doesn't have to focus exclusively on writing. It might focus on butterflies or it might focus on Houdini, but whatever direction you take, make sure you take it in a *direction*, without undue rambling. You'll get more attention from readers and potential publishing contacts with something that's focused. There are several group blogs on the Web, a good idea for busy people who don't have time to update posts frequently. Get to know the blogs by writers in your genre or category. Not only will you learn something about the life of a published writer and find like-minded people posting comments, you'll eventually want to network with the writers of these and similar blogs.

READINGS AND PRESENTATIONS

In "Ten Ways to Go From Good to Great" in chapter twelve, I recommended that you try to arrange public readings of your work. If you live in an area that has many potential places to read in front of an audience, do this as often as possible. If you travel, try to arrange something, perhaps through a friend or acquaintance in the other city, at a venue there. You can do this when you visit family or when you go back to visit your college or when you're on a business trip. If you don't read from your novel, you might want to offer some sort of informative presentation—a writing workshop, for instance—or, locally, you might approach the schools and ask if you can come in and work on writing with the students. You never know what these things will lead to, but they will certainly do two things: They'll help you get better as a writer, and they'll look really good in a query letter.

F. SCOTT FITZGERALD: LEARNING FROM ONE OF THE GREATS

Many of you know that F. Scott Fitzgerald became an instant literary sensation with the 1920 publication of his first novel, *This Side of Paradise*, when he was twenty-four years old. But many people don't know that more than ten years passed from the time he published his first story (a detective story in a student newspaper) to the time his novel came out, and that Charles Scribner's Sons turned his book down twice before finally accepting it for publication in late 1919.

Well before his first book was published, it was no secret to those who knew him that Fitzgerald aspired to be a famous novelist. Early in 1918, shortly after he left Princeton University and entered the army as a lieutenant, and more than two years before *This Side of Paradise* was published, Fitzgerald wrote his college friend Edmund Wilson to discuss the writing of various mutual acquaintances, then went on to describe the novel he was writing. To introduce it in the letter, Fitzgerald wrote out the title page for the book, then called *The Romantic Egotist*, and included this notation: "Chas. Scribner's Sons (Maybe!), MCMXVIII." He went on to say: "… if Scribner takes it I know I'll wake some morning and find that the debutantes have made me famous overnight."

SPELL OUT YOUR DREAMS

The remarkable thing about this letter is Fitzgerald's belief in the book's future. Not only did he put in writing the name of the company that eventually published his book, he described almost exactly what happened when the book was published: It became a bestseller, and he became famous, virtually overnight.

How did Fitzgerald set about publishing a best-selling novel? While it would be necessary to read several of the excellent biographies about Fitzgerald, as well as his published letters and diaries, to get the full picture, we can sketch out some of the things he did to pave his own road to success that might be helpful to other writers.

He began writing when he was away at boarding school and published his first story when he was just thirteen years old. At Princeton University, where his hopes to play football were dashed shortly after he arrived, Fitzgerald met and befriended writers with whom he could "talk and talk about books." Edmund Wilson, one of those writers, later wrote that they:

> ... saw in literature a sphere of activity in which they themselves hoped to play a part. You read Shakespeare, Shelley, George Meredith, Dostoevsky, Ibsen, and you wanted ... to learn their trade ... I remember Scott Fitzgerald's saying to me, not long after we got out of college: "I want to be one of the greatest writers who have ever lived, don't you?" ... he always ... pitted himself against the best ... and I am sure that his intoxicated ardor represented the healthy way for a young man of talent to feel.
>
> —*The Far Side of Paradise: A Biography of F. Scott Fitzgerald,*
> by Arthur Mizener

IF YOU GET SHOT DOWN ...

When Fitzgerald finished *The Romantic Egotist*, he showed it to a friend whose own publisher was Scribner. The friend read the novel, refused to show it to his editor, and even tried to talk Fitzgerald out of publishing it. But Fitzgerald persuaded another friend to submit the novel to Scribner for him. That friend's letter to Scribner said, in part:

> Though Scott Fitzgerald is still alive it has a literary value. Of course when he is killed [in World War I] it will also have a commercial value. Before leaving for France he has committed it to me...
>
> —*Correspondence of F. Scott Fitzgerald,* edited by Matthew J.
> Bruccoli and Margaret M. Duggan, with Susan Walker

No pressure, right? Nevertheless, Scribner turned the book down in a letter of four long paragraphs signed "Charles Scribner's Sons" (thought to be written by Maxwell Perkins, the legendary Scribner editor) that delineated the novel's problems while remarking on its originality. The letter concluded by suggesting the author revise the novel and show it to Scribner again. Fitzgerald swiftly made some revisions and resubmitted the book to Scribner, who just as swiftly turned it down flat.

... FIND YOUR ZELDA

In the meantime, according to Mizener's biography, Scott had met his future wife, Zelda, and, wanting to impress her, set about "the serious business of making a fortune," working for an advertising agency while writing short stories. Finally selling a story, he quit his job and "settled down to rewrite *The Romantic Egotist* according to a schedule which he had pinned to the curtain before his desk." When he finally bundled the completely rewritten manuscript off to Perkins, Scribner accepted the novel in two weeks and published it six months later to great success.

I tell this story to show you how Fitzgerald geared his life from a young age to the pursuit of books and writing. He may have aspired to be a football player and a playwright and even an actor, he may have worked for an advertising agency, he may have served in the Army, but at every turn he knew other writers and fervently made writing—his own and others'—a priority in his daily schedule, his thoughts, and his social life.

In the particulars of his story I find an example any aspiring writer can follow, because I don't know a published writer of fiction who doesn't regularly see other writers, discuss literature with other writers, or read the work of other good published writers, classic or contemporary. Even if you did not start writing at "a young age," you can use Fitzgerald's story for inspiration—the only difference is the age you'll be ten years after your first story is published. In other words, you can't be a great writer faster just because you're older. But you can get to a better writing place with time and an immersion in the work.

Here are some things you can do if you'd like to trace the path Fitzgerald followed as he set about forging his writing career:

- Write constantly.

- Know other writers wherever you are.

- Share and discuss your work with other writers.

- Read and discuss the work of others.

- Read contemporary and classic works of fiction and discuss and argue about them with other writers.

- Make your aspirations concrete by writing them down—"Chas. Scribner's Sons (Maybe!)"—and saying them aloud to others—"I want to be one of the greatest writers who have ever lived, don't you?"

Not only did all these actions undoubtedly improve Fitzgerald's writing and help him develop his craft to a very high degree, they worked to widen his reputation as a writer before his first novel was ever published. The letters and conversations he shared with other writers also undoubtedly yielded the names of book and magazine editors and publishers—as well as those of literary agents—that Fitzgerald could note for future use. But above all, everything he did served to bolster his idea of himself as a writer, and that kept him going, even in the face of despair and rejection, until his first novel was published.

RECOMMENDED READING

The New York Times Book Review. Published weekly and available nationally, the NYTBR is essential reading for anyone who's interested in contemporary writing.

The life and work of F. Scott Fitzgerald has inspired and touched countless writers. In addition to his novels, most famously *The Great Gatsby*, there are books about him that include his marvelous letters and other fascinating details about his life. Here is a sampling:

- *A Life in Letters: F. Scott Fitzgerald*, edited and annotated by Matthew J. Bruccoli
- *The Far Side of Paradise: A Biography of F. Scott Fitzgerald*, by Arthur Mizener
- *Correspondence of F. Scott Fitzgerald*, edited by Matthew J. Bruccoli and Margaret M. Duggan with the assistance of Susan Walker
- *The Letters of F. Scott Fitzgerald*, edited by Andrew Turnbull

RECOMMENDED WEB SITES

Salon (www.salon.com). Although it's not exactly free anymore (you can get day passes if you watch an ad), *Salon* has some of the best book coverage on the Web, from reviews and profiles to essays and commentary.

Backstory (http://mjroseblog.typepad.com/backstory). If you haven't yet found your own community of writers, here's a virtual community that will entertain and sustain you.

Zoetrope: All-Story (www.all-story.com). Online home of the short-fiction magazine founded by Francis Ford Coppola, *Zoetrope* offers three online fiction workshops: basic, advanced, and master class. In the ten-week courses, you'll workshop stories, discuss craft, complete exercises and assignments, and read the work of others.

Gotham Writers' Workshop (www.writingclasses.com). Offers too-many-to-count online writing classes and workshops. Having taught one once, I can confirm that they're well run and in-depth and that they attract writers who are serious about their work.

BookBitch (www.bookbitch.com). Long one of my favorite sites, Book-Bitch has lists of favorite book group books, reviews, links to every kind of book site under the Web, and a page called "Virgins" that's devoted to new authors.

CHAPTER FOURTEEN:

query letter babylon

Like many independent literary agencies, mine is small, with only two full-time people and one part-time person and no more than fifty active clients at any given time. Yet even we receive at least fifty query letters every week. Potentially, we could replace our entire client list—which has been nearly twenty years in the making—every week of the year. And at the end of every year, we've read, processed, answered, thrown away, cried over, winced at, yawned over, or gotten excited about nearly three thousand letters about as-yet-unpublished books. And that number doesn't include the e-mail queries that we officially don't accept but that nevertheless come in at the rate of twenty or more a week.

Out of those three thousand pleas, nearly 75 percent are about novels. And out of those, at least 90 percent are about first novels. That brings the number of queries about first novels to about two thousand every year. And in 2003, I accepted as a client one new novelist out of those two thousand. That's not 2 percent, or 1 percent, or even one-half of a percent. That's one-tenth of one-half of a percent.

Reading statistics like those must be thoroughly discouraging. Statistics often are discouraging: The number of people who apply to certain schools vs. the number who get in is always a discouraging number. Our chances of winning a million-dollar-plus lottery is another discouraging number, but many of us still buy tickets. So let's look at those numbers another way:

Eighty percent of those query letters about first novels should never have been sent.

That's right—a full 80 percent of the letters I read about first novels never should have been sent to me, or to any agent or editor. Either the writers were not ready to be published and their books were not ready to be agented, or they misdirected the query letter by writing me about the kind of book I don't represent.

So, if we subtract 80 percent from the two thousand first-novel query letters I and many of my colleagues see every year, we come up with a grand total of four hundred. Four hundred letters a year is only about eight letters per week. I would happily read to their end eight letters a week about first novels. Yet if I still only take on one writer of those four hundred, I have taken on one-quarter of a percent of the writers who write to me about their first novels. It's still a small percentage, but $1/400^{th}$ is considerably better than $1/2000^{th}$. (Try reading that sentence out loud and you'll see one reason why.)

WHO'S YOUR AUDIENCE?

Before we even get to the query letter, you're going to need to do some thinking. You've done a lot of work. In the first place, you've written an entire novel, no small feat by itself. You've suffered through the pain of having people read it, and bitten your nails to the quick waiting to hear what they think. Then you've gone through every emotion from frustration at the positive but inarticulate reader's response—"I liked it. It was good"—to pain at the critical person's response, to anger at the person who didn't understand it, to ecstasy at finding someone who did. You've formed a writing group, and you've rewritten the thing. You've gone to workshops, and you've had strangers read it and either help or hinder you. And then you've rewritten the thing again. You've set up readings and read parts out loud at cafés where the audience sat in a stony silence, and then you've gone home and rewritten the thing yet again. But you haven't asked yourself one tough question:

Who in the world will want to read this novel?

How can you, the author of the work, answer that question? Don't worry, you don't really need to answer it completely. You don't need enough information to fill a spreadsheet with demographic data. You don't need names and telephone numbers of potential readers. But you need some sense of who your audience might be beyond "everyone who reads fiction."

If you don't try to get at least a rough idea of your specific audience, you're not going to be able to figure out who will be the right agent to represent the kind of book you've written, and you're going to end up in the 99.95 percent of first novelists who get form rejection letters to every query they send out. What you want to do is target your efforts so your query letter falls into the small percentage of letters that are actually directed at the right person.

IN THEIR OWN WORDS: C.J. BOX

When C.J. Box, whose debut mystery novel, *Open Season*, kicked off a popular series featuring Wyoming game warden Joe Pickett, was first writing, he had doubts about who his audience would be.

> I thought *Open Season*, which was then called, unimaginatively, *Joe Pickett*, might have a regional audience and it was that imagined regional audience I was writing it for. The themes of the novel were so close to home, i.e., the effects of the Endangered Species Act, the protagonist a Wyoming game warden, the hunting culture, Wyoming, the setting a small rural town at the foot of the Big Horn Mountains. Because of the "smallness" of the world it portrayed, I assumed it might attract readers who either lived in the Rocky Mountains or were interested in them. I imagined selling copies of it out of the trunk of my car, like every local author I'd ever encountered. I never thought in terms of writing a mystery novel (I thought mystery novels were written by Agatha Christie) or writing the first book in a series. I thought about accuracy; portraying this world as I saw it from the inside out. It scared me to death that someone might read it and say it wasn't "real." So I shot small. Imagine my surprise.

DECIDING WHERE YOU FIT

If you are writing within a specific genre, like young adult, science fiction, mystery, romance, or Westerns, you have a better idea of whom your audience might be than someone who's writing a coming-of-age novel or any other kind of non-category fiction. Yet each of the established genres has gotten to be incredibly elastic and wide-ranging, so even you will have to figure out which segment of your category's audience is most likely to want to read your novel.

REVIEW YOUR "REVIEWS"

Go back and think about the other people who read your manuscript, and their reactions. Recall the reactions of audience members at any readings you may have given. Be honest with yourself as you contemplate the various reactions, separating kindness and sympathy from true galvanizing enthusiasm (if indeed any of them expressed that). Discard the kind and sympathetic—or, if you were unlucky enough to receive them, the cruel and indifferent—responses. In fact, go over the following checklist and write the names of your readers next to the word that most closely describes their responses. When you're done, discard all but the names next to all the words and phrases in the last two rows.

Word/phrase that most closely defines the response of _____:

cruel	cutting	hurtful
critical	baffled	embarrassed
confused	bland	uninvolved
indifferent	sympathetic	kind
helpful	thoughtful	amused
grateful	enthusiastic	excited
galvanized	moved to tears	eureka
wow	state of awe	laughed until I cried

Now meditate on those people who showed up on the bottom part of the list. What are they like? Who are their favorite authors? What are their favorite movies? Do they like to travel? Where do they like to go? Do they prefer malls to museums, club-hopping to opera-going, mud-biking to bird-watching?

Whatever they're like, these are your readers. If you thought you were writing edgy urban fiction for hipsters but the readers who liked it most were all fifty-something suburbanites, you'll need to be honest with yourself about your potential audience. Your honesty will help you narrow your search for agent, editor, publisher—whoever will help your book find its way into the hands of your future readers. Whoever your readers are, it's exciting to realize that there could be more of them out there. Your job is to find a way to reach them. There's a lot to do before you or they hold a bound copy of your book, but the first step in reaching them is to write a query letter to a literary agent.

WRITING THE LETTER YOU'RE NOT GOING TO SEND

Have you ever written a letter you knew you wouldn't send? That's the kind of letter your first query letter is going to be. You're going to write it, but you're not going to send it out to agents or editors. Why not?

Because you're going to use this letter to (1) make a better letter, and (2) make a better book. A query letter, like the best writing, has urgency and clarity. It's not dull, but it attends to the business at hand without fuss. It is, of course, a sales pitch directed with passion, belief, enthusiasm, or urgency at someone likely to buy the product being pitched. You're trying to find a reader for your book. And because every editor and agent is first a reader, you're going to write this letter to the reader who is most likely to want to read your book.

Figuring out who that is isn't as hard as it sounds, but it does mean you're going to drop the idea you had of doing a mail merge to every agent in annual directories like *Literary Market Place* or *Guide to Literary Agents*. (We'll discuss the ins and outs of coming up with a list of potential agents in chapter fifteen.) For the purposes of this letter you're not going to send, however, think about the reader you've identified as your ideal audience. He can be someone you know, someone who's read your manuscript, or someone you've made up. He can even be you. It doesn't matter. But you're going to write this letter with one person—that person—in mind, because you want your letter to sound focused, personable, and natural, not generic, vague, and stilted.

CLEARING YOUR THROAT

How to start your letter—by describing yourself or your book? Since most people can't decide, they try to make it easy on themselves by stating the obvious. This is the written equivalent of clearing your throat. Here are some opening lines from some real query letters I've received:

> I am writing to ask your agency to represent my unpublished novel.

There was no need for this writer to tell me that his novel was unpublished. Agents assume that people are writing to them about unpublished novels unless they are told otherwise, i.e., that it's a novel that was self-published or one that was published years ago and has gone out of print.

Here are some other ways of stating the obvious:

- My name is _____ and I am writing you regarding as to whether you might consider reviewing my manuscript for potential representation.

- I am a new fiction writer in search of an agent. I found your firm in *Writer's Market* and I thought we might fit together. The reason that I am in search of representation now is that my first novel is completed.

- I am seeking representation for my novel. I am writing to you because of your agency's reputation.

I was flattered when I read that last sentence. But after thinking it over, I got anxious because the writer didn't state what my agency had a reputation for. It really could have been anything.

Some writers try to open their letters with something profound to hook the reader, but because doing so is just another way of stating the obvious, it backfires:

> There is little joy to be found in a life steeped in depression.

Here's another favorite in the philosophical hook genre:

> A life can be defined by a single decision. Taking one path when you're young, and not another, can make all the difference in later life.

When I read that, I was grateful that the writer had thoughtfully explained in the second sentence exactly what he meant in the first.

These inept or at the very least ineffective opening sentences unwittingly tell me a lot, and in this way at least they're economical: I don't need to read the manuscript at all to reject it. To tell you the truth, I don't even need to read the whole letter. These opening lines tell me that the writer is prone to redundancy, which over the course of a full-length book is going to be very tedious indeed. They tell me the writer is somewhat timid, which makes me doubt that the prose will have the muscularity, urgency, or just plain confidence to achieve liftoff. They tell me that the writer doesn't have the kind of writing voice that makes the reader feel he is being spoken to personally. They tell me that the writer is given to half-baked generalities or is simply too lazy to wrestle his prose into something hard and bright and sharp as a diamond, with all a diamond's qualities of beauty, fire, depth, and the ability to cut glass.

EMPTY WORDS = NO HOOK: WHAT NOT TO DO

Don't follow the example of the following writers, whose letters were chosen randomly from the weekly haul, and who wasted their one-liners by using:

GENERALITIES AND CLICHÉS
- It's a book of literary fiction that focuses on a nasty tragedy, a novel of wry humor and tragic love.
- My first novel relates to specific ecological themes.

- It is a coming-of-age novel for women who come of age late in life.
- Fiercely independent [heroine] embarks on an identity journey, discovering love as humankind's greatest strength and its greatest weakness.

WORD COUNTS AND FORMAT

- Novel, mystery, suspense, 367 pages, double-spaced, finished.
- My novel is a 105,000-word descriptive, spiritual narrative formed on the memories of my own conversation, events, and experiences of the last few years.

LOCALE AND ERA

- The story is set in the 1970s and is about a rural Texas girl striving to escape her violent husband.
- It is a composition of commercial fiction set in both urban and rural locations, assembled in 340 pages in 26 chapters.

SHOPPING LISTS OF GENRES OR CHARACTER TYPES

- [Title] is a dark fiction/horror with elements of psychology, romance, mystery/thriller, dark-comedy, erotica, and fantasy.
- When an emerging New York artist disappears a few days before his exhibition opens he starts a chain of events that brings together crooked gallery owners, wannabe artists, professional forgers, ex-con smugglers, ecstasy drug dealers, and the FBI.

OVERCONFIDENCE

- Those that read the novel compare it to Kurt Vonnegut's.
- Consider a thriller with the flawed protagonist and satiric humor of a DeMille novel who finds himself in the middle of a catastrophe of Clancy proportions.
- My own style might be described as a dreamlike amalgamation of Nabokov, Wodehouse, Miller, Breon, Bulgakov, and Rabelais.
- Novelist Zoë Heller wrote *Notes on a Scandal*; my book is every bit as good.
- I've just completed my first novel, which I think you will find as compelling as anything by Doris Lessing or Philip Roth.

WASTES OF TIME

- I have hundreds of pages of plot structure, characterization, and time line on a trilogy I've always wanted to write.

- Though my story has existed mostly in my private journals, late night chain-smoking conversations among friends, and papers written in grad school, it is begging me to give it a broader voice.

BAFFLING

- What I am presently sending you started out many years ago as the beginning of a sprawling manuscript. I have been working on it for over ten years. I am in the process of dividing my enormous manuscript into sequential novels. ...

- I, a psychiatrist, have written a novel ...

- Wanted: An Agent who can represent Literary Fiction manuscripts that are somewhat large.

No one's inherently opposed to (a) novels that take ten years to write, (b) psychiatrists who write fiction, or (c) manuscripts that are "somewhat large." But non of these qualities are primary sales hooks. If they were, then generic novels—like generic ketchup, or paper towels, or salt—would have taken off years ago. Cover: black type on white background. Titles: *Novel That Took Ten Years to Write*, *Novel By Psychiatrist*, and *Novel That Is Somewhat Large*.

These letters are big on blather but describe books that are entirely free of distinguishing features. The authors of the books suspect this without admitting it to themselves—that's why they pad their letters with empty information and meaningless phrases.

TOP 10 QUERY LETTER NO-NOS:

10. Letters that have typos in the first sentence.

9. Letters that start with a nugget of wisdom: "Every step we take in life moves us in a direction."

8. Letters with faint or very small type. You can assume that just about everyone in publishing suffers from eyestrain.

7. Letters longer than one page.

6. Letters with overcomplicated directions for replying: "I'm going to Tortolla for the next three weeks. If you need to reach me, please call my cell number. Don't leave a message at my home number because I won't get it until I return." A simple street or e-mail address will do.

5. Photocopied letters with no salutation.

4. Letters that start, "I know how busy you are, so I'll get straight to the point and not take up too much of your valuable time." By writing this, you've already taken up a full sentence of my valuable time.

3. Letters that make grandiose claims: "My novel will appeal to women, and since there are 150 million women in the United States, it will sell 150 million copies."

2. Letters that say: "I've worked very hard on this novel." Does that fact alone make it a good novel?

1. And the number one query letter no-no: "I have written a fiction novel."

When an agent sees the above sentence in a query letter, he quickly draws the conclusion that a writer who doesn't know that a novel is, by definition, a work of fiction is a writer who isn't ready to be published.

BUILDING A QUERY LETTER THAT WORKS

By inference and bad examples, you've figured out that a good query letter:

- doesn't state the obvious—if it does, agents will think your book is all "telling," no "showing"

- is never longer than one page—if it is, agents will think your book is overwritten

- is not about you—if it is, agents will think your book will be too navel-gazing to invite the reader in

- never sounds generic—if it does, agents will think your book won't have a unique or appealing voice

- makes the book sound interesting—if it doesn't, agents will know the book isn't

Here's a letter that got my attention:

> Dear Ms. Rittenberg,
>
> I am seeking representation. I have won a few awards for fiction and poetry. My novel, THE CLEARING [later titled *A Certain Slant of Light*], is a supernatural love story told from the point of view of a young woman who has been dead 130 years. She's haunting a high school English teacher when one of the boys in his class sees her. No one has seen her since her death. When the two of them fall in love, the fact that he is in a body and she is not presents the first of their problems.
>
> Please let me know if you would be interested in reading part or all of THE CLEARING. I have enclosed a SASE. Thank you and I look forward to hearing from you.

Although Laura (yes, that's Laura Whitcomb, co-author of this book) began the letter by saying something that might not have been strictly necessary, she said it with admirable brevity. I didn't have time to stop in the middle of the opening sentence. Before I knew it, I had read the whole letter and written the word yes at the bottom. (If you could see the pile of rejected query letters in my office every week, you would see how the no is always written at the top of the letters. That's because I didn't reach the end.) Laura's letter wasn't written with fireworks, but it didn't need to be because the story as she described it briefly needed no embellishment. And she had enough confidence in her story to let the description be.

SET YOUR HOOK

The first paragraph of your query letter should skip the throat-clearing or at least keep the opening pleasantries to a bare minimum and get quickly to the one-line description. In that sentence you'll give the title of the novel and insert the genre if appropriate. Here's the first line of a letter I saw this year:

> [Title] is a coming-of-age novel about two young women trying to survive their first year of college and find their own identities.

To tell you the truth, that sentence would have been enough to describe the book, but the author went on for four more sentences in an attempt to make the novel sound dramatic. If she had taken out those four additional sentences, she would have had a serviceable description of the novel. However, she probably also would have had to face the fact that her novel was not inherently dramatic enough to interest agents and editors in a competitive marketplace. *It didn't have a hook.* Somewhere within herself, she knew this, and that's why she added the four sentences.

Look again at Laura's letter:

> My novel, THE CLEARING, is a supernatural love story told from the point of view of a woman who has been dead for 130 years.

The genre, the title, and the hook in one sentence. Laura added a few more sentences to flesh out the basic idea, but she didn't go on too long and, more importantly, she left the reader with a cliffhanger by saying:

> When the two of them fall in love, the fact that he is in a body and she is not presents the first of their problems.

Your hook should be your novel's distinguishing feature. A distinguishing feature can be something imaginative in the plot—the way Laura's book was a love story featuring a heroine who'd been dead for 130 years—or it can be sheer good writing. It can be something unique about the book or about the way you describe the book. But if the one-liner doesn't make anyone sit up and take notice, all the additional plot description in the world isn't going to help.

Your letter should not describe your book at length, should not drag the reader all the way through the plot and should not give away the ending. A real mood-killer is to use an overworked notion like redemption or a clichéd description like *It's about the human condition* when describing your book. Stick to the concrete. It's easy to see why someone might think that a one-line description is the same thing as a summary, but it's not.

LISTENING TO YOUR LETTER

If you're having trouble boiling the description of your book down to something that's vivid, cogent, and above all brief, it is very possible that your book is not, in fact, ready to be sent out. The letter might be saying, "The problem isn't with me, it's with the book you're trying to describe."

Here are some letters that were desperately trying to tell their authors that something was amiss:

- No single paragraph could sufficiently describe this novel, but I will try.

- Because of the large scope of the book this synopsis is a bit longer than what was asked. I attempted to shorten it, but I could not.

- My novel, the first in a series about a lawyer, is a hell of a ride. The entire novel, 716 pages, is complete and ready to ship.

- [The novel] is told by an unnamed narrator from a tiny shack with bad plumbing. In an aphoristic style, he recounts the epic tale of the rise and fall of ... a multilevel marketing company. ... Along the way, he takes time to criticize many horrendous but inexplicably popular things that have infiltrated society, making comments that are destined to be quoted at the bottom of e-mails and scrawled on dry-erase boards. ...

Have you tried to describe your novel and found yourself unable to stop? You need to ask yourself why that is. If the answer is "there's no other way to describe it," then your novel is in trouble. This is when you know you can use your query letter to help you make your book better.

MOVING RIGHT ALONG: A LITTLE BIT ABOUT YOU

In your second paragraph, you can give some brief and pertinent biographical information. Writing courses, publications, and awards are good. But more than a sentence summing up minor publications and writing study is not so good. A recent letter stated:

> I am a former English teacher who has published many poems in small journals and written book and visual art reviews.

Already too long, this line was followed by two more sentences. Again I had the opportunity to conclude that anyone who couldn't condense his pertinent writing experience into something brisk and interesting was not likely to have written a gripping or deeply absorbing novel. It is permissible to enclose a one-page list or a paragraph on a separate sheet noting all your credentials, publications, or awards, but a long *curriculum vitae* will probably be ignored.

Remember—the immediate task of the query letter is to get an agent or editor interested in reading your novel. It's not to showcase what an interesting, fabulous, credentialed, or kooky person you are. That will come later, when your agent needs to sell you as well as your book; we'll discuss this in chapter eighteen. But for now, you need to come across as professional, serious, dedicated, and confident. Too jokey a tone is wrong. Even if the letter is truly wry or funny or amusingly self-deprecating, it distracts us from the point: Have you written a book I want to read?

Anything you say about yourself should somehow, briefly and brilliantly, make us think we want to read your book. All Laura said of herself was: "I have won a few awards for fiction and poetry." Because she couldn't claim to have won the Pulitzer, hadn't invented nuclear fusion, wasn't married to someone famous and, more to the point, had never published a book, there was no point in giving a long résumé of her achievements.

Many query writers insert a sentence beginning, "Although I am an unpublished writer …" Doing so simultaneously states the obvious (you're writing about your first novel, after all) and dwells negatively on you—on what you haven't done. Remember that the query letter is looking to the future. The future is when someone is going to read your novel, and your job is to convince us that we will be that future someone. Say no more than one or two things:

- I received my M.F.A. from the Columbia Writing Program, where my novel was awarded the Prize for Singular Fabulousness.

- I've worked as a taxi driver and a mail carrier while writing and publishing short fiction in literary journals.

DON'T WEAR OUT YOUR WELCOME: THE CLOSING

Your third paragraph should be the sign-off paragraph. Wrap up the letter with a word or two about having enclosed a SASE and looking forward to a response, and sign off. Don't drag it out. Don't give your vacation schedule with your spouse's cell phone number. If you've used letterhead with your address, e-mail address, and telephone number, or inserted that information in a business-letter-appropriate fashion, anyone who wants to track you down will find you. Many agents nowadays don't even need you to indicate that you're making a multiple submission, because they assume you are. So stop talking, finish the letter with a complimentary closing, and hit "Save." Then prepare yourself for the next step: researching agents to find the right one for your book.

RECOMMENDED READING

Roget's International Thesaurus, 6th edition, edited by Barbara Ann Kipfer. Didn't use a thesaurus when you wrote your novel? If you can't find the words to describe it in your query letter, now's the time to get a copy of a *Roget's*.

What Color Is Your Parachute? by Richard Nelson Bolles. Why not use this classic career guide to help you prepare your work to persuade an agent to represent you and your book? The exercises it offers are designed to help you understand what you have to offer and could help you discover what's unique about your book and what might need work.

In addition to the following books, there are entire books devoted to writing query letters to literary agents, editors, and book publishers, but as I haven't read any of them, I can't recommend them. I suspect you'll find more advice in them about query letters for nonfiction than for fiction, however.

- *1001 Letters for All Occasions*, by Cory Sandler and Janice Keefe
- *Webster's New World Letter Writing Handbook*, by Robert W. Bly
- *Unsent Letters: Writing as a Way to Resolve and Renew*, by Lauren B. Smith

RECOMMENDED WEB SITES

Fiction Writer's Connection (www.fictionwriters.com/tips-query-letters. html). This Web site provides advice about query letters.

Query Letters I Love (http://queryletters.blogspot.com). On days when you think query letters are at best silly and at worst sheer torture, go to this blog, entirely devoted to query letters a Hollywood producer receives for film projects, to gain some perspective.

CHAPTER FIFTEEN:

the view from the other side of the desk

I have always found the question *How do I find a literary agent for my work?* to be a little unsettling. There's the obvious reason why agents find the question unsettling: Most of us have never had to look for one. Then there's the fact that most of us know we're listed in at least one directory or guide to getting published, if not in the telephone book, so we're not sure why we can't be found. But the question is unsettling because of the anxiety, hope, and despair at its heart—the same qualities found in the question *How do I find a needle in a haystack?*

WHY BOTHER WITH THE NEEDLE?

Now that you're ready to try to find a publisher for your book, you might be wondering, in addition to how to find an agent and what an agent can do for you, whether you really need one or not.

Do you just want to place your book, doesn't matter where, doesn't matter with whom? Just get it out there so you can, as it were, run it up the flagpole and see who salutes? You might be able to do that on your own, without an agent. Consult Richard Curtis's book, *How to be Your Own Literary Agent*, which I recommended at the end of chapter eleven. Just bear in mind that an unagented author might find it easier to place a book of nonfiction than a novel, and that placing your book is probably going to be a full-time job.

However, some established writers of genre material—romance, fantasy, science fiction—occasionally recommend to "newbies" that they try to get a book offer first and then get an agent to negotiate it. The pros and cons? One pro is that you might more easily attract an agent with an offer in hand than with nothing. One con is that you might attract an agent who just wants to see some money come in and who may not be attentive after that. Another is that an agent coming on the scene after the offer has been made has less negotiating leverage. He can probably improve whatever offer you get, but not always. You would have to research this agent as carefully as any other (we will discuss research later in this chapter).

Most of the mainstream publishers who publish fiction prefer to work with authors who have agents. Some regard us as necessary evils and some as go-betweens who reduce the amount of time they have to spend managing a writer's career. An agent can brief an author on all sorts of publishing matters so an editor doesn't have to spend time training new recruits. Because an agent's job is to handle the business end of things, the presence of an agent can help the editor and author keep their relationship focused on the creative end. Additionally, established agents have proved that they can regularly spot new talent, so editors have learned to rely on their prescreening techniques. No one bats .1000, but some have better averages than others.

Fantasy novelist Victoria Strauss has this to say about agents on the Writer Beware Web site (www.sfwa.org/beware), which she co-founded:

> Agenting is a skilled profession that requires specialized expertise, such as a good understanding of publishing contract terms, as well as personal contacts within the industry (publishing is still very much a back-room business) … if your goal is to sell to one of the large houses, your efforts are better spent searching for an agent than submitting direct to the few imprints that will

consider unagented work. It can take a long time to find an agent, but once you do, she can cut editors' response time to a minimum—and just as important, get your manuscript directly onto the desk of an editor who can give it serious consideration.

THE BENEFITS OF HAVING AN AGENT

So what can an agent do for you? First, when your manuscript is ready to go, the agent makes all the submissions to editors and absorbs the blow of the rejections. You can decide you want to hear every response or you can decide you never want to see another rejection letter again. No matter how you approach it, you will be free from the necessity of writing pitch letters, copying manuscripts, and going to the post office to send them off.

NEGOTIATING THE ADVANCE

Next, the agent fields any offers for your book. When an editor wants to publish your book, she makes an offer of an advance. An advance is a sum of money the publisher pays for the right to publish your book. But the money is not unencumbered. The complete expression is *advance against all earnings.* That means that the money your book earns will go into your royalty account until it adds up to the amount the publisher has advanced you. If the amount of earnings exceeds the amount of your advance, you will receive royalties. If the amount of earnings never adds up to the amount of your advance, you won't see any more money. But neither will you have to pay back the difference between the money your book earned and the money you were advanced.

When an editor prepares to make an offer for a book, he will almost certainly offer more to publish a book sent in by an agent than a book submitted by an author—an unagented author. The editor knows that the agent knows what the publishing house is capable of paying. And the editor who wants to buy the book doesn't necessarily want to alienate an established agent by making an insulting offer, because that agent might have a big project on the horizon that the editor will want to see. Nevertheless, editors are entirely capable of making disappointing offers for agented books every day of the week. They just might not be quite as disappointing as the ones they'd make if there weren't an agent involved, and an agent will almost always obtain some kind of an improvement.

THE CONTRACT

After the offer comes the contract. A publishing contract is marginally less boring—and marginally more readable—than, say, a mortgage agreement or a lease. And that's not saying much. One thing I can guarantee: Even if you've studied law, there are parts of a publishing contract that may as well be written in Urdu for all the sense they'll make to you. Agents have read countless publishing contracts, and they are pretty familiar with the kinds of things publishers won't change and the things on which they'll be flexible.

Every good agency has established "boilerplates" with different publishers. That means that the agents sold books to a specific publisher in the past and, in the course of the negotiation, got the publisher to agree to make certain changes in its standard contract. Those changes are then carried over, for the most part, to the next contract the agent negotiates with the publishing house. You will enjoy the benefits of those altered contracts when you sign with an established literary agent. And you should know that many publishers have two standard contracts: one for authors with agents and one for authors without agents. Which do you think is the more favorable?

PROTECTING YOUR RIGHTS

An agent can also, in the course of a negotiation, hold back certain subsidiary rights on your behalf. An author who signs a publishing contract without an agent will sign over to the publisher all ancillary rights to the book—film and television, dramatic, magazine, electronic, foreign translation, paperback reprint, book club, audio, you name it. An agent

the view from the other side of the desk

can help an author retain certain of those rights, typically film, television, dramatic, audio, and foreign translation rights. The agent then attempts to sell those rights on your behalf, and if he is successful, you'll have more contracts to sign and more checks to deposit.

ROYALTY PAYMENTS

After your book is published, you'll be sent royalty statements twice a year. These are statements of account that list sales of your book and show how far you are from paying back your advance. Or how close. Or, ideally, how much money you're making. Your agent reads these statements and might enter the data into a computer accounting program so he can keep track of your sales. Your agent will also be able to spot errors in these statements and get the publisher to correct them. These statements aren't particularly easy to read—some people find them more impenetrable than contracts—but the Association of Authors' Representatives (AAR), through its indefatigable Royalty Committee, is steadily getting publishers to make their statements more comprehensive and more standardized, to everyone's benefit.

MEMBERSHIP BENEFITS

Any agent who is a member of the Association of Authors' Representatives (AAR) enjoys the benefits of the work done by the AAR's Contracts Committee. Members of this committee regularly meet with publishers to discuss certain aspects of the publishers' contracts. The committee's work has resulted in several changes to the standard contracts of various well-known publishers, and those changes benefit everyone, members and nonmembers alike. In addition to that work, however, the committee provides AAR members with contract checklists that help agents negotiate better terms in any publishing contract. Aside from the AAR, the Authors Guild offers contract review and advice to its members. There are organizations for writers of mysteries, romance novels, science fiction and fantasy, Westerns, and many more. Some of these organizations will offer advice and support as well.

HOW TO FIND THE RIGHT AGENT FOR YOUR BOOK

If you've decided you do want to get an agent for your work, how do you begin to find that elusive needle in the proverbial haystack?

The one thing you need to keep uppermost in your thoughts is this: Agents and editors are, above all else, readers. When we sit down with the manuscript of a novel, most of us hope to experience the wonderful sensation of getting lost in the pages of a book and being unable to put it down that made us book lovers in the first place. Finding an agent is like finding someone who will be the person most likely to enjoy your book. When you think about it, you know that your best friend will like a certain type of book, your mother another type, your carpool partner a third. Yet there are times when you like a book so much you tell everyone to read it, no matter what their taste. It's likely that, with a novel you yourself have written, this is going to be one of those times. But you're going to have to curb your enthusiasm and think hard and realistically about whether the agents you're researching are going to be the right readers for your work.

MAKING A TARGETED LIST

This is a research project—not a needle-in-a-haystack project at all. In the previous chapter, you tried to develop a profile of your ideal reader. Now take that ideal reader and try to come up with a list of some actual books that person might have enjoyed reading. Try for a list of ten titles published in the last five to ten years. Got it? Okay, now you need to figure out who the agent was for each of the books on your list. Here's how:

1. **Get a copy of each of the books on your list and look at the acknowledgments page.** You can do this at the library or in a bookstore without checking out or buying the actual book. See if the author thanks or acknowledges his literary agent in some way. Put that agent's name on your list.

2. **If the book doesn't have any acknowledgments, call the publisher of the book and ask for the subsidiary rights department.** Tell them you'd like to know the name of the agent for that book. If, for some reason, they don't want to give it to you, tell a white lie and say that you're interested in the film rights. If they give you the name, put it on your list.

3. **If you strike out with the publishing house, go to the Internet and see if the authors of the books have Web sites.** You might find the agent's name there with a direct e-mail or Web page link. Don't fire off an e-mail to the agent, however. Just put his name and contact information on your list.

4. **If you didn't find the agent's name on the author's Web site, there are many other places you can look on the Internet.** You can go to search engines like Google, Yahoo, and Answers.com and type in something like "Philip Roth literary agent." There are also a few sites where you can put in a writer's name to find his literary agent. They're not comprehensive, but you might find what you're looking for at one of the following sites:

    • **Agent Query (www.agentquery.com).** A handsome, well-laid-out site you can search in many ways, this site is one of the best of its kind.

    • **Publishers Marketplace (www.publishersmarket place.com).** You can search for an agent by putting in the name of a writer even if you are not a member.

    • **Bill's List of Literary Agents and Their Authors' Books (www.wrhammons.com).** Bill Hammons tries to keep up-to-date with literary agents and the writers they represent. While his list isn't comprehensive, it's a heroic effort and a real service to other writers.

    • **WritersNet (www.writers.net).** Writing resources, news, and discussion for writers, editors, publishers, and agents.

5. **Lastly, especially in the case of less well-known writers, you can e-mail them directly and ask for the names of their agents.** They might have an e-mail link on their site, or you might find their e-mail address in another listing. Sometimes you won't hear back, but you never know when someone will be happy to hear from a fellow writer and want to offer a helping hand.

MAKING A BLIND LIST

If you haven't been able to come up with the names of any contemporary authors whose readers might like your work, don't despair. You just need to start looking for agents in a different way. You're going to try to find an agent by searching for the kinds of books they represent and narrowing the list down to the ones who might be likely to represent the kind of book you've written.

There are at least two annual guides that provide a wealth of information to help you make a good list. They are:

- *Jeff Herman's Guide to Book Editors, Publishers, & Literary Agents.* I don't know anyone who doesn't like Jeff Herman's book. Much more than a listing of names and addresses, it offers advice on everything from writing a book proposal to negotiating a contract, and its listings of editors and agents are full-blooded profiles that tell you everything from the person's telephone number to his pet peeves and the names of the authors he's worked with. Even if you have already developed a list of agents, you'll need to consult this book.

- *Guide to Literary Agents,* edited by Joanna Masterson. This annually updated directory lists more than six hundred literary agents with their areas of interest and has articles on writers conferences and other topics of interest as well as interviews with a handful of literary agents. Another invaluable guide.

In addition to using these guides, you can search for agents at the following Web sites:

- **Association of Authors' Representatives (www.aar-online.org).** Searchable database of AAR members by name or keyword. For instance, you can type in the word romance and get the agents who have that word in their member profile. Unfortunately, however, you will get agents who include that word in the categories they do *not* represent as well as agents who do represent that category. But it's a start.

- **Publishers Marketplace (www.publishersmarketplace.com).** I include this again because you can not only search by author name, but by keyword, genre, or subject.

There are many more Web sites that list literary agents, but I've looked at a host of them and have found that the above-listed sites and directories are the most reliable, comprehensive, and up-to-date. They contain more information than a name and address and can better help you to establish a list of agents who might respond to your work.

HONING YOUR LIST

You've discovered something else while you've done all this research, something you may have known all along but may not have acknowledged: Your novel is not all things for all people—no novel is. Many writers fantasize that their first novel will be universally adored, bought, read, and reread. It's an important fantasy—it may keep you going when all logical indications beg you to stop—but it's a fantasy that, once it's served its purpose, should be put to rest. Doing the research suggested in this chapter will help you to focus on the people who should be exactly right for your book. Paradoxically, narrowing your list and finding the just-right person, whether agent or editor, can do more to ensure that your book will be widely read than flinging hundreds of mail-merged letters into the vasty publishing deep.

DUE DILIGENCE

If you've really thought about your potential readers and tried to match your book to an agent who sounds as if he might really respond to it, you should have a list of no more than ten agents at this point. Don't run to the post office yet! It's time for the next stage of your research: finding out as much as you can about each of the agents on your list.

As you developed your list of agents' names, you came across more data about them than their contact information. If you didn't dive into it then, now's the time. Do any or all of the agents on your list have Web sites? Go to them and read every page. If not, read their profiles in the directories listed above. Do an Internet search using Google or Answers.com and see what you can find out. Don't just click through the first reference—go to five or ten at the very least. If you find a message board where other aspiring and/or published writers discuss the agent in question, you've hit pay dirt because you'll be able to post your own questions and get feedback from those other writers.

Here's what you're going to be looking for at this stage of your research:

1. **Are they members of or recommended by any trade organizations?** The only professional membership organization for literary agents in the U.S. is the Association of Authors' Representatives (see the sidebar on page 204 for more about the AAR). But here are some other organizations that can vouch for an agent's credibility or warn you away from those who have exhibited unethical behavior:

   • **Romance Writers of America (www.rwanational.org).** The RWA is an incredibly well-run organization that holds annual conferences and has an active membership. On their Web site, under "Industry Resources," you'll find a list of "RWA Recognized Agents."

   • **Preditors & Editors (www.anotherealm.com/pre deditors).** This site not only lists agents, it will rate an agent as "Not Recommended" if the agent meets certain negative criteria. As a result, some agents refuse to be listed here. Such a refusal might or might not in itself be a warning sign—you'd do well to dig deeper if you don't find the name on this list.

- **Science Fiction & Fantasy Writers of America, Inc. (www. sfwa.org).** Another excellent site with extensive resources for writers—not only science fiction and fantasy writers—this site has a section about literary agents and what they should and should not do.

2. **Has the agent sold books to well-known or reputable publishing houses?** If every book on an agent's list is published by an obscure publisher—defined as a publisher you've never heard of or one whose books you can't find in any bookstore—that agent might not be very effective. The SFWA Web site, in the section mentioned earlier called "Writer Beware," describes the "Amateur, Incompetent, and Marginal" agent (www.sfwa.org/beware/agents.html). While the article doesn't name names, it gives you a good feel of what to avoid, such as agents who charge up-front fees or have a poor sales record.

3. **Can you get a referral?** Now is the time to call or e-mail all your writer friends and try to find someone who might know one or more of the agents on your list. You may have stumbled on such a connection in your research, in which case it's time to ask if you can use that person's name when writing to the agent. But try (diplomatically, of course) to pin down the depth of the relationship, because agents get a surprising number of letters that start "So-and-so suggested I write you about my novel"—and they have no idea who So-and-so is!

FINALIZING YOUR QUERY LETTER

Remember the statistic in the last chapter, that 80 percent of first-novel query letters should never have been sent? Some of those letters shouldn't have been sent because the novels they described weren't ready, by a long shot, to be published. And some were misdirected. In this day and age, there is simply no excuse for misdirecting your query letter. By misdirecting, I mean:

- not bothering to find out if the agent is taking on new clients or considering unpublished writers
- not researching the agent's areas of interest or specialty
- not paying attention to the agent's submission guidelines
- writing to an old address

In addition to the names, addresses, and track records of your ten target agents, you're going to study their sales records and submission guidelines as if your life depended on it. Then you're going to write ten query letters. While they'll be substantially the same, each will be tailored to the person to whom it's addressed so it sounds as if you are writing to someone you know or have met.

Through the course of your agent research, you've had a chance to think a bit about each of the names on your list. Agents aren't public people—ideally, we stand in the shadows behind the author—so it may be difficult to picture those on your list or to get an exact idea of who they are and what makes them tick. But if you've written a novel, you've imagined and brought to life whole characters from a few traits or a few words. Apply your imaginative novelist's mind to what you know about each agent and see what you come up with.

Just as the letter isn't about you—*it's about the book*—it's not about the agent, either. Yet while you shouldn't say in your letter what you *think* the person you're writing to is like—the recipient will find that disconcerting, if not creepy—thinking of the agent as a person or a character will make it easier for you to write a letter that sounds like you at your most comfortable and confident. In other words, you'll write a letter that will sound like a writer an agent would be thrilled to represent.

NEATNESS COUNTS

To make sure your query letter is putting its best foot forward, check it against this list:

- Is the letter free of typos?
- Is the recipient's name spelled correctly?

- Are you sure the address is correct? If you only looked in one place for the address, you can't be sure. Don't call the agency to verify the address—we get too many of those calls, and they eat up our time—but look through several directories and Web pages for confirmation.

- Do you have good quality paper for the letters? It doesn't need to be fancy. Just good.

- Do you have access to a laser printer or a printer that's not running out of ink?

- Is the letter no more than one page long?

THE (IN)FAMOUS SYNOPSIS

It seems that every article, guide, or Web site about getting published suggests that you prepare a synopsis of your novel. And that many agents (and publishers) ask that you send a synopsis of your novel when making your query. There just doesn't seem to be any way to get around the necessity of the synopsis. But I have to admit that I almost never read them, and neither do many of the fiction editors at the big mainstream publishing houses.

Let me rephrase that: We don't like to read them because we would rather read the real thing—the novel itself. If we've read the first chapter or the first fifty pages or the first three chapters, and we've been charmed by the voice or gripped by the story or gotten obsessed with the main character, we're going to want to read on, so we will ask for the remainder of the manuscript if we don't have it.

But synopses serve several purposes. If an agent's guidelines ask that you send a synopsis of your novel with the query, it might be because that agent routinely uses plot synopses to determine whether he'll find the book salable. I suspect this is more common in the traditional reaches of genres like science fiction, romance, or mystery, especially where the agent is selling to houses that have fairly strict writing guidelines.

On eHarlequin.com, the Web site of the big romance publisher, an author who wishes to submit a manuscript is asked to submit "a synopsis of your story that gives a clear idea of both your plot and characters and is no more than two single-spaced pages"; the site further states: "Stories that contain scenes or plotlines that bear a striking resemblance to previously published work are in breach of copyright law and are not acceptable." It's clear that the editors at a house that publishes so many books in a similar vein need to see a synopsis to avoid plot and character overlap as much as possible—and to make sure no one's plagiarizing anyone else.

KEEP IT SIMPLE

Note that in the Harlequin example above, the synopsis should be "no more than two single-spaced pages." And there's the rub with the synopses most of us see: They are far too long. In fact, most people try to cram the two-page version into their query letter, making the letter far too long, and then enclose an additional synopsis of five or ten or twenty pages.

Most editors would be happy with a page, or a paragraph. Jackie Cantor, an executive editor at Berkley who was Diana Gabaldon's editor for years, told me she never reads synopses: "I'd rather read the book. It's the writing I'm interested in." Claire Wachtel, an executive editor at Harper-Collins who does read synopses as long as they're accompanied by part of the manuscript, signed Anita Shreve's first novel based on one hundred very well-written pages followed by a synopsis. Claire told me, "It was the writing in those first hundred pages that got me, not the synopsis. If the writing's there, you can fix anything. If I don't like the writing, I don't care what the plot is."

And yet there are all those submission guidelines asking for a synopsis. Earlier we discussed the one-line hook, as well as the necessity of keeping your query letter to no more than a page, which requires keeping the description of your novel down to no more than three or four sentences—the one-line hook and a couple of sentences to flesh it out and leave us wanting more. Expand the short pitch from your query letter into a two-page synopsis. Hit the

the view from the other side of the desk

high points, include only the top characters, skip some of the subplots, and wrap it up. And stick to the story—don't go off on a tangent in the synopsis by comparing your work to that of other writers or discussing marketing. Try writing the synopsis as if you were relating the plot to an avid reader, the kind of person who says, "What happens next?" Write the synopsis now and save it in your computer or keep a copy so it's ready when you need it.

THINKING INSIDE THE BOX: FOLLOWING SUBMISSION GUIDELINES

Each agency has different submission guidelines, and it's essential that you follow them strictly. For instance, my agency's listing in *Literary Market Place* (*LMP*), a huge directory covering publishers, printers, agents, and any other business connected to publishing, says, "Query letter & first chapter with SASE; no e-mail queries." That means the following:

- You must send a query letter before being invited to send the entire manuscript.

- You don't have to include the first chapter, but you can. However, pay attention: It doesn't say "first three chapters."

- You must include a self-addressed, stamped envelope (SASE) or you will not receive a reply.

- You must not send your query by e-mail.

Here's another agency's requirements: "No unsol mss, query first with SASE. Submit letter or three chapters via mail." And here's what that means:

- "No unsol mss" means no unsolicited manuscripts. An unsolicited manuscript is one that the author sends without first writing and asking if the agent would like to read it.

- "Query first with SASE" means you must send a query letter with a self-addressed, stamped envelope and ask whether the agent would like to read your manuscript.

- "Submit letter or three chapters via mail." This is a little confusing. You're told to "query first," then told to "submit three chapters" or a letter. What to do? Luckily, this agency's listing also says: "See Web site for guidelines," then provides a link to the site, where the guidelines are more detailed and much clearer.

Here's one other agency's submission guidelines as listed in *LMP* shorthand: "Fiction: query, bio, synopsis & first fifty pages of completed novel. No reading fee or other fees; query first with SASE. Do not send downloads unless requested." And here's the translation:

- If you wish to solicit their interest in a novel, you need to send a query letter with your biographical information, *curriculum vitae*, or résumé; a synopsis; and the first fifty pages of your book. However, note that they say "completed novel." That means they don't want to be solicited about novels that aren't yet finished.

- "Query first with SASE." Didn't they just say that you were supposed to send a letter, a bio, a synopsis, and the first fifty pages? What do they mean? What they mean is that the query should consist of the query letter, the bio, the synopsis, and the pages. It should not consist of the entire manuscript.

- "No reading fee or other fees." That means they're a reputable agency because they won't charge any upfront fees.

- "Do not send downloads unless requested." Although this agency accepts queries via e-mail, the queries should not contain large attachments that need to be downloaded.

When guidelines ask for "three sample chapters," you should send the *first* three—not, say, chapters twelve, thirty-seven, and fifty-three. You would be surprised how often people do this, usually with a note explaining, "My best writing is found in these chapters." Think about it: When you recommend a book to a friend, do you say, "You're going to *love* chapters twelve, thirty-seven, and fifty-three"? Or do you say, "You're going to love this book"?

Read the guidelines and follow them slavishly. Everyone's overwhelmed with submissions, so if you ignore the guidelines, you only make it easy to say no to your query.

INSTANT TURNDOWN: FOUR STEPS TO THE FASTEST REJECTION POSSIBLE

1. Send in a complete manuscript without being asked.
2. Make sure it's a first draft.
3. And single-spaced.
4. And bound with steel rivets.

DON'T PHONE IT IN ...

Some people don't bother doing any research or following any submission guidelines at all—they call instead of writing. We get a couple of varieties of this call, such as:

> "Is this a literary agency?"
> "Yes, it is."
> "I've written a book and I don't know how to get it published. Can you tell me what to do?"

We usually direct them to the library with the suggestion that they look for directories and guides to getting published. Then there are the callers who know what a literary agent is but haven't done any research to determine whether our agency is likely to be interested in the kind of book they've written. These conversations are not very comfortable for either party:

> "What kind of book is it?"
> "It's a fiction novel."
>
> Or:
>
> "It's a novel about extraterrestrials in the White House."
>
> Or:
>
> "It's a five-hundred-page poem."

Or worse, they launch into a long—if not endless—plot description. I will never know if these descriptions have an end because in almost every case I conclude the conversation quickly by saying, "I'm sorry, but it doesn't sound like the kind of book I represent."

... BUT IF YOU DO, MEMORIZE YOUR LINES

Although I don't recommend making a query call, you may have decided that's the most comfortable or efficient approach for you. If so, try not to be an "almost." These are callers who have researched the agency they're calling, yet when they get the agent they've targeted on the phone, they're so surprised they become tongue-tied. They stumble around, saying things like, "Wow, I didn't expect to get you on the phone," and "I forgot what I was going to say." This is perfectly understandable, but they had one shot, and they just blew it.

There is something they could have done to save themselves: They could have written a script of their pitch and rehearsed it before calling. The pitch should cover a few points:

- State whether or not you've been referred to the agency you're calling.

- Be specific about what you have written. "I've written a book" just isn't specific enough. Neither is "I've written a novel." Name the category. Don't force the agent to drag it out of you.

- Ask if the agent would like to read the manuscript.

- If the agent says yes, say thank you. If you're speaking to an agent who is somewhat senior, do not at this point ask for the agency's mailing address. If you have to say anything, just say you'll send it soon. Don't get overexcited and say you'll overnight it for morning delivery, unless the agent has asked you to.

- Have a little something in reserve about your writing background in case the agent asks. Don't try to squeeze it in if the agent sounds busy. If the agent says yes to your request to read the manuscript, he's not asking for anything else at that moment. You will, of course, include the pertinent information in your query letter.

- Hang up the phone. Don't call back a minute later and ask the assistant for the mailing address. If you've done your research thoroughly, you won't have to waste time—yours and theirs—in this way.

- When you send the manuscript, you still have to enclose a complete query letter—not a note that says, "As discussed." The letter will of course have something in it about the conversation, but other than that it should have all the information you would have written if you hadn't called.

RECOMMENDED READING

Handsome Is: Adventures With Saul Bellow, by Harriet Wasserman. This memoir by long-time literary agent Harriet Wasserman sketches her professional and personal relationship with the Nobel Laureate.

The Publishing Game: Publish a Book in 30 Days, by Fern Reiss. Fern is not only practical, organized, and energetic, she's the ultimate cheerleader. You should not try to self-publish without the help of her book.

RECOMMENDED WEB SITES

Persist and Publish (www.freewebs.com/alabamaworley). A self-described "study group of novelists who are committed to getting published," this site offers a wealth of helpful information, such as articles on "Etiquette in Contacting Agents" and "The Steps in Finding an Agent," as well as links to articles on writing cover letters and synopses. An excellent and frequently updated resource.

Absolute Write Water Cooler (www.absolutewrite.com/forums). If you're thinking of self-publishing, you might want to look here before you dive in or sign anything. Check out the New Never-Ending PublishAmerica Thread (NEPAT) under "Bewares and Background Check."

CHAPTER SIXTEEN:

becoming an agented author

You've mailed a query letter to an agent. Better yet, you've mailed ten query letters to ten different agents. Each letter was slightly different from the others because in your research you discovered different things about each agent and tailored each letter accordingly. You also discovered that each agent has his own style, has represented different kinds of books, has a different depth of experience, and seems to require a unique approach.

Now you wait. It's easy for me to *say* you should think of something else while waiting, but I don't know how easy it is for you to do. On the one hand, you should get on with your life; on the other, you probably shouldn't leave the country, since publishing people tend, when dealing with the new-new thing, to want instant gratification, and if you're not around to return the message, they might move on. Like all busy people, they rely on momentum to take them into new projects or through a big one, since it goes without saying they're perpetually overextended. So if you're slow to respond to their enthusiasm, you might lose their attention until the Ferris wheel comes around again.

THE WAITING GAME

Chances are that you'll be able to go to Timbuktu and back twice before you start hearing back from people. And chances are even greater that everyone you've written will reject your query. If they write back at all. Statistically speaking, it's unlikely anyone will pick up the telephone to call you, much less to offer representation. Even should everyone answer, it could be four to six weeks before you hear a peep out of anyone.

The best thing to do while you're facing eternity alone is to prepare a second list of ten agents. Follow the same steps in compiling it that you followed for the first list—matching tastes or interests, getting referrals, researching each agent and agency. Start getting your new query letters ready, tailoring each one, again, to the person to whom it's addressed. Make sure you have a couple of fresh copies of your manuscript ready—just in case. Then go to the movies. Take up yoga. Adopt a kitten. Do whatever it takes to keep yourself refreshed and busy so you won't fall prey to black despair or Holly Golightly's "mean reds."

WHEN AN AGENT DOES CALL

Let's say—pie-in-the-sky time—that three of your A-list agents have asked to read your manuscript. You've sent it off to all three, and you've told each that two other people are reading the manuscript. (It's important to be as specific as possible. "I've had some people interested," a writer told me recently as I was leaving the country on a business trip, "let's talk after you're back." When I did call her after my return, she called back a day later to tell me she'd signed with someone else. If I'd had more specific information from her, I could have given her work a higher priority. The good news is that she signed with an excellent fellow agent.)

Then, let's say that anywhere from a few weeks to a couple of months after you've sent the requested manuscript, you hear back from one of the agents: He wants to represent your manuscript. What do you do? Do you say yes right away, on the spot? Or do you say you've got to think about it, not to mention that you've got to give the other two agents who are reading the manuscript a chance, and tell the agents who haven't answered your letter that you've been offered representation? Ideally—meaning, in the most businesslike scenario—you thank the agent profusely for his interest, but ask him for a day or two to give your answer, because you've got to get in touch with the other agents involved in the submission.

In addition, you can ask some or all of the following questions to help you come to a decision:

1. **What kind of publishing house do you think will want to publish my book?** The agent won't be able, of course, to tell you who will publish your book, but his answer will tell you whether you and he see eye-to-eye on what type of book it is. If you've written a romance that would be perfect for Harlequin and he wants to show it to Farrar, Straus and Giroux, a very literary hardcover publisher, you've got to question whether he'll be the right agent for you.

2. **What kind of commercial potential do you think my work has?** You may want to hear that he thinks it will be a number one original mass market paperback bestseller. But if you've written a literary coming-of-age novel, you should be realistic enough to recognize blowing sunshine when you see it.

3. **What's your process like?** Do you give me input and ask me to revise my manuscript before sending it out? Do you like to talk to editors about my work first, or do you send it to people you know who you think will respond to it? Some agents will be entirely comfortable with these kinds of questions and some won't. Sales strategies and styles vary from book to book and are influenced by timing, intuition, relationships, and serendipity, so it's not always easy to predict what the process will be like. However, if you encounter agents who won't answer these questions at all, be wary. Especially if they are charging up-front fees, they may not have a sales process because they've discovered the real money lies in the fees, not in sending out your manuscript.

becoming an agented author

4. **Will you send me copies of rejection letters if I want to see them?** The only correct answer to this is yes. Not everyone wants to see rejection letters, of course, but the decision should be yours, not the agent's.

5. **Should I come to New York to meet editors?** The agent will probably tell you that this will not be necessary, and he will be right. With fiction, the decision to publish comes down to the book, not your pretty face or sparkling personality—although those could help a lot later.

6. **Do you have your clients sign an author/agency agreement?** Some excellent agents do not have their clients sign an author/agency agreement. Most do. It's my opinion that the presence of this agreement underscores the business aspect of the partnership and is therefore necessary. (I'll discuss author/agency agreements in greater detail on page 226.)

7. **What can I do to help you help me?** There isn't one correct answer to this question, but if the agent says "absolutely nothing," you might wonder what kind of a partnership requires nothing from one of its members. At the very least the agent should say, "Write wonderful books."

In my experience, most people say yes immediately over the telephone. That's fine when I'm the only agent who has the manuscript and the writer has researched me and decided I'm the agent he wants for his work. But when I'm one of several agents who have a work under consideration, and I receive word that the author has signed with someone else without giving me the courtesy of an interim telephone call, it always strikes me as incredibly unprofessional.

If the agent who's calling is the only one with the manuscript, you should certainly feel free to say yes immediately if that's what you want to do. (If you get a call like this from an agent you haven't researched, you should ask to sleep on your decision overnight, during which time you'll feverishly research the person, consult with your friends, spouse, shrink, or accountant, and get a tarot reading.)

But, if your manuscript *is* with two other agents, you have an obligation to at least call them—they might have begun reading it, and if you're going to sign with someone else, you don't want them to put any more time into your book. If you're going to give them a chance to represent you, you want to give them a heads up so they know they've got to hurry and make their decision. Any good agent should understand and accept that you need a little time to make a decision like this and should recognize how professional it is that you want to give the others a chance to come to a rapid decision.

If you've left it with the offering agent that you're going to talk to the other two agents, you should agree on some rough ground rules, mainly about the timing. You might ask when the agent would like to hear back from you. You might promise "by Friday," "after the weekend," or "by tomorrow." When you call the other agents, chances are you'll talk to an assistant or need to leave a voice mail. Be succinct. Say, "I sent my manuscript to Ms. Jones at her request last month. It was a multiple submission, and I've had an offer from another agent. Would you please let me know the status of my manuscript with your agency?" Responses will range from utter silence to "We've already sent it back" to "I'm halfway through and I love it! Can I have until tomorrow?" Utter silence has the advantage of making your decision easy. Try not to dwell on the fact that your manuscript, the one you worked on so hard and the one that agent *actually asked to read*, was met with … utter silence. If you get the next response—"Oh, we just turned that down"—try not to dwell on the fact that your manuscript has been rejected, because it has also been accepted by someone else.

Another type of response you might get is a scolding: "But I just got that two days ago! How can you possibly expect me to have read it by now, or even to read it by Monday? You're not playing fair and I don't think I want to work with someone like you." Ouch. It's never fun to have your wrists slapped like that, but it was really the agent in this case, when all the players got the manuscript at the same time, who wasn't playing fair. In a competitive business, the players are always at risk of being caught napping, and you, the author, can't do anything about that. You should just be happy your book was exciting enough to cause such distress.

Moving up the scale of palatable responses, you could well be met with a polite, if slightly opaque, "What good news for you. Thanks for letting me know, and good luck." Upon receiving this kind of answer, you are not permitted to ask whether the agent has or has not read your book and what he thought of it. Your answer is going to be a simple "Thank you."

IF EVERYONE LOVES YOU

The toughest scenario will actually be the one where—you should be so lucky—one or more of the other agents has read or is reading the book and wants to offer representation. We agents see this as the equivalent of entering a beauty contest, and we have mixed feelings about it while recognizing it as a fact of our professional lives. The onus is on you to handle the contest professionally.

Set certain rules for yourself. You've already followed through on a couple: You let each agent know that other agents were looking at the manuscript at the same time, and you told the first offering agent that you needed to give the other agents an opportunity to respond.

Having behaved professionally to this point, there's no reason to stop. Keep communicating. Let's say you're in the very lucky position of having three agents who want to represent your work. Hear each of them out, ask the questions listed above, and tell each of them, "Thank you. I need to sleep on this, but I'll make my decision tomorrow morning, and I'll call you before the day is out." Then do it. Make your decision. You've got three good offers—you've identified these agents as qualified and effective—so how wrong can things go? As I've said before, if you've done the research ahead of time, there aren't as many questions to weigh. You're left with one: How do you feel about each of them? Your brain has done its work—now you have to let your gut decide. When you wake up in the morning, you'll know.

After you've called and accepted the offer of the one you want to work with, you're going to take a deep breath and make the other calls *immediately*. Just try to keep the conversation short and repeat these words as necessary, even as you are hanging up on a screamer: "Thank you for your interest in my work."

THE COMPATIBILITY FACTOR

Ultimately, when it comes to choosing an agent, you're going to have to decide exactly what kind of style you think is most effective. Years ago I heard that a well-known television talk-show host fired her first agent because everyone in the business liked that agent. Word on the street was that the host believed she would be better served by someone who was feared and possibly hated. And who's to say she was wrong? On the other hand, I recently sat on a panel with several well-known novelists. One, who has made a great deal of money from his first book and less from the two that followed, expressed regret that he has never had an agent who was nurturing and supportive in the way described by the other novelists there. It was clear he started out wanting an agent who could get him the most possible money but, once the first book was an enormous success, grew disenchanted with that style of agenting and wished for more career guidance than she'd given him.

The decision is yours to make. If you want someone you feel you can talk to, you need to know that about yourself. If you want an aggressive agent who might have stepped from the pages of *Glengarry Glen Ross*—someone who might not call you very often, and will certainly not buy you a coffee, until you become a "closer" (in this case, a novelist whose book sells and sells well)—that's your call. If you've done your research ahead of time and narrowed your list down to agents who, no matter what their style, are known to be effective, you won't need to spend time wondering whether the agent runs a fly-by-night agency or an established one. You'll just need to decide if the person's style is going to work well for you.

How can you really tell if it's going to work? You can't. But most writers who have had bad agent experiences will admit that, when first signing with the agent, they were so elated to have someone offer to represent them that they ignored little signs that turned out to be alarms they should have listened to.

THE AUTHOR/AGENCY AGREEMENT

The author/agency contract is designed to make clear and lasting the terms of the business partnership. It spells out certain basic terms of the agreement:

1. **What the agent will represent.** This book only? Every book you write? Screenplays and other writings?

2. **The time frame of representation.** The most natural term is the one that proceeds until one or both parties decide to terminate. You're usually asked to give written notice and wait thirty days. But if the agent wants to terminate, he has to do the same thing.

3. **The commission connection.** The agency will continue to receive commissions on any contracts it negotiated on your behalf, whether you continue to work together or not.

4. **The commission and how it's paid.** Commonly 15 percent, sometimes 10 percent, the commission is deducted from amounts paid to you in the name of the agency as they come in. If you receive a ten-thousand-dollar advance, half of which is paid upon signature of the contract, and half of which is paid upon publication of the book, the commission will be deducted from each payment. No agent should deduct the entire commission due from the first payment.

5. **Other commissions for which you're responsible.** These are chiefly the commissions paid to co-agents in foreign countries and in Hollywood. Traditionally, the basic agency commission will be split evenly with the film agent so each agent receives 7.5 percent. Foreign co-agents,

however, receive 10 percent, so typically the contract will require a 20 percent commission on foreign sales so each agent is paid 10 percent. Recently, film agents have begun asking for this arrangement, so some new contracts are requiring a 20 percent commission on film deals—10 percent for the original agent and 10 percent for the co-agent.

6. **Expenses for which you're responsible.** It's common practice to have authors provide copies of the book or manuscript that the agent can use in selling. It's usually cheaper and more efficient to have the agent make the copies and charge the fee back to you, whether by sending an invoice or deducting the amount from any payments that come in. Some agents charge for postage or overnight shipping and long-distance telephone charges. The contract should list whatever expenses you've agreed to bear.

The contract will also stipulate how both parties agree to handle disputes and might ask the author to "indemnify and hold harmless" the agent against any kind of claim for copyright infringement, libel, or any other like matter that arises out of anything you've written that the agent has represented. Agents must have this protection because they don't hire fact-checkers or legal teams to read your manuscript before sending it to publishers. They have only your word that the work is original. You will see this clause in any publishing contract you sign, for the same reason.

The controversy over factual problems in James Frey's *A Million Little Pieces* brought to light this fact of publishing. His agent and publisher proceeded on the strength of his word that everything in his book was true. When he signed a contract with Doubleday, he assumed full responsibility for every word in his book. The public debated whether the publisher should have questioned details in the book more closely, but the fact remains that Frey was entirely responsible for what he wrote in his book and represented as fact.

I don't recommend that you sign a contract that locks you into the relationship for a specific period of time. That's not to the advantage of either party: If you would both like to continue for as long as it takes to sell your books, there's no point in having to renew the contract every year or two. And if either or both of you decide to call it a day well before the time period has expired, it would be tedious to have to wait. However, there are agents who require you to agree to a time period. There are also agents who want you to agree that, if you sell your book within a year or two *after leaving that agency,* you will pay them their commission. I don't recommend agreeing to this.

Once you've read the agreement, get in touch with the agent with any questions you have. Many people ask a lawyer to look it over for them, which is a good idea. If you decide to negotiate for modification of some of the terms of the agreement, try to do so without hostility, since your aim is to form a good working relationship. I can't speak for what other agents will agree to change in their author/agency contracts, so suffice it to say that you'll have to decide what you can and can't live with before you sign.

IF EVERYONE PASSES

Let's say you do hear back, and every one of the ten agents you wrote to sends a rejection letter. Since you have a second list, you can make a second submission of query letters. And while you wait to hear back from the second group, you can make a third list and research everyone on the list the same way you did for the first and second lists. In this way you'll keep yourself busy and hopeful while waiting to make the right match. It goes without saying, too, that you'll be working on a new book now that you've got the first one off your desk.

But what if you can't bring yourself to go on sending query letters out? What if you've found the whole thing too heartbreaking, too nerve-racking, too debilitating, or too exhausting? If that's the case, you've got some decisions to make:

1. **Too heartbreaking?** Was your faith in your novel so weak that one round of rejections killed it? Or did your heart break because it was suddenly clear to you that your book really was not ready to be published? This might be the one that goes into the drawer. If not, get

together with a supportive friend who will remind you of what good work you've done and encourage you to get back on the horse.

2. **Too nerve-wracking?** If you discover that this whole waiting game makes you feel too dependent and out of control, you might be a candidate for self-publishing, where you'll be able to handle or oversee every detail of your book's publication yourself. If you choose this route, consult as many guides and articles as possible, discuss the option on Internet message boards, and check out self-publishers with places like the Better Business Bureau. In addition, these two Web sites—Science Fiction & Fantasy Writers of America, Inc. (www.sfwa.org) and Preditors & Editors (www.anotherealm.com/prededitors)—carry warnings and alerts as well as articles about how to spot scam publishers.

3. **Too debilitating?** Maybe you sent it out at the insistence of friends and family, even though the thought of strangers reading your book was an agony to you. If that's the case, you might not have the stomach to go through with publication, which is in many ways even more demanding than the attempt to find an agent or a publisher. You should consider having your book privately printed and circulated among family members and friends.

4. **Too exhausting?** You might need to think twice about writing as a career, while patting yourself on the back for writing an entire book. If the act of writing and completing a book was satisfaction in itself, there's no shame in deciding not to pursue publication.

IN THEIR OWN WORDS: ADAM FAWER

Adam Fawer, a former dotcom executive who had previously written only for business publications, had always wanted to write fiction. His first novel, *Improbable*, was published in 2005.

> After the longest weekend of my life (the weekend *they*—the editors, the all-powerful, the dream makers—were reading my book), the news wasn't good. My

agent gently informed me, in an encouraging, don't-give-up-now voice, that no one wanted to buy my novel. I was stunned.

I don't think I believed that it was over until I got the e-mail my agent forwarded from one of the rejecting editors—and all I can say is *ouch*. It was filled with eviscerating criticisms that have since been burned into my brain. I must have read that e-mail fifty times. The first time I was numb. The second mildly annoyed. The third irritated. The fourth angry. The fifth enraged. And then it got ugly.

It took about twenty-five readings before the criticisms started to sink in. Gradually, I saw where the editor was coming from. He wanted something different than what I had delivered. Not better, necessarily (or at least that's what I told myself), but different. Okay, I thought, I can give him something different.

It wasn't until I was into the second month of rewriting my novel that I realized not only were most of his criticisms right, but the resulting book *would* be better than the original. If only I could finish it. At first I thought I only would have to rewrite the first 20,000 words, but after I completed an entirely new first act (50,000 words), I realized I had only just begun.

Five painful months later, I emerged from the rubble of book number one with a brand new 134,000-word novel loosely based on my first effort. It contained only about 25,000 words of the original text. But it was better—and more importantly, my agent sold it.

RECOMMENDED READING ...

Breakfast at Tiffany's, by Truman Capote. For what the "mean reds" are like.

Glengarry Glen Ross, by David Mamet. Why? Because it's a play about ruthless, scamming salesmen who are desperate to make a commission. A good read when you're feeling down about the agents who reject or ignore you.

... AND VIEWING

Wonder Boys, directed by Curtis Hanson, based on the novel by Michael Chabon. Michael Douglas plays an aging writer who can't finish his enormous manuscript. If waiting to hear back from agents is difficult, and reading rejection letters is worse, see this film to comfort yourself with the knowledge that at least you were able to finish your book.

RECOMMENDED WEB SITES

Science Fiction & Fantasy Writers of America, Inc. (www.sfwa.org). This indefatigable and ever-helpful Web site has a sample author/agency contract with explanations of each of its clauses.

PublishLawyer.com (www.publishlawyer.com). Another helpful site, created by a publishing attorney in Maryland. Clicking on the "articles" link will bring you to a list that includes a good article on "The Author-Agency Agreement."

CHAPTER 17:

working with
an agent through
thick and thin

Not only did you write an entire novel, you rewrote it—seven times. You found other writers and made time in your life to meet with them regularly and to read their work as they read yours. You wrote a query letter—and then rewrote it —and then rewrote your novel—and rewrote your query letter twice more. You networked to get referrals to agents, and you researched many others, developed a list, and began submitting your novel. The word submission took on a whole new meaning as you suffered the humiliation of being ignored or rejected, of having your name misspelled or not used at all, of having your work pigeon-holed or misunderstood or lost.

Yet somehow, perhaps by using the same passion, grit, determination, and creativity that made you a writer, you persevered, and you got an agent you trust, respect, and believe in. You trust he'll find a publisher for your novel. You respect his ability, his track record, the other writers he represents. You believe his commitment to your work. And you're ready to sit back and wait for the call that says, "Random House wants to publish your book!"

Not so fast! There's plenty to do before that call comes. To put it another way: There's plenty you can do to help make that call come faster and with greater enthusiasm.

WHAT YOU CAN DO TO HELP

First off, you will probably need to rework your novel yet again. With editors under greater pressure to find books that are ready to go, and with their time chopped up into innumerable meetings, agents now routinely work editorially with their clients well before an editor gets involved. Yet all too often I've met and represented writers who respond to an agent's request for changes with the remark, "I'd rather wait to make more changes until I have a real editor."

If that's a polite way of saying you don't agree with the suggestions, that they really don't ring true to you and you're afraid of breaking what worked well enough to attract the attention of an agent, that's fine. You'll have to communicate these feelings to your agent, and try to convince him that your instincts are correct. If he doesn't agree, it's quite possible you've signed up with the wrong person. I've heard the horror stories: "An agent told me to set my football novel in a ballet studio." "An agent told me to rewrite my coming-of-age novel as a pirate historical." "An agent told me he could sell my book faster if I made every paragraph no longer than three sentences and reduced its 500 pages to 150." You'll need to determine whether the advice seems particular to your novel or particular to the agent's area of specialty—such as pirate historicals.

A good revision is one where you find creative solutions to problems your trusted readers have identified in the work, not one where every suggestion is slavishly and literally carried out. So if the agent has raised a series of questions or concerns about the book, he's not saying he wants everything changed or he'll wash his hands of you. He's asking you to make a good or promising book better. Make it the best you can make it. If you resist the suggestions even though you know your novel needs some work, however, you're only hurting yourself and your novel's chances in the marketplace.

Perhaps you have a romantic fantasy of how publishing works: You meet your editor, who is wearing a well-cut tweed suit, for lunch at a hushed and understated midtown restaurant, where she tells you a few things you could do to make your novel better, has a couple of martinis, and tells you over coffee how bright your future is. I do know at least one writer who had a lunch like that as recently as twenty-five years ago, but it's no longer common—if, indeed, it ever was. Or perhaps you have the "diamond-in-the-rough" fantasy of publishing: that editors sit at their desks, which are lit only by a green-shaded lamp, poring through manuscripts in the hope of finding something brilliant within the many badly typed pages lying before them. In a world dominated by e-mail, overnight delivery, and instant messaging—indeed, instant everything—does this seem likely?

I think you're getting the picture now. So, when your agent says, "I'd like to see another draft. Could you get the action moving before page 100, and reduce the number of characters by a third?" you are going to get to work. Have you taken Laura's excellent advice on rewriting from the first half of this book? Have you gone through the "Ten Ways to Go From Good to Great" in chapter twelve? If so, you've become an excellent judge of writing advice and can sort the good from the bad when it comes to your own work. You've also developed the ability to be tough on yourself and look dispassionately and objectively at your work, especially after periods of rest from it.

This isn't a race. It's taken you this long to get this far. Why should your manuscript suddenly be rushed into the arms of editors? A premature submission might result in the kinds of rejection letters that say, "I'd be happy to take a second look should the author revise," but it's rare that the second look results in a contract to publish your book. It does happen, but more often the editor has lost her initial enthusiasm for your writing, or has even forgotten what she saw in it the first time around. If you think about it, the only two winners of a premature submission are the U.S. Postal Service and Kinko's!

BIO NOTE

The next thing you can do to help is to write a terrific bio note for your agent. You may have described yourself briefly in your initial query letter and you may even have enclosed your résumé or *curriculum vitae*. Yet neither of those things includes the kinds of facts about you that make you sound really interesting—like someone the publicist assigned to your book could talk up when trying to get publicity for it. So don't do the usual list of dates and jobs. Write about yourself as if you were a character in a Russian novel. Or have a friend interview you to pull out the kinds of things in your background you take for granted but others might find fascinating. Find bio notes of some of your favorite authors and see what makes them interesting. Many books just have a line or two about the author on the jacket, but the more successful and well-known the writer, the more likely you'll find a variety of bios on the Web or in the library.

Recognize that it's to your advantage as a novelist to be or to have been a jack- or jill-of-all-trades. A varied life experience speaks of many qualities. It tells us that here is someone who's seen enough to take us places we haven't been. It indicates that writing has been more important to the person than the development of another, more stable or conventional career. If the variety of odd jobs, residences, and aborted careers is due more to the fact that you had no direction or life plan or even that you were in the grip of an alcohol or drug addiction, don't be ashamed. These are the forces that have shaped you, that have given you empathy or insight, an appreciation for or experience of the kinds of characters more conventional people—like agents and editors—don't meet regularly. These experiences may have made you less likely to waste the time you have left than someone who's lived comfortably or without much incident, trouble, or change.

When you're published, you'll be the kind of writer who is more likely to garner "off-the-book-page" publicity than the person who graduated with a degree in creative writing or got an M.F.A. from the University of Iowa. And you will undoubtedly be the kind of writer that readers empathize with, care about, and want to see in person at readings and other events if you've had life experiences that have proved difficult, tragic, or just plain colorful.

Raymond Carver, author of short story collections including *Cathedral* and *What We Talk About When We Talk About Love*, and winner of Guggenheim and National Endowment for the Arts grants and fellowships, was one of the most influential American writers of the later twentieth century. Bruce Weber, in a *New York Times Magazine* profile, wrote that before Carver became established as a writer, he "picked tulips, pumped gas, swept hospital corridors, swabbed toilets, and managed an apartment complex." Carver himself told an interviewer in 1978 that he was also "a saw mill hand, a delivery man, a retail clerk, and an editor at a publishing firm." This peripatetic existence—part writing, part alcoholism—endeared him to his readers, who felt he could speak and write about real people in an authentic way.

In writing your bio note, you should try to display your appreciation for the varied experiences that have brought you this far. At the bookstore or library, make it a habit to read book-flap bios. Most are dull or brief, but some have at least a nugget of information that's unusual or striking. Read interviews with your favorite authors and note the things about their lives or pasts that interest you most. If you have a friend interview you, let her draw out the quirky, unusual, touching, or courageous notes you've disregarded simply because you're used to them or because you were afraid they were the kind of details that would put off those grandees of publishing.

Your agent might not include your bio note exactly as written when submitting your manuscript. He might instead draw from it to enliven the cover letter or when telling editors about you when pitching your book. After Dennis Lehane, author of *Mystic River*, signed with me, I asked him to write and tell me more about himself. Using what he wrote, I was able to write a cover letter when I submitted his first novel, *A Drink Before the War*, that read like this:

As we discussed, I am very pleased to enclose *A Drink Before the War*, a raw, fresh first novel by Dennis Lehane.

Dennis is twenty-five, a native of Dorchester, Massachusetts, and has worked as (among other things) a chauffeur, a strip club DJ (for three days), and a Behavioral Therapist for emotionally, physically, and sexually abused children. (You'll see the significance of this when you read the novel.) He is now absolutely a writer, and in the last eighteen months he's written this novel, four screenplays, a dozen short stories, and the beginning of the next novel featuring the same detective team. Several of his stories have won contests and one of his screenplays has attracted the attention of James Woods. He is now teaching writing at a college in Miami and working closely on the new novel with poet and novelist James Hall.

You have this exclusively, and I think you'll find it as exciting as I did. I look forward to talking to you about it very soon.

The unusual mix of jobs and the author's youth, combined with his productiveness and his connection to at least one well-known writer, were important elements in creating interest in the editor's mind. That letter didn't sell the novel—the novel sold the novel—but even today, interviews with Dennis Lehane go back to some of those biographical details (his work with troubled children, his Ritz-Carlton chauffeur's job) over and over again. Interviewers are fascinated by aspects of his past that seem influential on some of his book's themes or characters.

An agent's job is to provide an editor with as much ammunition as possible so that her job of convincing other publishing house staff—sales, marketing, publicity departments—will be more effective. An agent's job is to know how to sell you as well as your book. Selling yourself isn't easy, but if you can give your agent some good, raw material, he will be able to put it to excellent use.

KEEPING TABS ON YOUR AGENT

How do you know what your agent is doing? How do you find out? How do you know what his strategy is—if he has a strategy—and whether it will succeed?

Agents have different styles and keep their clients informed in different ways. One agent I know sends a weekly e-mail update to her entire client list in which she recounts the editors, producers, or foreign publishers she lunched with or met with that week, any sales she made, and any submissions she made. She is a paragon among agents and basically makes the rest of us look bad. However, we all need something to which we can aspire!

Other agents send a submission list to their clients, listing every editor who has or will get the manuscript. Others show proof of their activity by sending a copy of every rejection letter; some add a note saying who will see the manuscript next. Some call with each editor's response; others wait for the author to call and inquire.

And some, alas, never say a word. I have heard too often of writers who, after a year's silence, asked at least to be sent copies of the rejection letters the agent had received. And even that request went unanswered. In such cases, it's clear the author has no choice but to terminate the relationship immediately. And it doesn't need to be a year's utter silence. On the other hand, I've talked to writers who've told me they never hear from their agent, only to admit when pressed that they haven't made any attempt to get in touch with their agent but expect the agent to get in touch with them at regular intervals.

KEEP IN TOUCH

Establish with your agent the best means of communicating. After first taking on a client, for instance, I like to talk on the telephone, not rely exclusively on e-mail. E-mail is an excellent way to communicate all manner of information, but before getting to the e-mail-only stage I like to get to know the sound of the writer's voice. In the voice I can hear a greater range of emotion than I can glean from e-mail, and it's often easier to resolve a problem or put a worry to rest in one conversation, when the same issue might require the exchange of half a dozen e-mails or more. Many writers hesitate to call their agent because they're aware the agent is busy and they aren't likely to get them on the telephone immediately. But a whole series of e-mails, even brief ones, can equally eat up time.

So how to decide when to call, when to e-mail, when to write, and when to send something overnight or via messenger?

E-MAIL WHEN YOU:

- have news to impart
- have one or two brief and specific questions
- need to send a document electronically or as an e-mail attachment
- have been told by your agent that that's his preferred method for *all* communication

WRITE WHEN YOU:

- have a change of address
- have to send any kind of official paperwork, whether it be a contract, a tax form, or a power of attorney
- have written a new story or book and your agent has asked you to mail it rather than send it electronically

CALL WHEN YOU:

- want or need to discuss any aspect of your career in greater or less structured detail
- need to go over a list, an author's questionnaire, or your manuscript
- have a simple procedural question or clerical matter that can easily be handled by an assistant
- have some very good gossip

USE AN OVERNIGHT SERVICE OR MESSENGER WHEN YOU:

- returning a signed contract or tax form
- sending flowers

Whatever form of communication you use, try not to ramble. Long, unparagraphed, misspelled e-mails are not likely to get an immediate response. The agent may not easily be able to sort out what it is you need to know, or may need time to digest the contents and form an answer. People in publishing

working with an agent through thick and thin

generally don't like e-mails that are written entirely in lower case. As one editor said, "How lazy can you be?" Try to make your e-mails easy to answer by setting questions off with space before and after or with bullets.

After you and your agent have worked out your communication style, keep in touch. While not everyone returns calls promptly, the squeaky wheel gets the grease. Yet a screeching wheel is vastly annoying, so try to be the one that works beautifully when oiled periodically. There's nothing more difficult for a busy person than having to repeat himself. If you don't respond to the attention you do get, you'll get less. If you're responsive—if you think of ways to make your business partner's work more interesting; show a lighter side; improve your work; continue your efforts with getting published in literary journals, magazines, and quarterlies; meet other writers—you'll be a joy to have around, and your agent will want to pay you even more attention.

LET YOUR AGENT DO HIS JOB

It's hard to know, at first, when to stay out of your agent's way and when to jump in. But before we discuss submission strategies in the next chapter, there is definitely one thing you should not do: Don't make any submissions on your own.

Sometimes a writer will call and say, "A friend of mine read my manuscript, and she loved it so much she wanted her editor to read it, so she sent it to him. I thought you'd want to know." It's true that we do want to know. But it's unlikely to make an agent happy to hear this, for a number of reasons:

- Your agent may have promised the manuscript to a different editor at the same house.

- Another editor at the same publishing house may already have the novel under consideration.

- If the editor does turn out to be interested, the agent's negotiating leverage is considerably weakened by his inability to set certain expectations in the editor's mind from the start.

- Another editor at the same publishing house may already have rejected the novel.

- The agent may not have wished to submit your novel to that editor because of issues involving other clients. This may be difficult to swallow. But think about it: If you've gotten an agent for your Western who has something of a specialty in Westerns, he'll have to juggle at times. Perhaps he has another client whose work, ready at the same time, might be overshadowed by yours. He might have a strategy that includes submitting these novels to certain people in a certain order. He might have planned to send yours to someone more senior than your friend's editor. Or he might have planned to send your manuscript to someone less senior—sometimes, junior editors are more enthusiastic, and with first novels, the editor's enthusiasm is an important driving force.

So if you do meet an editor who expresses interest in your work, refer her to your agent—and let your agent know right away. Similarly, don't withhold information about writing-related activities. Have you given any readings lately? Submitted stories, essays, or pieces of your novel to journals or magazines? Begun a new novel? Accepted a magazine assignment? Tell your agent! It could be just the ammunition he needs.

DON'T BE A "WHAT-HAVE-YOU-DONE-FOR-ME-LATELY?" CLIENT

It's true there's not much you can do while your book is "out there." But try to refrain from calling only to ask, "Have you sold it yet?" When you call, try to bring something to the table. First of all, it should be obvious that if there had been an offer, you would have heard about it. However, there are times when an editor expresses great enthusiasm to your agent, says she's going to buy the book, and then—nothing. Not even a returned call or an e-mail. At other times an editor might call or write to say that she'd brought the manuscript up with her editor-in-chief and been shot down. In any case, many seasoned agents don't call an author the instant an editor makes that I'm-going-to-try-to-buy-it claim, because we've all been burned often enough that we don't want to get our client's hopes up only to have them shot down.

We usually do, very cautiously, let the author know of an editor's interest, if only to give him the pleasure of knowing that *someone* out there loved the book. There are times when the agent needs the author to answer questions the editor has about the book or the author's plans for a next book. And there are times when the editor wants to have a conversation with the author about editorial input and direction.

These conversations are invariably stressful, but when there's no way to proceed without such a conversation, the editor and author get on the phone. The editor is usually in a positive frame of mind because she liked the book enough to initiate the conversation. But the author is usually a wreck because he is terrified of saying the wrong thing, or thinks the editor didn't understand the book, or (back to that "waiting for a real editor" mind set) doesn't want to promise to make the changes until the editor actually buys the book. These authors are essentially offended by the very idea of this conversation. In the cases I know of where they weren't offended and entered the conversation with an open mind, the book sold to the interested editor.

RECOMMENDED READING

Read interviews, profiles, and biographical notes about the top writers in your genre or category. A librarian can be a great help in putting this together.

As Ever, Scott Fitz—Letters Between F. Scott Fitzgerald and His Literary Agent Harold Ober, edited by Matthew J. Bruccoli, with Jennifer Atkinson. This book is out of print, but if you can find it, you'll have a great model to follow in F. Scott Fitzgerald's business dealings with his literary agent.

RECOMMENDED WEB SITE

Carver: The Raymond Carver Web Site (www.whitman.edu/english/carver/ carver.cgi). The epigraph at this site is a quote from Carver himself: "If this sounds like the story of a life, okay." A writer's life, that is.

CHAPTER EIGHTEEN:

getting to yes

By now you've learned the best way to communicate with your agent. He may call, e-mail, write, send copies of rejection letters, or use all these means of communication with you. But how does your book get on editors' desks, and what's going to happen next?

Let's discuss submission strategies first. There are any number of ways to sell a book, and rarely does the sale of a first novel happen in a truly predictable way. The elements of the equation that add up to a sale are: (1) your book, (2) your agent's contacts, (3) the needs of the market, and (4) serendipity.

The first and most important part of the equation is your book. Your agent's submission strategy will rely on what kind of a book it is and how much he believes in it. An agent takes on a first novel for any number of reasons:

1. It's a page-turning commercial novel he's sure he'll sell.

2. It's a good piece of genre writing.

3. It's beautifully written and executed.

4. It's the beginning of a brilliant career.

5. It came with the endorsements of several highly regarded writers of the same kind of fiction.

Having decided your novel is (1), (4), and (5), your agent may choose to make a multiple submission. Unlike the kind of multiple submission an unknown writer makes from a list of names he has collected from directories and referrals, your agent's multiple submission will be based on personal knowledge of each of the editors on the list.

Developing a submission list is fun. It's one of the challenges that make our job so stimulating. If we're reading a manuscript and liking it a lot, chances are we're already making a mental list while reading the manuscript. We're matchmakers, and in addition to the editors' names and addresses we have in our address books, we keep a lot of ephemera about each editor we know in our heads. Even when we read novels that have already been published by editors we know, we're cataloguing the elements of the work at hand and combining them with what we know about the editor who saw it into print. So when we decide to take a manuscript on, we have a pretty good idea of who might want to publish it.

Even after you and your agent have decided you need to revise the novel before it goes out to editors, your agent will be formulating the submission list. There are any number of ways we do this. When we lunch with editors, as discussed earlier, we find out what kinds of things they've already published, what kinds of things they'd like to publish, and what kinds of things their bosses are asking that they publish. If everything aligns, we can pitch your novel over coffee. (Why wait until the coffee comes? Because one rule of sales is, "When you've gotten to yes, shut up." If you don't stop the pitch when they say "I want to read it—send it to me," you may unwittingly give them time or reasons to reconsider. If you can get them to say yes just as the check comes, you've made a presale and you can wrap things up and get out of there before they have time to think it over.)

Other ways we add names to the list include:

*   going through our contacts or submission lists from previous sales to refresh our memories about who's interested in what

- reading *Publishers Weekly* for job changes, launching of new imprints, profiles of editors and publishers, what's new on the best-seller list, and its surveys of specialty markets like mysteries, romance, young adult, and other genre fiction
- reading *Publishers Marketplace* to find who's buying what from whom
- calling other agents to go over the list and see if we've overlooked anyone

GETTING IT OUT THERE

When your manuscript is ready to roll, your agent goes to work. First, he'll call all the editors on the list who expressed interest in it to alert them the novel is on the way, and he'll call the others to pitch the book and ask if they want to be included in the submission. The list is in formation up to the very last minute due to job changes, unexpected meetings, and calls from editors who've heard that a hot new manuscript is going out, asking to be included.

Then, the agent writes or puts the finishing touches on the cover letter, personalizing each one as necessary. This letter, like your query letter, should never be longer than a page. It will include only a brief description of the novel—not only are overlong plot descriptions boring, but the novel is going to have to stand on its own merits—and as much ammunition about the author, (his *curriculum vitae*, contacts, and overall salability) as the agent can gather. Increasingly, editors are forced by their sales and marketing departments to compare a new novelist's work to the work of well-known or best-selling writers, so we have to come up with the kind of pitch Buck Henry did so wittily in Robert Altman's film *The Player*—something in the spirit of: "It's *Run Lola Run* meets *Infinite Jest*," "Michael Crichton meets *A Beautiful Mind*," or "*The Lovely Bones* as told by Emily Dickinson."

The manuscript is then put into a crisp new manuscript box that's labeled at the foot. Many agencies use colorful boxes that will stand out on an editor's crowded shelves. In effect they're branding their product by doing this, and an editor can tell at a glance where a manuscript comes from—one well-known agency uses handsome matte orange boxes, another shiny red, a third bright yellow. In my office we devote a lot of attention to the label that's placed at the foot of the box, choosing a font for the title that somehow conveys the style of the writing, and making sure the title and author's name are readable from across the room, where it will be buried in a stack of other manuscripts.

Into the box go the manuscript and any other materials that will help the editor make a favorable decision: essays the author may have published in prominent publications, a list of short story publications, even a list of the author's well-known or published friends and acquaintances who have promised to blurb or review the book when it comes out. The manuscript will be a good clean copy, as will the accompanying material. If we receive bad copies or unreadable or messy lists or reviews (of, say, an anthology the author has contributed to), we retype them so they look as sharp as possible. The box is then closed, and the cover letter is placed on top, then rubber-banded to the box. Most places record each submission, and we want the information they need to log in the submission to be easily available. We also want the editor to be able to quickly review the submission before making the decision whether to open the box and start reading then and there, assign it to an assistant to read, put it on the stack of manuscripts to be read, or put it or the first fifty pages into her bag or briefcase to take home or to read on the train.

Some editors insist that agents inform them if they're submitting a project to anyone else in their vast corporate empire of two dozen separate publishing imprints. I don't, as a matter of policy, ever inform an editor of this, simply because one man's meat is another's poison—meaning that one editor may love the book and another may hate it, and the editor who loves the book doesn't need to know that it was turned down by one of her distant colleagues.

LIMITED MULTIPLE SUBMISSIONS

While first novels that feel commercially "hot" to an agent will undoubtedly be sent to a dozen or more editors, many manuscripts are initially sent out on a limited multiple submission. This is where the agent chooses only three or five editors to read it simultaneously. The agent may employ this strategy with a manuscript, such as a literary coming-of-age novel, that marks the beginning of a serious writer's career but that might not stand up to a lot of hype or a high-pressure multiple submission. The editor should know that there's enough interest that she's not alone in wanting to read the manuscript, but should be allowed to read the manuscript with a certain degree of calm in order to appreciate its quieter or more serious qualities.

EXCLUSIVE SUBMISSIONS

In a clamorous marketplace it's essential to employ a strategy that will get a novel the closest possible attention. That, and those stacks of manuscripts in every editor's office, may lead an agent to go against expectation and make an exclusive submission of a novel. In this case the agent calls the editor at the top of the submission list, pitches the book, and, if the editor displays a great deal of enthusiasm in expressing her wish to read it as soon as possible, promises that she can have it alone—exclusively—for a brief period of time before it's submitted to other editors.

Another reason to make an exclusive submission is that the editor may have met the writer at a conference, seen an earlier draft of the novel, referred the writer to the agent, or read a short story the author published, and called the agent first to express her interest in the writer's work. Or, since this is a business of relationships, the agent may owe the editor a favor, or may even wish to make an exclusive submission of a prestigious or hot commercial novel to curry favor with an editor. No matter what the reason, an exclusive submission conveys the idea that the agent has chosen this editor for her particular skill and ability and wishes to present her with something special.

A manuscript on exclusive is likely to be read more quickly than a manuscript that's sent out widely or indiscriminately. But the agent must set up the rules of the submission at the beginning. The editor may be given the weekend to get a head start on reading the manuscript, after which the agent will automatically send it out to other interested editors. Or the editor may be given a period of ten days in which to read the book, get other readings from colleagues, and make the offer.

In either case, after making an exclusive submission, it's important that the agent follow through on the time constraint set at the beginning: If the editor has been given the weekend, the agent must get an answer on Monday. If no answer is forthcoming, or even if the editor says she's enthusiastic and wants to get some of her colleagues or her boss to read it so she might put together an offer, the agent must be prepared to widen the submission immediately to the other interested editors on his list.

If any more time passes, it becomes awkward: Suppose that the agent lets the editor have another week in order to get her ducks in a row, then, with no offer in hand, sends the manuscript out to the other editors. Two days after the other editors receive the manuscript, the first editor finally comes through with an offer.

What is done in this case? It depends on several factors, but it ultimately depends on you, the author. If you like the offer, like the sound of the editor and feel the house is right for you and your book, you can accept the offer on the spot. If your agent has been clear with the other editors—that the editor who had it on exclusive for a brief period of time hadn't made an offer or rejected it before the manuscript went out on a simultaneous submission—you have every right to take the bird in the hand and leave it to your agent to explain to the editors what has happened. They might be slightly annoyed, they might have begun reading the book and may like what they've read, and they may even yell, but they also know that it's business as usual. No one did anything wrong and those are the breaks.

Another course of action would be to turn the first offer down and wait to see what the other editors have to say. What's the risk here? It's obvious: You might not get another offer. In that case you'd be in the position either of going back to the original editor, hat in hand, and saying, "We were wrong, can we have the offer back?" or of having your agent continue to submit the novel until he finds another interested publisher. The first course of action has been known to work, but it's also been known to backfire. Sometimes the editor is miffed that her offer was turned down and wishes to wash her hands of the author who didn't appreciate her enthusiasm and the work she put into making an offer. Sometimes she'll revive the offer but lower the amount of money, because she knows you've struck out elsewhere and she realizes she can now get your manuscript at what amounts to an end-of-season price reduction.

ON THE TABLE OR HOLDING THE FLOOR

One way to handle the scenario in which you've gotten an offer but wish to hear what other editors have to say is to have your agent ask the editor if she'll leave her offer "on the table" for a certain period of time while you solicit other offers. Your agent can finesse this by saying that while you're pleased to have the offer, the editor knew that, when the clock ran out, the manuscript would go out to other editors. The editor could either refuse to let the offer stand or agree.

If the editor agrees, she will likely say it will only stand for a certain period of time. But no one with any negotiating skill wants to look like a doormat, so it is more likely that she will agree only if you and your agent accept her bid as a floor. A floor, when accepted, becomes the first bid in an auction. The auction proceeds without the initial editor, because by placing a floor and having it accepted, the editor is granted another privilege: the option of topping. After the bidding ends, your agent will call the floor-holder to relay to her the highest bid, and if the floor-holder wishes, she can win the auction by topping with an offer 10 percent higher than the last bid. A floor-holder with 10 percent topping privileges does not participate in the auction, but the agent keeps her informed of its progress.

Floor offers pose something of a dilemma because the other rule of the floor is that, should no auction occur, you are obligated to accept the floor offer as your advance. Therefore, if you and your agent accepted a floor offer that you wouldn't like to accept as your final advance, you'd be stuck. On the other hand, if the floor offer is too high to serve as a reasonable opening bid, it might scare away other bidders and you'd find yourself without an auction when there might have been an exciting one. The right floor is one that can kick off an auction if there's going to be one, and if there isn't going to be one, it's the offer you're going to be happy to get for your first book.

While some agents routinely make exclusive submissions, many make them only rarely. That's because they've found the best way to get the highest advance for your book is by getting multiple bids. Sometimes you get only two offers. One is higher than the other, and the lower bidder declines to raise his bid. You then have to decide which offer to take. You might assume anyone would take the higher offer, but it doesn't always work that way. Some authors take the lower offer because it comes from a publishing house they particularly admire. And sometimes the lower offer comes with other terms that make it more attractive than the higher offer. As usual, there will be several factors you'll have to weigh and discuss with your agent before making your decision.

But the big money for first novels comes as the result of an auction. What does a book auction look like, and how can you have one for your book?

AUCTION FEVER

Your manuscript has been sent out to a dozen editors and already, just a day or two later, your agent is getting calls from editors who didn't get the manuscript and want to see it, as well as from editors who've already started reading it and are calling to find out if anything is happening with it. They want to know if other editors have called, if anyone's made an offer, and if your agent is going to set a closing date, which is the date by which everyone who's interested needs to make an offer. If your agent is already getting these calls, chances are very good indeed that he's going to set a closing date as soon as possible. Assuming the editors got the manuscripts on Friday so they could read over the weekend, and that they started calling Monday and more calls came in on Tuesday, your agent may set the auction for later that week—say Thursday—or for the middle of the week after. If more than one editor makes an offer, there will be an auction.

The agent sets a closing date and calls, e-mails, or faxes the interested editors with the rules. They might go something like this:

- The closing date for *Great American Novel* is Thursday, Sept. 21.
- First offers must be received by my office by noon that day.

- The auction will be conducted in rounds.
- Only North American publication rights will be available.
- The author reserves the right to base his final decision on factors other than strictly financial ones.

This puts everyone on notice and sets the general rules for the auction. But don't assume everyone follows the rules!

PREEMPTIVE OFFERS

First, there will undoubtedly be an editor who calls before the day of the auction and tries to make a preemptive offer. That's an offer that, ideally, is so attractive that it takes the book off the market before anyone else can bid. Your agent cannot shop a preempt —meaning he can't call the other interested parties and ask if they were planning to make a better offer. (When I say *cannot*, I mean that it's unethical. I don't mean that no one does it. Unfortunately, people do.) A preempt is usually offered with a very tight time frame of, perhaps, five or ten minutes. This is done to forestall shopping. A preempt is a take-it-or-leave-it offer. The agent must call the author and ask him if he wants to accept on the spot. If he says yes, the agent calls the editor and accepts the offer for his client. If you and your agent decide to turn down the preempt, your agent will invite the editor to come to the auction and put in her bid with everyone else.

LET THE BIDDING BEGIN

Book auctions aren't held in person the way auctions for antiques are. They're held on the telephone. On the day of the auction, the editor who tried to preempt may be the first to call. If she's smart, she'll make her first offer much lower than the offer with which she tried to preempt your book. You might find this upsetting, but don't worry—she'll raise it if there are other, higher offers.

With her offer, no matter how low or high, the auction has begun. The next thing is to collect the first bids of all the interested editors. It will be a tense morning. What if no one else calls? What if only one other editor calls? You're going to have to wrap your mind around these possibilities. Your hopes will have gotten high, and your confidence may have been strong the day you turned down the preemptive offer, but today you might have to talk yourself through the more disappointing outcomes before your agent's telephone—and yours—rings again. Comfort yourself with the notion that, at the end of the day, you will have a publisher for your novel.

Let's say it's a good day because the telephone does ring again—five more times. At noon your agent has in hand no fewer than six offers for your first novel. One is low, two are the same, and three are higher. This is the end of round one. To begin round two, your agent puts the bids in order and calls the low bidder to tell her what the highest bid was. The low bidder can either drop out of the auction or make a new offer that's higher. If she's going to bid again, you and your agent have to wait for her bid before calling the other editors. When you've gotten the new bid, your agent calls the next lowest bidder and tells her where she stands. In the case where you have two identical bids, the agent calls the editor who made the first bid. When an editor makes a new and higher bid, your agent calls the next editor. And so it goes.

When all five low-bidders have responded by raising their bids or dropping out, your agent concludes round two by calling the highest bidder from the first round and filling her in. If that editor chooses to make a new offer that's higher than all the others, her bid will kick off round three.

MORE RULES OF THE AUCTION GAME

There are some pieces of information your agent must reveal to the offering editors and some he is under no obligation to reveal.

1. If your book only receives one bid, your agent must reveal this fact to the bidder. The bidder then has no obligation to improve her starting bid. However, your agent may be able to persuade her to improve it.

2. If there are other bidders, your agent is under no obligation to say who they are while the auction is going on, except in the case dis-

cussed under the next point. Although they know better, sometimes editors ask who the other bidders are, hoping to catch the agent off guard. Your agent shouldn't tell the editor who's competing against her because there remains the possibility that the bidding editors could get together and rig the auction in some way.

3. If two editors from one large publishing house both make bids, your agent is under some obligation to inform each that another person from her corporate parent is also bidding. Some corporations won't allow two of their employees to bid against one another.

4. In order to allow you to choose the offer you want, which may not be the highest offer, your agent must state at the outset that you reserve this right. If he doesn't, you're obligated to accept the highest offer of the auction, whether you want to or not.

5. Your agent is under no obligation to reveal your personal information to any publisher.

6. At the end of the auction, the losing editors—the underbidders—will ask your agent who won and who their competitors were, and while your agent isn't strictly obligated to reveal this information, most don't see any reason to conceal it. If they did try to conceal it, the editor would suspect something out of order—such as the fact that the agent had fabricated the other bids, which some have been known to do.

WHEN NOTHING HAPPENS

The fact remains that with your first novel, you just want to get the damned thing published, so you don't care so much about advances, auctions, and all the rest. But what if your novel just isn't selling? What if contact with your agent has dwindled to the copies of rejection letters you're getting every month or so in the mail?

This is a dispiriting time. And this is when you have to constantly reconnect with your belief in your own work. If your agent is steadfastly enthusiastic, the one kind of call you shouldn't make too often is the one where you say, "Do you think anyone will like it?"

Of course you will occasionally need to voice those doubts. But try to understand not only the role but the motivation of your new business partner. As a non-publishing small-business owner once said to me, "It's a numbers game. You're going to hear the word no a lot more often than you'll hear the word yes."

So, to your agent, a series of rejections isn't nearly the crushing blow you might find it to be. You may want sympathy, and you may get it, but don't be surprised if your worries and self-doubts are sometimes met with bafflement. The agent may have a number of manuscripts circulating at once. He wants your book—and all the others—to sell as much as you do. If he didn't think anyone would like your book, he wouldn't have taken it on.

A whole bunch of rejections isn't easy for anyone, but they're a lot easier for your seasoned agent to take than they are for you to take. That's one of the reasons you got an agent! Agents take real pleasure in conquering the doubters and proving the naysayers wrong by selling your novel to an enthusiastic, smart editor. Big, overnight-sensation auctions are exciting for everyone, even the bidders, but in many ways it's even more satisfying to see a book through to successful publication after a number of turndowns.

So take your cues from your agent's attitude. If he remains positive, refresh yourself with that attitude and go back to work on your next book. If, on the other hand, you find a consistency in the rejection letters' criticism that makes you believe you could successfully rework your manuscript, ask your agent if he'd like you to do so. I would recommend bringing this possibility up after several—not, say, fifteen—editors have said essentially the same thing about the book. If you wait too long you may as well start over again with a new book, because the pool of willing readers will have gotten too small.

Also, in spite of the fact that editors and agents will say they'd be happy to reconsider should the manuscript be reworked, too often, upon such a resubmission, the reader finds the bloom has gone off the rose and declines the book. To explain this, we can point to a few factors:

1. **Taste is fickle.** The editor's initial enthusiasm has simply faded. She may not even recall why she liked the book in the first place.

2. **Your craft isn't up to the task.** The editor may simply be disappointed with the revision. It could be that she had a vision for a book you can't write or don't want to write.

3. **The editor's mandate has changed.** She may have been told to concentrate on acquiring fiction more commercial or more literary than the novel you have written.

4. **The editor is less hungry.** This could happen after an editor has published a big book successfully or after she has published a string of successful books. In these cases, the editor may have new books to publish by the successful authors, or may have begun to receive submissions of a sufficiently high caliber that she's become far more selective than she was at the time of the first submission.

PRESSING AHEAD

As you can see, having an agent is no guarantee that the road to publication will be completely free of obstacles. But hold on to the thought that a seasoned, reputable agent takes great pride in placing a book he believes in. Ideally, he will have the kind of tenacity in selling a project that you have in writing it.

If the submissions of your novel continue to result in rejection, and if the submissions of a revised version fail as well, don't assume your agent has given up on you unless other signs point in that direction as well: unreturned phone calls, unanswered e-mails, a lack of interest in or no plan for what to do next. If your communication with your agent remains good and if you hear him say he's still interested, have faith. Don't give up. Get to work on your next book.

That's what one client of mine did to great effect. I'd taken on her collection of short stories but hadn't been able to place it. Undaunted, she wrote a novel; unfortunately, though that, too, got good readings from excellent editors, it failed to sell. Yet while it was under submission, she began a new one and sent me a chapter every month. Though that's not the way writers and agents usually work, they can, and in this case it just seemed right. After each chapter I was on the edge of my seat until the next one came. Eighteen months later, the author had a terrific new book, and after she'd polished it, I sent it out to editors. It sold like gangbusters: A two-day auction with six bidders resulted in a mid-six-figure advance for this hardworking writer who didn't let a few rejection letters, two babies, and a teaching job slow her down.

BREAKING UP IS(N'T) HARD TO DO

What if you read all the signs of disinterest from your agent, yet feel you've grown as a writer and have a strong new book to show? You called. You wrote e-mails describing your new book. You even sent the manuscript in and never got a response.

Don't beat a dead horse. You gave him a chance. Now it's time to move on.

If you are going to go, it's important to go *now*, with a new book no one has seen. Don't let an apathetic agent—should he respond at all—take your manuscript out to a few people just to see what happens. A manuscript that's made the rounds is as tired as last year's Payless shoes.

First, you must make a clean break from your current agent. How do you do this? You will need to go back to your author/agency agreement, if you signed one, and read the termination clause to see what you need to do. Be aware that, even after terminating, you may be obliged to reimburse your agent for any expenses that were listed as reimbursable in the agreement.

In addition, there is an obligation that may come into play if you change agents while your manuscript is still under consideration with editors. Let's say that your first agent had not received rejection letters from every submission—that there were, in fact, two or three outstanding submissions when you switched agents. And let's say, further, that your new agent discovers that one of those editors wants to make an offer for your book. Your new agent is perfectly within his rights to negotiate with that editor. But should you accept that editor's offer, you will be obligated to pay your original agent her full commission. In the end, you may have to pay two commissions, one to each agent. So if you're feeling unsure about whether to continue with an agent, make the break before having him submit a new work.

STARTING OVER

Put your query-letter-writer-and-agent-researcher hat back on and pick up the pieces. Should you describe your experience in being agented and having your first novel rejected? Many writers include this information in their query letters because they think it shows they have been singled out before or that they are experienced in the ways of publishing. Or they simply think they should be honest or that someone will want to hear their story.

Keep this story out of your new query letter because, as noted earlier, we're all looking for something new and exciting. New and exciting is exactly what your new book is. But including the tale of woe about your first agented book will create an atmosphere of guilt by association. We'll see that story in your query letter and we'll think, not only has this writer already failed, but he's complaining about it. We'll regard your career as an uphill battle and our enthusiasm will die on the vine. It's quite possible that your first agented book should have been the one that stayed in the drawer. Whatever the reason for its failure to sell, keep the tale of woe out of the query letter.

Should you ever tell this story? Yes—when a new agent wants to take you on. After you've agreed to work together, you can tell what happened, because there may be information in the story that your new agent will need before approaching editors. He'll need to know who saw your first novel and whether anyone tried to buy it and failed, or whether anyone took particular pains to praise your writing or to discuss your work with you. He'll be able to evaluate all this information and either ignore it or put it to use.

REALITY CHECK: DOING THE MATH

Most first novels are not sold at auction. They're not usually sold on the first round of submissions, or to the first editor they're sent to, or even in the first month or so that they're out on editors' desks, and there might just be an advantage to this. The higher the advance that an auction brings, the more pressure on the book and consequently on the author. In reality, advances for first novels are usually under $50,000, with most hovering around $10,000 to $20,000. The $5,000 or $7,500 advance is not unheard of, either.

While $50,000, even $40,000, sounds wonderful, it will only support you if you write fast. If you've spent four years on your novel, your agent has spent six months submitting it, and your book won't come out until eighteen months after it's accepted, that's six years from start to finish. Fifty thousand dollars divided by six equals a salary from your writing of $8,333.33 per year. A $15,000 advance with the same time frame brings $2,500 a year, and a $7,500 advance brings $1,250 per year. So even though you'll probably need to keep your day job, it's easy to see how a more modest advance—a sum of money that your publisher gives you in the hope that sales of your book will pay him back—can earn out more quickly than one that was pushed up by auction fever. When royalties from sales of your book add up to the amount of your advance, you've "earned out." But how does that happen? How do they figure it all out, and how in the world does anyone make any money at this?

THE FORMULA

Before making an offer to buy a book, an editor will prepare some kind of pricing formula. Every company's formula is different, but according to Brian DeFiore, who was an executive at several different publishing houses before becoming a literary agent, the formula is generally composed of such costs as the author's advance; paper, printing, and binding costs; printing plant fees; the costs of jacket art, marketing, warehousing, and shipping; and overhead (such as building leases, employees' salaries, and all the other expenses of running a business). The formula helps publishers arrive at an estimate of how much money they'll need to spend to purchase the rights to the book and to produce it, which will be balanced against the number of copies the publisher hopes and expects to sell. Book sales are not as predictable as, say, sales of Coca-Cola, but a publisher's experience and knowledge of the marketplace will help find the right ballpark for a book's advance.

Most mainstream publishers offer, through agents, a contract that stipulates your book will receive a royalty of 10 percent of the cover price on each and every copy sold. The offer usually includes an escalation in royalties that goes like this: 10 percent of the cover price on each of the first five thousand copies sold, 12.5 percent of the cover price on each of the next five thousand copies sold, and 15 percent of the cover price on every copy sold thereafter. These are royalties on sales of hardcover books. Sales of trade paperback books—trade paperbacks are the larger, nicer paperbacks—fetch a royalty rate of 7.5 percent of the cover price on each copy sold. And sales of mass market paperbacks—sometimes called rack-size paperbacks, these are the smaller, cheaper paperbacks you can buy in supermarkets, newsstands, and airports, as well as in bookstores—are often granted a rate of 6 percent (and as low as 4 percent) of the cover price on each copy sold. Sometimes you can get the publisher to go up to 8 percent after, say, 150,000 copies. Established agents can often get the mass market royalties to start at 8 percent and escalate to 10 percent or more.

After several years of creeping price rises, the price of hardcover novels hasn't gone up appreciably in recent years. Putting aside the publisher's formula, how many copies would your $24 hardcover novel have to sell before you'd start making money? If you've gotten an advance of $20,000—$10,000 after you signed the contract (and when I say *after*, I mean something like two months after, not the day or the week after) and the balance of $10,000 when the book was published—you'd make money over and above your advance if it sold ten thousand copies. If every copy was sold in a regular bookstore, and if every one of them went home with a customer and stayed there (in other words, if not returned to the publisher), your book would have earned $27,000 against your advance of $20,000, and your publisher would be happy. If you were to write another novel as good as the first, you'd probably get another contract with a higher advance from that publisher.

Knowing how essential it is that your book make money so you can earn out your advance and secure future, more lucrative contracts, you should be inspired to focus on the publication process and get involved in helping the book achieve its sales potential. We'll examine this process and see what you can do to help in the next chapter.

RECOMMENDED READING

"Advances & Royalties—How Authors Are Paid" (www.brandewyne.com/writingtips/authorspaid.html). This article is best-selling author Rebecca Brandewyne's simple explanation of how books earn money.

"The Big Misunderstanding About Money" (www.sabrinajeffries.com/big-misunderstanding-about-money.php). This article for aspiring writers by a hardworking romance writer has an excellent chart that breaks down what certain types of books might expect to earn.

RECOMMENDED WEB SITES

WritersServices (www.writersservices.com). This site is run by Chris Holifield, who has a great deal of publishing experience. The site's useful articles on the business of publishing include pieces on advances and royalties and pricing, among many other subjects.

Publishers Marketplace (www.publishersmarketplace.com). Subscribe to its free weekly e-newsletter, called *Publishers Lunch*, if you want a quick rundown of what kinds of books are selling each week for approximately how much. If the flood of sales starts to depress you, however, just cancel your subscription. There's such a thing as too much information.

CHAPTER NINETEEN:

becoming a published author

Your editor is just the tip of the iceberg that is the publishing house. Behind her is not only the entire editorial staff, from publisher and editor in chief to editorial assistants, but the departments devoted to publicity, marketing, sales, contracts, production, and subsidiary rights. In another building—usually in another state—is the warehouse and distribution center, which stores the books and fills the booksellers' orders.

How does it all come together, and how do you end up with a book in your hands, copies in the stores, and reviews in the newspapers? It's a long story—sometimes it takes nine months, and sometimes it takes eighteen to twenty-four months—with many players. After years of working alone, and then a period of time working with your agent—your business partner—you're going to be working with a whole team of people whose job it is to get your book published.

After you've accepted the offer, the publisher will issue a contract that covers the terms of the offer your agent negotiated, as well as a score of other issues. It often takes four to six weeks for a large publishing house to send a contract to your agent. And after he receives it, he'll want to negotiate many of those points with the publisher. After all, the contract is written by the publisher, so it's likely to be weighted in the publishing house's favor. Your agent's job is to attempt to redress the balance and make the contract as favorable to you as possible.

THE PUBLISHING PROCESS: TRYING TO KEEP UP

Once you've signed your contract, the publishing process officially begins. This process can be exciting—having your book published is what you've waited for, what you've dreamed about—but it can also make you feel very much out of control of your book. There is so much to think about, and so much that seems to be sprung on you—"We don't like the title, can you change it?" "The heroine's name is wrong." "What do you think of this cover concept? You don't like it? Oh, that's too bad, because the book is being printed now."—and on and on and on. Good communication with your editor can make all the difference, but there are nevertheless many surprising and potentially painful moments along the way to publication of your first novel.

Let's try to lay out some of the milestones on the road to publication so you'll have a better idea of what to expect—and a better idea of how much you'll want to get involved at each step.

1. EDITORIAL

After you've signed and returned the contract, your editor will probably get in touch with you. You'll get a telephone call or, more frequently these days, an e-mail from the editor introducing herself and telling you what the next steps are going to be. The editor will probably want to discuss her reaction to the novel and her ideas for revision. She'll tell you how she works—whether she'll send you a manuscript with her notes in the margins, or an editorial letter, or whether she'll expect you to take notes from the conversation and embark on a rewrite immediately.

After that, you're not really on your own. Your contract carries a delivery date—something like a deadline. And it is for real. During the negotiation, your agent will usually discuss the delivery date with you and ask whether you can realistically live up to it. Your agent will probably have some idea of how much work your editor thinks you'll need to do, and you'll have some idea of what your life is like and how much time you're going to be able to devote to revision. Be honest with yourself about how much time you're going to need. Take into consideration the following factors:

- how well you work under pressure
- how much thinking or meditating time you need to ponder the improvements your novel will need
- how much writing and rewriting time you'll need
- the month or season your book will be published (If you know this, you can work backwards by nine months or more to allow time for editing and production.)
- the necessity of getting this book done so you can embark on your next novel (If you want a career as a novelist, you have to get the momentum going and keep it going.)

Once you've set a realistic delivery date, it's important that you meet the deadline. Your editor will have attempted to set a schedule of editing all the manuscripts that are coming in so she can turn to yours within a reasonable period of time. She'll also have told the managing editor when to expect the edited manuscript. The managing editor will have noted the date on her schedule so she'll be prepared to hire a freelance copyeditor to take the job around that time. The publisher will have found a place for your novel on a future list. In other words, the contract, with its delivery date, sets the publishing wheels in motion, and it's expensive to put the brakes on. Get your book in on time.

When your editor has decided (usually a month or two after you hand in the revisions) that your manuscript is *acceptable*, an important contractual term, she will schedule it with the production department. An acceptable manuscript is one that is delivered in the correct format—whether it be two printed copies or one computer file and one printed copy, with double-spaced text, page numbers, and title page—and that lives up to the publisher's expectation for how good it will be when it is finished. It's rare that a novel, upon delivery, will be rejected for being unacceptable, because novels are usually sold after they're finished. But if the book was sold based on a few chapters or a partial manuscript, the finished product could be found, in the publisher's eyes, disappointing.

Before this point the publisher will have determined when the book will be published. Nowadays contracts stipulate that a publisher will publish the book within eighteen or twenty-four months of the date of the contract. It used to be that it took nine months from manuscript to published book. It doesn't actually take any longer today. In fact, a book could conceivably be published in a week—printed, bound, and shipped to stores. But the big houses now need to plan further in advance to get all the pieces to come together to make a book's publication a success.

2. ART AND PRODUCTION

From the moment you hand in your finished book and your editor accepts it, with all its revisions, your book will be in production. Let's look at some of the people and departments involved.

Copyeditor

Once your manuscript is officially accepted by your editor, a copyeditor goes over it with a fine-toothed comb to find grammatical and syntactical errors, typographical errors, errors in fact or chronology, even inconsistencies like the fact that your heroine had red hair on page 3 but raven tresses on page 57. The copyeditor also develops a style sheet for your book that specifies standardized spelling, capitalization, indentation, how you handle dialogue, the correct spelling of characters' names and other proper nouns, etc.

You'll be asked to go over the copyedited manuscript, answer all the copyeditor's questions, and get the whole thing back to your publisher in ten days or two weeks. Authors usually find this an interesting experience, sometimes trying, sometimes amusing, as copyeditors try to "regularize" a writer's prose style, and the writer fights back to preserve vernacular or other examples of consciously nonstandard English. Most publishers have developed a house style that the copyeditors they hire are instructed to follow. If your writing has deliberate idiosyncrasies that clash with the house style, try to pinpoint them in advance of the copyediting so the copyeditor knows which changes you'll find acceptable and which ones will interfere with the voice of the book. Whatever your response to the copyeditor's marks and suggestions, it's important to study them carefully and respond promptly.

The Book Designer

This is the person who, working with the copyedited manuscript, designs the interior of your book. Not only will she choose the font in which your book will be set, the book designer will make the following decisions:

1. the font of the titles and subtitles—also called display font

2. whether your book will have running heads (These, as their name implies, run across the top or bottom of each page. Some books don't have them at all. Some use the author's name on one side of the two-page spread, and the name of the book on the other. Some use the chapter titles, if the chapters have titles.)

3. the paper to be used (Although the head of production will typically make this decision, the designer needs to know what kind of paper will be used in the book so she can assess the readability of the font on a particular type of paper. The decision about paper is based on expense, availability, quantity needed based on the size of the print run, and the possibility of obtaining more paper should the publisher do well enough with your book that it needs to go back to press. Paper is expensive and orders for it are put in well in advance of need.)

The Jacket Designer

The production head usually works with a stable of freelance jacket or cover artists. He knows their different styles and how well they meet deadlines. He'll get one on board for your book and send the manuscript over. Some designers read the whole book and some only read the description of the book, or just enough of your manuscript to get a feel for the atmosphere of the book or to know something about the main characters or the setting. They may be given some guidelines—"This is a hot young novelist—we want something really edgy," or "Give us something that will make readers think of *The Da Vinci Code*"—or they may be given free rein.

When the designer produces a sketch, the production head, the editor, and others in-house look it over. Sometimes it's rejected before the author ever sees it. Some designers hand in more than one treatment for the cover so the publisher can choose a direction. The design usually comes with some notes about the colors and finishes that are to be used and any special effects, such as raised type or a cutaway on a paperback cover. When the publisher has something acceptable, your editor will show it to you.

Most publishers do not allow the author to have approval over the jacket art. Each sketch is expensive to obtain, and if the author has contractual approval over the cover design, he might reject three or four or seven possibilities before approving anything. Therefore, although your editor usually asks when showing you the cover art, "What do you think?" or "How do you like it?" she's not technically seeking your approval. I nevertheless recommend my clients take several steps when responding to cover art:

1. **Understand your cover's ultimate purpose.** The cover of a book is an ad, not a work of art to hang on your wall. Go into a bookstore and look at the hundreds of books trying to get your attention. Some book jackets stand out by screaming, some by proclaiming news, some by breaking new ground, some by sheer beauty, and some by whispering. How is yours going to stand out?

2. **Prop the sketch up and walk away from it so you can look at it from across the room.** Can you see it? Can you read the title? Your

name? What does it say to you? What do you think it will say to a stranger?

3. **If you don't like it, try to analyze why you don't like it.** Think about whether you'd like it if the title font were different, if different colors were used, or if the art were tweaked in some way. Try to think of something good to say about it.

4. **Finally, write to your editor.** List all the things you like about the jacket. Then list the things about the jacket that you don't understand or that are wrong or misspelled. Ask a series of questions: Can we see it with an orange typeface instead of a brown one? Can the designer make the font bigger? Can we try a version where the tennis ball isn't bleeding? Because you are not a designer, you are not telling anyone how to design a jacket. You're asking for tweaks. Breaking your request to see a new sketch down into little steps is much more effective than an e-mail that says: "I hate it."

Following these steps will greatly increase your chances of getting an improved jacket sketch, if not a completely new one. It's just possible that not everyone at the publishing house loved the original sketch, and if you can articulate some of the problems you have with it, you might help everyone see how to improve it.

The Printer and Binder

The head of production is also responsible for contracting with a printing company and bindery. Some printers provide binding; some don't. Most publishers routinely work with one or two printers for all their jobs. In order to get a book printed, the production head must book a slot in the printer's schedule well in advance of the actual printing. This is another reason why delivery dates and schedules are important. If publishers lose time at a printer's, there's no guarantee another slot will be available immediately.

Although most publishers have a good idea of the number of copies they will print of your book, the final number is dependent on advance sales written by the sales representatives as they take orders from booksellers and wholesalers. If advance orders are disappointing, the number of copies ordered for the first print run will be scaled down accordingly. If the orders are higher than everyone had hoped, the print run will be increased. The final number is determined shortly before the book is sent to the printer.

With the book designer's specifications, the production head will choose a method of binding, whether sewn or glued, for your book. If a large printer does the job, it will handle every step of the process, from printing the sheets to forming them into signatures (sheets folded together), and cutting them into pages, binding and covering them, and wrapping them with jackets. Other printers send the folded and gathered sheets to a separate bindery for finishing.

Before your book is printed, however, and after everyone agrees on the look of the book, it's time to ramp up the involvement of the other departments.

3. MARKETING

The duty of the publisher's marketing department is to persuade the bookstores that the publisher is putting a lot of energy behind your book. If the booksellers know that, it's easier for them to believe the marketing will bring bodies into their stores. More bodies in their stores mean more sales. If yours is the book they think will bring people into their stores, they'll order more copies of it.

Lisa Gallagher, senior vice president and publisher of William Morrow & Company and former head of marketing there for several years, planned many campaigns for first novels. She says:

> The marketing campaign is about getting attention for your book—whether from the booksellers, the media, or the consumer. Ultimately it is about driving book sales. Every book should have a marketing plan prior to publication. This is the publisher's rationale for buying the book in the first place, with a particular audience or readership in mind, and the plan is how to reach them.

The marketing campaign has two stages—the first is aimed at the book trade, and the second at the book's potential readers. Lisa says that while publicity is key for a nonfiction book, the circumstances are slightly different for a first novel.

> It's important to get booksellers reading early in the hope of winning their support. The chain of enthusiasm begins with the editor who acquired the book. Manuscripts are then distributed throughout the house, including the marketing, sales, and publicity departments, and the enthusiasm of all the in-house readers is communicated to the booksellers during the sales call.

Meanwhile, the editor and agent are busy trying to get well-known writers to endorse the book. Any blurbs they gather will appear on the book jacket, but if they come in early enough, they can be used on advance readers' copies (ARCs), which we'll take a closer look at on page 270, and in mailings, e-cards, and any advertising.

Standing Out

Placement in the big chain stores is something the publisher must pay for, in much the same way that General Mills pays for the best shelf placement for Cheerios. There are many levels of in-store placement—front table displays, window displays, positioning at the end of an aisle—so a book doesn't need to be a mega-bestseller for the publisher to put some marketing dollars into placement. Yet since most first novels don't have the marketing budget of a best-selling author, other promotional tools can be even more important.

Other Promotional Tools

The marketing department, together with publicity, sales, and, of course, the editorial department, determines whether the house will spend the money to make ARCs, which are like fancy bound galleys. They often look like a trade paperback version of your book, with a description on the back as well as an outline of any advertising, publicity, marketing, or sales plans the publisher may have come up with. (But beware of some of this information: Typically, the announced first printing—the number the publisher claims it will print—is not the real first printing. It's used to flush out as many orders as possible before publication. As noted earlier, the number of prepublication orders the publisher receives is really what determines how many copies will be printed.)

The marketing department, again in tandem with sales and editorial, might design in-store displays, like decorated cardboard boxes—charmingly called dumps—in which to display multiple copies of your book. They'll offer posters or bookmarks to booksellers, and sales incentives, such as higher discounts for more copies ordered. They might put your book into an in-house promotion, say, making it the lead fiction title for the spring list, which signals confidence in the title to the sales reps and the booksellers.

They'll also promote it online. HarperCollins, for instance, offers AuthorTracker, where members sign up to receive e-mail alerts about news of their favorite writers; First Look, where the publisher offers ARCs to review before publication; and Invite the Author, where book groups can win a telephone interview with an author. Although these promotions are aimed at consumers, they prove to booksellers that the publisher is leaving no stone unturned in its effort to find buyers for its books.

4. PUBLICITY

After your editor, you will, if things go well, have the most contact with your publicist. Some months before your book is published, you'll be assigned a publicist. Her job will be to get your book reviewed as widely as possible. She'll also, theoretically, book you on radio or television shows, arrange bookstore or library appearances, try to get you invited to regional or national book conventions, make every effort to get non-book-page articles and interviews done on you, and in every way possible talk up your book to people who might be able to promote it.

If your publisher does plan to do ARCs, you're lucky, because they're expensive and not every book gets them. ARCs are the best tool for getting word-of-mouth going. Laura Whitcomb's publisher decided to put out five hundred ARCs of *A Certain Slant of Light* and then brought Laura from Oregon to New York for BookExpo America, the annual booksellers' convention, to sign them and give them away. These ARCs are also sent to an editor's or marketing head's or publicist's "big-mouth list," people throughout the industry and beyond who are considered tastemakers or enthusiasts, people who will talk about the book if they get it early enough, because they're the kind of people who like to be in the know. You should make your own big-mouth list. You're not going to be given many copies of the ARC, but you might come up with people of interest to the publisher, or people who might be likely candidates to give your book a blurb.

The Authors' Questionnaire

Very early in the process—often at the time you get your contract—you will receive an authors' questionnaire to fill out. This is not the kind of questionnaire where you rate your feelings on a scale of one to ten and answer a handful of yes-or-no questions. It's a lengthy document that contains everything from your date and place of birth to how you got your idea for your novel to your publication history to a list of every bookstore where you might be known, every writer who might be persuaded to blurb your book, and every newspaper or magazine that might be convinced to run a review. The authors' questionnaire provides you with a unique opportunity—possibly the only one—to promote yourself within the publishing house. It might seem like a chore—it is—but it's extremely important that you hand in a complete authors' questionnaire. You can be creative with it in such a way that it's a reflection of you as a novelist as well as of your fiction. You might find it helpful to print out the blank questionnaire found at this link, http://copylaw.com/forms/authors.html, and use it to practice on until you get one from your publisher.

The marketing department people will read your authors' questionnaire, which is another reason it's important that you make it terrific. Once they've read it, they'll have an even better idea of the target market for your book and who your readers will be. If you worked hard on determining this well before you ever wrote to a literary agent, much less found a publisher for your book, and if you make it clear in your authors' questionnaire that you know the answer to this question, your publisher's marketing department will have an easier job of coming up with creative ways to promote your book.

Face-to-Face Meetings

You must go to your publisher in person five months or so before the book comes out and ask your editor to arrange a meeting with your publicist and someone from the marketing department. Call it a brainstorming meeting and come armed with ideas and things you can do to help the book. Say you can guarantee forty people at a signing. That you've got a prominent best-selling author who's promised a blurb. That your company or first cousin is buying one hundred copies to give out at Christmas. That your novel's Web site is up and running, that you're running a contest on it where the winner will win a trip to Tahiti, or that you're developing a game based on your book that visitors to the Web site can play and win a prize. That in return, you'll get their e-mail addresses and end up with a mailing list. Think of something positive and encouraging to bring to the table.

If the house is behind your book, you'll get the meeting. If it's not, your editor may attempt to turn down your request. You should persist, even if it means that you end up meeting with your editor only to find the publicist is just "dropping in to say hi" and the marketing person had a family emergency. But whatever shape the meeting takes, use it to form face-to-face relationships with every person on the team. Exchange business cards and find out how much each wants to hear from you. The person running the meeting might suggest that you keep exclusive contact with your editor but put everyone else in the meeting on the "cc" list. Afterward, ask your editor if you can stop and shake the hand of the production head or the copyeditor or the sales manager or anyone else you can think of so you can express your appreciation in person.

A meeting like this might not generate anything exciting or new or tangible. But the best intangible a meeting like this can produce is this one:

Everyone on the team is charged up enough by you and your novel she goes the extra mile and does more than budgeted in terms of money and time. And that's a gift. If you get that from your meeting, you've gotten a lot.

The Press Release

The publicist's pitch starts with a pitch letter and perhaps a press release. Unfortunately, not every book gets even these minimal accompaniments. That's why it's important for you and your agent to be in touch with your editor and publicist to find out whether they're preparing these materials. Many agents I know recommend their authors ask to see the official press release and to offer to help write it or rewrite it. I very strongly recommend that you put your imprint on everything describing your book that leaves the publisher's offices—press release, jacket copy, catalog copy—you name it. I guarantee that if you don't see it, you will later find out it was riddled with mistakes.

The way to do this effectively is, of course, with diplomacy and tact. Either you or your agent should start with your editor. Don't ask, "Are you doing a press release?" Ask, "When will we see the press release?" Your editor will let you know when it should be ready. Then tell her you'd like to see it to see if there's any way you can help. If that doesn't work, tell her you're doing your own mailing and wanted to crib from what the publicist had already done.

Try to approach this in the spirit of teamwork, pointing out that everything is better—from the novel on—if there's another pair of eyes looking it over. The fact is that I have known great publicists who write fabulous pitches, but I've also known publicists who were functional illiterates. You've got to get involved. If you don't, you'll only be sorry later. Don't let up on getting your hands on the press release. Be a squeaky wheel. Don't accept no for an answer. You can't let your book go out into the world without this. Since most first novels' publicity campaigns consist entirely of a mailing to one hundred book review editors, this is a vital piece of paper, sometimes the only thing that will get anyone to pay any attention to your book at all.

The reality is that most publicists are overworked, and most first novels don't get much publicity. Publishers, as the quote earlier from Lisa Gallagher indicates, don't see as much value in publicity for first novels as they do in publicity for nonfiction, so the author tour for first novels is going the way of the dodo bird. Bookstores want to have authors who will bring people into the stores and buy books. First novelists don't yet have a wide audience, so it's not likely people will come in droves to every bookstore in which they appear. But there are ways around this. We'll discuss more of what you can do to help in the next chapter.

IN THEIR OWN WORDS: JIM FUSILLI

Jim Fusilli, author of *Tribeca Blues* and other Terry Orr novels, is the pop music critic for the *Wall Street Journal*. He also served as the mystery reviewer for the *Boston Globe* for a year, so he understands the power of a well-written press release.

Ask the publisher if you can write your own press release. Do two—one for local media, the other for national. In the local release, play up your ties to the community. When I was reviewing for the *Boston Globe*, you wouldn't believe how many releases I received that didn't lead with the author's New England roots. In the national release, lead with what distinguishes you from other authors: "Medal of Honor winner Joe Blow" is better than "Joe Blow." Also, make sure the publication date is in the lead. If you've got a blurb that sings, get it in the first graf too. Keep the release short and to the point.

Remember, the purpose of the release isn't to tell the reviewer how fabulous you are. It's to get him to lift your book out of the pile of books that arrive daily to his desk and read it. A tight release that speaks to the reviewer's needs will almost always do that.

Outside Publicists

Many writers, not just first-time novelists, wonder whether they should hire an independent publicist to work with the in-house publicist on getting word of the book out to as wide a media audience as possible. Most authors who choose to do this are happy, even though it's expensive, because it gives them the satisfaction of knowing they did everything they could to make the book a success. And a recent study by RainToday.com, a marketing firm, indicates the investment is worth it. As Jim Milliot noted in *Publishers Weekly*, authors who worked only through their publishers reported average sales of 4,500 copies for a first book and royalties of $25,000, while authors who hired a marketing or public relations firm averaged sales of 10,000 copies and earned royalties of $55,000. While the RainToday study looked specifically at authors of nonfiction books, the findings are significant if only because market research of this kind is almost unheard of in publishing.

Although some publishers and their publicists might bristle at the idea of an author hiring an outside firm, it is a viable option. If you do choose to go this way, understand that you'll have to line up a good independent publicist several months or more before the book is published to allow him to be most effective. Susan Richman, a veteran publicity executive, advises:

> Before making the decision to hire a freelance publicist, you should sit down with your editor and try to get a frank picture of what the house plans to do for your novel. If the publisher is very excited about the book and says they're planning to put a lot into it, a freelancer would be superfluous. But if it wasn't targeted to be a book they were putting a lot behind, a freelance publicist would be very helpful.
>
> You would probably want the early stuff—sending galleys out for review—to come from the house, and have the freelancer handle the later things—like trying to arrange an interview in, say, a woman's magazine if your novel appealed to that audience. But marketing plans are set well in advance, so you can have a conversation with your publisher about their plans and have plenty of time to hire a freelancer if that's what you need to do.

5. ADVERTISING

Publishers and editors have one pet phrase that drives me crazy: Advertising doesn't work. As any red-blooded American knows, advertising does work. Yet to advertise properly—to saturation point—is an expensive proposition, and publishers just can't afford it. I would love to see them make a virtue out of the fact that they don't advertise, however, the way that "No Ad" suntan lotion does. They could promote a book by saying something like this on the cover:

> You will not see any advertising for this uniquely beautiful first novel. If you are holding it in your hands right now, it proves you're a discerning individual who doesn't need an advertising blitz to help you recognize quality when you see it. Don't put it down—bring it to the cash register immediately so you can take it home with you and begin reading it tonight.

Ads for books run every day in the newspaper, so it's clear that publishers believe in some advertising. One way they like to use advertising is to announce their enthusiasm for a book to the trade. A full-page ad in the *New York Times Book Review* is as much a signal to booksellers as it is to readers that the publisher believes it has a big book on its hands. But that one ad could blow an entire marketing budget, and whether it actually leads to measurable cash-register sales is questionable. Ben Sevier, an editor at St. Martin's Press, sees it this way:

> With the price of major newspaper and magazine advertising being prohibitive, publishers often find that their marketing budgets can be put to better use elsewhere, like bigger runs of ARCs, co-op [where a bookstore and a publisher share the cost of an ad or an appearance], and marketing programs with organizations like Book Sense [a program for promoting books developed by the American Booksellers Association] or Baker & Taylor, Inc. and Ingram Book Group [book wholesalers]. Publishers sometimes announce advertising in a general way—"National Print Advertising"—and then upon publication tailor that advertising in the way that makes the most financial sense based on factors like the size of the initial distribution of the book, or whether some or all of the money might have better effect elsewhere. There's no hard-and-fast glossary as to which marketing phrase means exactly what kind of advertising we'll do—the best marketing plans are flexible and tailored specifically for the individual book's unique market.

6. SALES

The unsung heroes of publishing are the sales representatives. These dedicated men and women must love books, because there are other things they could be selling that would undoubtedly pay them better. Even with the spread of the chains of superstores, where buying has been centralized and put into the hands of a few people at the home office, every publishing house has sales reps who are on the road much of the year, driving from store to store to meet with bookstore owners or managers and tell them of the next season's books.

Catalog Placement

The sales rep's main selling tool is the publisher's catalog. The rep generally sits down with the bookstore's manager or chief buyer, and together they pore over the catalog. Let me rephrase that: Together they speed-read and speed-talk through the catalog. The reality is that each title gets much less than a minute—sometimes mere seconds—of a book buyer's attention. The rep has to get his pitch ready well before ever setting foot in the bookstore. He will not want your help in preparing this pitch. From hearing about your book at the publisher's sales conferences to reviewing any marketing and publicity plans to, as often as possible, reading the manuscript or bound galley, the rep has been forming a sense of how to sell your book, and equally of how hard his sales manager wants him to push it—or not. With all this behind him, he enters the bookstore and tries to get the buyer's attention for each book in the catalogue. If the buyer isn't impressed with what he hears about your book, he'll express it in one word: "Pass." If the buyer of a small independent bookstore is interested in your book, he'll express it in three words: "I'll take two." Two copies of your book. That's it. And that's a perfectly normal sale.

Given this reality, you probably don't need any more encouragement to insist on seeing the catalog copy before it goes to press.

The best sales scenario for your little first novel is to find out that certain reps have read it and fallen for it. If they love your book, they'll go to their accounts—the bookstores—and use their relationships, their selling history with that store, and their passion to make sure they get as many copies of your book out there as they can. When this happens, it's thrilling, because generally those sales reps have arrived at this decision on their own. Yes, they've seen the house's level of enthusiasm. They've heard that early readers thought your book was great. But sales reps have been there, done that. They've heard books hyped every season and seen nothing come of it. They're pretty good at seeing through false hype and arriving at their own conclusions. So if you hear from your editor that a sales rep or two really loved your book, take it seriously. Light a candle. Think good thoughts. You'll be discouraged from contacting the sales rep yourself, but there's nothing to stop you from sending an appreciative note or e-mail to your editor and asking her to pass it on.

Now that you have an idea of the different parts of a publishing house and how they work to get your book before the public, let's look at what happens on publication day—and what you can do to make the most of it.

RECOMMENDED READING

Bookmaking: Editing/Design/Production, by Marshall Lee. If you really want to know what goes into publishing a book, this is the bible.

Thinking With Type: A Critical Guide for Designers, Writers, Editors, & Students, by Ellen Lupton. Although there is more in this book about fonts and how to design and use them than you ever could have imagined, it's appealing and accessible. Anyone interested in words on the page will find something of interest here.

Chip Kidd: Book One: Work: 1986–2006. A gorgeous retrospective of the work of one of the most influential book jacket designers in American publishing.

RECOMMENDED WEB SITES

Publishers Weekly (www.publishersweekly.com). The book industry trade publication has its own site with a lot of useful information, but you have to be a subscriber to see all of it. I don't recommend that aspiring novelists subscribe to the magazine because they'll easily be overwhelmed by the endless stream of OPBs (Other People's Books). Look at the site when you need specific information you might find there.

Book Sense (www.booksense.com). The Book Sense program was developed to help independent booksellers compete with Amazon and the chains, giving the indies strength through numbers.

Barnes & Noble Discover Great New Writers (www.barnesandnoble.com). The URL is too long to reproduce; go to B&N's site and scroll down the home page until you see "Exclusively from B&N." There you will find "Discover Great New Writers."

BookAngst 101 (http://bookangst.blogspot.com/2004/11/mad-max-survey-editors-on-marketing.html). Follow this link for a uniquely realistic and informative Q&A between BookAngst 101's originator, Mad Max, and three anonymous editors on the subject of publishing and promoting a "mid-list-ish" novel with a first printing in the seventy-five-hundred- to fifteen-thousand-copy range.

U.S. Department of Labor (www.bls.gov/oco/ocos232.htm). There's a thorough article on the bookbinding industry at this site.

Borders Original Voices (www.bordersstores.com). The program, begun in the 1990s, highlights exceptional emerging writers in four book categories—fiction, nonfiction, picture books, and young adult—and one music category. These awards aren't reserved for first-timers the way B&N's Discover awards are, but at Borders, the winner in each category receives five thousand dollars. Visit the Web site and click on the red "Original Voices" box.

CopyLaw.com (http://copylaw.com/forms/authors.html). The URL brings you to a blank authors' questionnaire. Print it out and use it for practice so you'll be ready when your publisher sends you one.

Jim Fusilli (www.jimfusilli.com). Visit Jim's Web site for an article about his eye-opening experience reviewing books for the *Boston Globe*—and to view an example of a terrific author Web site.

CHAPTER TWENTY:

publication day—and beyond

For some of the nine months to two years you'll wait from signing the contract to seeing your book in bookstores, you'll be busy. You'll rewrite your book, address your editor's notes, respond to the copyeditor's comments, and proofread the galleys. There will be a long, quiet period after you sign off on the copyedited manuscript. That's a difficult period because you fear everyone has forgotten about you and your book. You can use that time to build a Web site and network to see if you can find published writers to blurb your book. Many writers advise that this is the perfect time to begin your next novel if you haven't already started. Even if you don't finish it before publication of your first one, it will be good to have it under way.

PUBLICATION DAY

What exactly is a publication date? It is not the day the books arrive from the bindery or the day you get your own first copy. Originally the date meant the last day by which every bookseller who had ordered the book would have it in stock. That's why the publisher will typically receive books—have "books on hand"—six to eight weeks before the actual date of publication. Nowadays, in the U.S., publishers frequently drop the whole notion of a specific publication date and just assign the book to a month. Nevertheless, publicity and marketing efforts are geared to bear fruit—readings, reviews, interviews—right around the book's approximate date of publication.

A book that the publisher expects to become a bestseller will be assigned a specific publication date because of the sales strategy known as the one-day laydown. While this is rarely done for first novels, you should know what it means—and if your editor tells you they're going to do a one-day laydown for your novel, you should shout "Hallelujah!" because it means they're pulling out all the stops. The publisher informs every bookseller who has ordered the book of the laydown date. The books are shipped ahead of time, but the boxes are marked with the date and the instruction that the cartons are not to be opened before that date.

An intensive advertising and marketing campaign, including author appearances and radio and television appearances and advertising, heralds the laydown date in an effort to get everyone into the bookstores that day. The most obvious example of this is the publication of any Harry Potter novel. John Grisham and Stephen King receive this treatment, and recent years have seen first-time novelists like Elizabeth Kostova (*The Historian*), Susanna Clarke (*Jonathan Strange & Mr. Norrell*), and Alice Sebold (*The Lovely Bones*) receive it to excellent effect as well.

Even though your book might not get this treatment, you shouldn't feel slighted: You've got plenty of company. Even without the one-day laydown or a media juggernaut, there's a lot you can do to make the publication of your first novel as satisfying as possible. You don't need to go off on your own and try to arrange things without telling anyone. But you won't want to sit back and wait, either.

THINK LOCALLY

One of my first publishing bosses said to me, "A publisher can broadcast, but the author needs to narrowcast." Lisa Gallagher, senior vice president and publisher of William Morrow & Company, recommends that you, with your publisher's support and help, give extra emphasis to your local area booksellers. Make sure the publisher sends readers' editions to these booksellers with a note or—as Jim Fusilli recommended in the last chapter—a special release tailored for local interest. You can then make the rounds of the stores in your area, introducing yourself to the managers and asking for their support, whether it's in the form of a reading or simply of a placard announcing a new book by a local author. Follow up with thank-you notes to keep your name in front of them and to leave a good impression. Then follow up further with specific questions: Have they found a slot for you in their reading schedule? Have they seen the good review that appeared in *Publishers Weekly*? (These typically run one to three months before publication.) Make it clear that you want to help ensure that your reading will draw an audience to the store. That will make it easier for them to find time for you and may encourage them to talk your book up to their customers.

READINGS

If you know a good number of people in your hometown, or if you can guarantee an audience of thirty or more people at your local bookstore, you can usually persuade both the bookstore and your publicist that it would be worth their while to book you for an appearance, whether it be an author signing, a reading, a Q&A, or a magic act. Keep in mind one obvious fact: *Bookstores want to sell books.* If not enough people buy your book, you won't be able to publish the next and the one after that. So step up to the plate. Put a mailing list together. Go meet the manager of the bookstore personally. Offer to supply the wine and cheese if that's what it will take to get your friends into the store. As soon as you have this conversation, write or e-mail your agent and your publicist (write one and cc the other) to let them know you've made the contact, and give complete details of name, telephone number, job title, address of the store, and possible dates.

After securing a date, get busy. If it's three months away, send a "Save the Date" e-mail or postcard to everyone on your mailing list. Having a signing lined up is another way you can extract a press release from the publicity department. Tell them the bookstore manager wants to borrow from it for her own publicizing efforts. Make an effort to attend other signings at the bookstore where yours will be held. You're supporting the place that's going to support you, and you're getting a feel for how they handle these author appearances. If there's anything you really don't want to see happen when you appear, ponder how to head it off at the pass. Does the person introducing the authors not seem to enjoy speaking in public, mumbling the author's name and the title of the book before shoving the microphone at him? Tell the manager your cousin has begged to be allowed to introduce you. Do there never seem to be enough cups or napkins? Bring your own. You get the picture. Don't assume anything.

SPECIAL INTEREST GROUPS

If you've written a book that will appeal to special groups, find out as much as you can about that constituency and how and where their books are sold. Many booksellers specialize in mysteries, and they hold annual conventions, like Bouchercon World Mystery Convention, to meet authors, publishers, and fellow booksellers. If you've written a mystery, you'd do well to send yourself to Bouchercon and network like crazy when you're there. There are conventions for romance writers, thriller writers, and science fiction authors as well. The American Booksellers Association (ABA) holds BookExpo America every year, a national convention where publishers display their future books and booksellers come from all over the country—not for the faint of heart. More approachable are the ABA's regional conventions, where, as the name implies, you'll be able to play on any regional appeal you or your book might have.

THE WORLD WIDE WEB

Although no one really knows how successful they are, there are endless opportunities to promote your book on the Internet. Adam Fawer, author of *Improbable,* contacted a dozen or more bloggers who he felt might respond to his thriller—which was based on probability theory and quantum physics—and suggested they interview him. He got an excellent response, and more than one took the opportunity to conduct their first-ever author interviews with Adam.

It's pretty obvious that you should have a Web site, but what should be on it? Should it be a regular site or a blog? Before you put up a site, think about whether you'll realistically update it often enough to make it interesting. (If you won't be able to, consider forming a group blog or site with a few other like-minded writers who will share the workload.) Make the site simple and attractive and make it easy for visitors to buy your book with a "Click here to buy the book" button that will send them to Amazon.com, Powell's, Barnes & Noble, or your publisher. Have a section devoted to your schedule of appearances, and another for visitors' comments. If you post comments on the site, keep them focused and interesting, and avoid horror stories about your publisher and other negative posts. More effective would be positive comments about other published books, readers you've met or corresponded with, or the dedicated booksellers you've encountered. As the saying goes, you catch more flies with honey than with vinegar.

If you don't build a site of your own, there are add-on opportunities growing on the Web. Google has introduced the Google Books Partner Program where, with your publisher's participation, you can promote your book online. Searchers can view a small portion of its content, and Google will show them where it can be bought. Amazon.com offers a variety of ways to help you promote your book in its online store, such as through Amazon Shorts, where established authors can publish a short downloadable piece on a page that promotes all their other titles.

THE BASICS

An inexpensive promotional tool is a postcard mailing. Get postcards designed and printed with your book jacket and mail them to as many people as you can think of. Use them to invite people to readings or just to alert them of your book's availability. You can also easily have bookmarks made—offer them to your local bookstores to put near the cash register, and bring them with you when you travel. Some people make stickers; others make buttons, magnets, T-shirts, or matchbooks. Every little bit helps.

BACK TO REAL LIFE

When you dreamed of publishing your first novel, what did you hope would happen? Probably the same thing F. Scott Fitzgerald hoped for: overnight success. You might also have hoped for a great review in the *New York Times*. Make that plural—great reviews in both the daily *Times* and the *New York Times Book Review*. Another hope you may have harbored was for Oprah to single out you and your book and tell everyone in the country to read it. It happens—Alice Sebold's *The Lovely Bones*, Jonathan Safran Foer's *Everything Is Illuminated*, and Elizabeth Kostova's *The Historian* were all first novels that received excellent reviews and climbed the best-seller lists. Unfortunately, however, it doesn't happen as often as we would like.

No matter how well your book is received, books and the way they're made are mysterious to a great many people, and you can't expect everyone to understand what went into the moment when your book appeared in the window of a bookstore. That's why many writers get calls like this from friends, mothers-in-law, co-workers, or neighborhood busybodies: "Did your book come out yet? Because I went to the bookstore and couldn't find it. The manager had never heard of it. It doesn't look like your publisher is doing anything for it." It's upsetting to get a call like this, and I've never known a first novelist who could shrug it off with ease.

Most people who make this call to the first-time author did something wrong. They didn't look in the right place. They didn't ask the right person. They didn't spend any time at all in the bookstore. They got the title wrong. They got your name wrong. They asked two months before your book came out but didn't tell you until after it was out. They neglected to mention that the bookstore manager informed them they could get the book any time if the customer wanted to order it—and that they refused to order it. They didn't tell you they were making the story up because they hoped you would send them a free copy. Or they didn't know that the bookstore hadn't paid its bills to your publisher for two years running and was therefore on credit hold, not receiving any books from your publisher until they paid their bills. Best of all, they couldn't remember which bookstore it was, where it was, the name of it, or the name of the person they talked to.

There's only one way to respond to a call like this: Get the name and address of the bookstore and, if possible, the manager or head buyer's name and number, and send or e-mail this information to your editor. Then drop it.

When things start to slow down, make a new writing schedule for yourself. Try to savor each tiny bit of good news—an independent bookseller e-mailed to say he loved your book; the Knitting Book Club is offering it to its members; you've been asked to give a reading at the Barnes & Noble in your mother's hometown—but put your energy into your new book. Look ahead. If you look back, do so for only two reasons: to see if you can learn from your experience, and to savor the good things that happened.

HOW TO AVOID THE SOPHOMORE SLUMP

The publishing industry regards second novels with a mixture of hope, wariness, and resignation. If the first one didn't get buzz that led to good sales, publishers know the second outing will be a little harder. It's easier to promote a first novel, because readers and booksellers are intrigued by new voices. In addition, second novels often aren't as good as first novels. Why is that? Several reasons:

- The author wrote his first novel slowly and diligently, but thought it would be easier the second time around and rushed the process.

- The author had a big success with his first novel and decided not to accept any editing on the second book.

- The author wrote the first novel in the Eden of the unpublished writer and wrote the second in the Hell of the writer who is still smarting from the one bad review his first novel got.

- The author got a large amount of money for his first book and felt too much pressure to write a big hit with the second.

Let's say, however, that the second novel is every bit as good as the first—if not better. Yet sales of the first novel weren't great. Why? Maybe Barnes & Noble promised your publisher a bigger order if the publisher did a larger first printing and threw some marketing money at the novel, so your publisher printed twenty thousand copies instead of ten thousand. And then took returns on thirteen thousand copies, leaving you with a net sale of seven thousand. Seven thousand copies is not such a bad first-novel sale, except that you got a fifty-thousand-dollar advance, which has not been earned back, and the returns far exceeded the industry standard of 40 percent. With that twenty-thousand first printing, your publisher's sales reps were under pressure to get booksellers to take three or four copies, where they would normally have taken one or two.

Now that your second novel is under consideration, your publisher knows that every bookseller who had a disappointing result with your first novel will be cautious of over-ordering. What's going to happen? It can go either way. If you have a good relationship with your editor and others at the publishing house, and if you have indeed written a novel that's better than your first, your publisher probably will want to continue publishing you in the hope that sales will get a little better with each book. They might not want to "overpay." But if your agent can get them to offer you an advance that's not an out-and-out insult, you should dance with the one what brung ya. They've invested a great deal in your career not only in terms of money, but in terms of the energy it takes to introduce a new writer to readers, with the implicit promise that there will be more good books coming from the new writer's direction soon.

However, if you've been shrill, demanding, unhappy with everything the publisher did or attempted to do for your book—or did not do when you thought it should have—*and* if your sales are disappointing, *and* if your new book is not appreciably better than your first, you should prepare yourself to be dumped. Ironically, of course, if you've behaved this way, you're not likely to see what you did wrong—you're too busy parceling out blame.

"HE'S A PRODUCER"

I gave several novels by one of my clients to a former boss of mine, a longtime publisher who was himself the son of two famous publishers. When he saw that the novels had come out about a year apart, he wrote me: "He'll be a success: He's a producer." I hadn't ever heard anyone put the success of a writer down to such a quality before. But his point was blindingly obvious. Given the unlikelihood that you'll become a famous best-selling novelist with the publication of your first book, you're going to have to work to get there, if that's where you want to get. You're going to have to work to make any kind of a career out of writing. Getting one book published may be the realization of a lifelong dream, but it doesn't usually pay the mortgage.

If, in the long process of writing a book, making it better, finding an agent, and getting published, you learned to regard what you were doing as a full-time job—as often as not a second full-time job—you are well on your way to building a career for yourself. Look around you. How many truly successful people do you know who achieved success by putting a year into this and a year into that? That's why the route to success is often likened to a ladder. Even if the masses don't take you seriously as a writer, you've got to take yourself seriously as a writer if you're going to take the next step on that ladder.

If you're having a hard time moving on, think of a world without books. Think of what it would be like if you weren't compelled to write, if no one was able to write, if your own life hadn't been enriched by book after book, many of them brilliant but not many of them perfect. In *The Giver*, by Lois Lowry, we gradually come to realize that the people of the Community have no color, no music, no memories, and no books. Any of these things raise emotions in the heart, and—"back and back and back"—emotions had been found to be dangerous, as anything uncontrollable can be threatening. It goes without saying that the Community had no writers.

Every writer is the fulcrum for hope. A good story well told is the expression of hope for order in a chaotic world. It's the expression of hope that people will communicate with one another, will open their hearts to one another. It's the expression of hope that a human being can leave something lasting that might touch the generation that comes after. Writers—and their writing—can be dark or light, cynical or idealistic, misanthropic or loving. It is their prerogative—their mandate—to express the full range of human emotion. Without writers, I suspect all the color would gradually drain from the world, leaving us in grayness.

IN THEIR OWN WORDS: KATHRYN HARRISON

Kathryn Harrison, the author of half a dozen novels, including *Envy*, *The Seal Wife*, and *Poison*, as well as the best-selling memoir *The Kiss*, still doesn't find publication easy.

> Publication is hard. With the first book you have no perspective on the industry. Your book has been a huge part of your life, it's loomed large on your horizon, yet fifty thousand books a year are published and only a small percentage will get attention, so it's likely the debut of your book will be a non-event for the rest of the world. It's the final death-throe of something that was alive—it was alive as long as it was manipulable, changeable, reworkable—but it's dead to you now and any attention it gets is like an autopsy.
>
> I love the private act of writing. My favorite time is before anyone's read it; after that, the editing and publishing are a gradual process of letting go of something dying, like shedding a skin. The only way to insulate myself from that death is to fall in love with a new project. If you're working on something new you'll be less likely to be impressed with the good reviews the book gets or devastated by the bad ones.

FALLING IN LOVE AGAIN

The second time around might not be easier, but if, like Kathryn Harrison, you've fallen in love with a new idea for your next book, it might *feel* easier. After coping with the business end of publishing for months, you'll probably be so happy to be back in your writing room that it won't feel like work. You'll take pleasure in the fact that your craft has gotten better, without losing sight of the fact that the ability to write and write well can be continually improved across a lifetime. Whether the second novel is easier or not, you're still going to have to do all or most of the things you did to make the first one better: Share it with your writing group, read it out loud, put it away, print it out, read it through, mark it up, tear it apart, and rewrite it several times.

This time around, though, you might be able to show your early drafts to your agent or your editor, depending on how those relationships have shaped up. You might have the kind of agent who will work with you editorially. While many agents do this nowadays, not all of them do—not all of them are willing, and it isn't really a requirement of the position. Even if you have an agent who is willing to give feedback to work in progress, don't send him a draft riddled with gaping plot holes and underdeveloped characters and ask him to tell you how to fix it.

Remember that your agent's job is to hold on to your belief in your work so he can get you the most favorable possible contracts and relationships with publishers. Those good contracts and relationships are meant to encourage the publisher to think of new and creative ways to "grow" you as a published writer. So if you rush a manuscript over to your agent with the request that he read it and help you fix it, you're only putting a possible damper on the agent's enthusiasm for your work. He has other clients, so you might try to imagine what his week would be like if he had a stack of rough drafts on his desk, all from writers wanting him to spend the time it would take to go through several versions of each until the writer got it right. He wouldn't have much time left over to make the telephone calls and hold the meetings that are used to further your career.

You've formed a business partnership, and a good business partner doesn't ask the other to carry the entire burden of the project. So go back to your writing group. Go back to the process that you learned in this book to take your manuscript from good to great. Hold the readings. Join the workshops. Put the novel away for six weeks. Print it out and read it through. Only after you've done all those things should you show it to your agent. But just think: You won't have to try to find an agent for this one. You already have one. And you've got a new career: You're a published writer.

RECOMMENDED READING

How to Get Happily Published, by Judith Applebaum. Applebaum runs a book marketing company called Sensible Solutions, Inc. that is based on the principles she outlines in this book. Especially valuable—here and at the book's Web site, www.happilypublished.com—are her tips on how to boost your book's sales.

"Performance Anxiety," a 2002 *Village Voice* article by Joy Press (www.villagevoice.com/specials/vls/178/press.shtml). Press identifies "second-novel syndrome" and interviews several well-known authors about its effects.

A Life in Letters: F. Scott Fitzgerald, edited and annotated by Matthew J. Bruccoli. In this volume, intended as "the standard one-volume edition of Fitzgerald's letters," Fitzgerald discusses his second and third novels, *The Beautiful and Damned* and *The Great Gatsby*, and in so doing maps his growth as a published writer.

Publicize Your Book! by Jacqueline Deval. From a former director of publicity for several major publishing houses, this book tells you what really goes on in the publicity department and how you can work with whatever publicity you get, as well as how to develop your own. Excellent for first-time authors.

RECOMMENDED WEB SITES

American Booksellers Association (www.bookweb.org). The online home of the organization that sponsors both BookExpo America and Book Sense.

Here you'll find links to all of its regional booksellers' organizations and calendars of conventions and other events. Once you locate the region most relevant to you and your book, click through to that division's site and you'll find application forms for attending the annual conventions.

Google Books Partner Program (http://books.google.com/googlebooks/ author.html). This link takes you to Google's author resources page, which tells you about the Books Partner Program and other programs of interest to published authors.

Writing-World.com (www.writing-world.com/promotion/james.shtml). Check out the article titled "40+ Ways to Make Your Next Book Signing an EVENT!" by Larry James. It can't hurt and it might help.

21st Century Publishing (http://julieduffy.com/writing/promote_online. htm). Julie Duffy's site, directed at print-on-demand authors, offers helpful promotional tips in an article titled "Promoting Your Book in Online Groups."

The Lipstick Chronicles (http://thelipstickchronicles.typepad.com). The blog of four women mystery writers—Harley Jane Kozak, Nancy Martin, Susan McBride, and Sarah Strohmeyer—gives a good glimpse into the lives and creative processes of some up-and-coming writers.

EPILOGUE

We hope that this book has demystified the writing and publishing process and given you the kind of information that will help you find your way to successful publication. It's important to know that you're not alone, that other writers, famous or not, have the same ups and downs, worries and doubts and exhilarations, as you do. We hope you feel inspired not only to write, but to write well and to write better. Our wish is that you've gained the confidence in your work that will enable you to approach publishers and agents without fear or self-consciousness.

Getting published is a daunting proposition, and its complexities could fill several books. If you write because you can't *not* write, as Dennis Lehane said in the foreword, giving up just won't be an option. If you stick with it, you'll be able to make a career of writing. One book proves you're a writer, but a string of books—that's what makes you an author.

—Ann Rittenberg and Laura Whitcomb

INDEX

ABOUT THE AUTHORS

ANN RITTENBERG

Ann Rittenberg, the president of her own literary agency (www.rittlit.com), has worked in book publishing for more than twenty-five years. She lives in Brooklyn, New York, with her husband and three daughters. This is her first book.

LAURA WHITCOMB

Laura Whitcomb's first novel, *A Certain Slant of Light*, was chosen for the Barnes & Noble "Discover Great New Writers" program, and the movie rights were sold to Warner Bros. studio. The book was also recorded as an audio book for Listening Library and will be published in Italian, Chinese, and Japanese. She lives in Portland, Oregon.

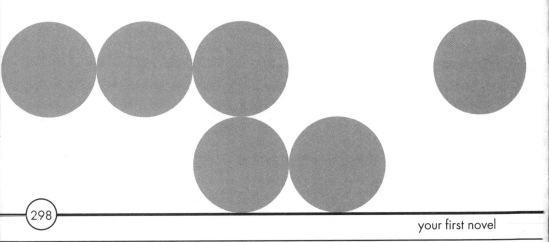